Drug War Deadlock

Drug War Deadlock

The Policy Battle Continues

Edited by
Laura E. Huggins

HOOVER INSTITUTION PRESS
Stanford University   Stanford, California

The Hoover Institution on War, Revolution and Peace, founded at Stanford University in 1919 by Herbert Hoover, who went on to become the thirty-first president of the United States, is an interdisciplinary research center for advanced study on domestic and international affairs. The views expressed in its publications are entirely those of the authors and do not necessarily reflect the views of the staff, officers, or Board of Overseers of the Hoover Institution.

www.hoover.org

Hoover Institution Press Publication No. 539

First printing, 2005
12 11 10 09 08 07 06 05   9 8 7 6 5 4 3 2 1

Manufactured in the United States of America

The paper used in this publication meets the minimum requirements of the American National Standard for Information Sciences—Permanence of Paper for Printed Library Materials, ANSI Z39.48-1992. ∞

Library of Congress Cataloging-in-Publication Data
Drug war deadlock : the policy battle continues / edited by Laura E. Huggins.
        p.   cm. — (Hoover Institution Press publication ; no. 539)
    Includes bibliographical references and index.
    ISBN 0-8179-4652-7 (alk. paper)
    1. Drug abuse—Government policy—United States.   2. Drug control—United States.   3. Drug abuse—Government policy—Europe.   4. Drug control—Europe.   I. Huggins, Laura E., 1976—   II. Series.
HV5825D7777   2005
362.29'1561'0973—dc22   2005009380

CONTENTS

FOREWORD

President Richard Nixon officially declared a "war on drugs" in 1971. This declaration of war escalated in the 1980s, and the debate over its justification became pronounced. For two decades forceful arguments have arisen on both sides of the drug debate, with traditional proponents of a legalistic, rules-oriented, societal-values approach on one side and advocates of individualistic decision-making and libertarian arguments on the other. Today, what was once an almost unspeakable prospect—the decriminalization of illegal drugs—has been proposed by respected figures across the country. As arguments for decriminalization, harm reduction, and legalization become more strident and calls for zero tolerance and harsher penalties more vociferous, it sometimes seems as though the divide between the two camps has become an unbridgeable abyss.

The question of a society's drug policy remains important. Does the apparent stalemate prevailing in the United States represent an optimal position? If the debate heats up once again, what arguments and facts should citizens and government leaders take into account? What should our drug laws look like? Should the possession and sale of drugs be against the law, and all drug violators be imprisoned; or is treatment for addicts and abusers a wiser policy? Do adults have the right to use drugs for recreational purposes, and should they be permitted to purchase drugs legally in state-controlled commercial establishments? Should we criminalize or decriminalize?

Such questions have inspired exceptional scholars and experts, including several fellows at the Hoover Institution, to offer constructive arguments in shaping the drug debate. We are pleased to present herein *Drug War Deadlock*. This primer provides a summary of the widely varying perspectives in the debate over controlled substances in the United States. In selecting and presenting examples from the current literature, this volume strives to provide an educational tool that interested parties can use to make informed assessments of the situation.

Drugs are pervasive in our culture, and many believe that our drug policy is flawed. However, the alternatives can be confounding. Legalization, decriminalization, and harm reduction are not uniformly understood concepts—a fact that leads many to opt out of the discussion. This primer hopefully lays the foundation for a bridge across the great abyss dividing American opinion on drug policy. The next step in construction of that bridge must be resumption of a productive national dialogue.

We hasten to acknowledge the support of Jack and Rose-Marie Anderson. Jack is a member of Hoover's Board of Overseers and encouraged me to continue to include drug policy as an important topic for the Institution to address.

John Raisian
Director
Hoover Institution

INTRODUCTION

Penalties against possession of a drug should not be more damaging to an individual than the use of the drug itself.

President Jimmy Carter
Message to Congress,
August 2, 1977

Let us not forget who we are. Drug abuse is a repudiation of everything America is.

President Ronald Reagan
White House Speech,
September 14, 1986

Recent polls suggest that most Americans regard the war on drugs in the United States as a failure. Yet this futility has not generated much momentum for alternative antidrug strategies. Policy makers also seem divided about the future direction of drug policy. Federal officials, for example, continue to pour money into fighting drugs while states are passing medical marijuana initiatives and rolling back mandatory minimum sentencing—indicating a push toward more lenient drug laws. Is it time to escalate the war on drugs and if so should the focus be on interdiction, education, or incarceration? Alternatively, should our current course be reversed toward strategies such as legalization, decriminalization, or harm reduction?

The dynamics of our drug policies are a complex puzzle to which there are no simplistic solutions. *Drug War Deadlock: The Policy Battle Continues* presents a collection of readings from scholarly journals, government reports, magazines, think tank studies, newspapers, and books in order to address the drug debate in a comprehensive manner. Each part is composed of opposing articles written by many of the foremost authorities in their fields. Moreover, supplementary snapshots are often included to further explore the issue at hand. This approach does not attempt to tackle every issue relating to illegal drugs; rather the aim is to offer the reader a concise view of divergent viewpoints pertaining to drug policy.

Although the concern over drugs has receded somewhat from the spotlight it received in the late 1980s and early 1990s, they are still seen as a significant danger by most Americans. According to the Pew Research Center's recent survey of attitudes on illegal substances and drug policies, the public continues to rank drugs among the major problems facing both the nation and local communities. Ninety percent said drug abuse is a serious problem, with more than a quarter calling it a national crisis. Concern is particularly evident among the African American community, where 43 percent of blacks rate drug abuse as a national crisis, compared with 26 percent of whites. Regarding the drug war, more than four times as many people believe the nation is losing ground on drugs (54 percent) compared with those who say the drug war is making progress (13 percent).

It has been estimated that the U.S. government spends approximately $33 billion annually on prohibition enforcement and arrests 1.5 million people on drug-related charges. Yet it is unclear whether the battle has lowered drug use, crime, or poverty rates. Despite the United States' multibillion-dollar effort to curb the supply of illegal drugs, marijuana, cocaine, heroin, and many other drugs continue to flood America's streets. In fact, drug trafficking has become a multibillion-dollar industry—one that serves as an integral part of the world economy. Proponents of the drug war claim that the rate of use would be much higher today and would be accompanied by higher crime rates had the drug war not gone into effect thirty years ago. Others suggest that the criminalization of drugs has turned nonviolent offenders into criminals, spawned a crime wave similar to the days of prohibition, and threatened constitutional liberties.

Although drug use has swelled over the past few decades, drugs are not a new phenomenon. There is evidence that people have been ingesting mind-altering drugs for more than 10,000 years, but only for the last few hundred years have societies attempted to control the distribution of such substances through criminal law. In the United States, discussions over the use and abuse of drugs can be traced back to the early 20th century. The contemporary debate, however, emerged in the 1980s when the government, out of frustration and anger at being unable to curb drug abuse, stepped up efforts by imposing harsh criminal penalties for possession and sale of illegal drugs.

Part one of this volume probes the history of America's drug war from both sides of the battlefield and offers the reader a basic understanding of U.S. drug policy while providing background information on current statutes and legal requirements. The legal basis for drug violations in the United States is immense yet law enforcement operates under significant constitutional restraints. This inherent tension between society's desire for security and the value we place on liberty will be explored throughout the remainder of the book.

The objective of part two is to delve into the significant divide over the moral implication of drug use in order to get at the foundation of the policy debate and identify underlying points of contention and places where empirical analysis might change one's view. People's philosophical beliefs guide their conduct and therefore play a role in their perspective on illegal drugs. Many prohibitionists, for example, assert that drugs should be banned simply because drug use is immoral. Legalizers, on the other hand, believe that drug laws are hypocritical and infringe on individual rights. These positions are not always explicit in the policy debate but they undeniably shape drug policy. Investigating questions of morals, values, and beliefs is central in any consideration of drug legalization. To determine a wise and sane drug policy we need substantial evidence, but ultimately, our decision as to what works best will likely be based on ideological inclinations. Even if we all were to agree on the facts, we wouldn't agree on weighing certain values over others.

This section also investigates such questions as whether adults have a moral right to use drugs for recreational purposes. John Stuart Mill, one of the most influential thinkers of the 19th century, believed that people can only restrict the freedom of others in order to protect themselves, and that society can only exert power over its members against their will in order to prevent harm to others. But will the harm to others from drug legalization be greater than the harm that exists from keeping drugs illegal?

The important question of the nature and limits of power that can be legitimately exercised by society over the individual will continually be revisited throughout this primer. Part three addresses this and other questions relating to illegal drug use by profiling a few opposing perspectives from esteemed scholars, distinguished members of the media, and respected law enforcement affiliates. The primary goal of this section is to provide a peek into the contrasting sides of the drug debate.

The issue of whether or not to move toward legalizing the production, sale, and possession of illegal drugs has become a hot spot within the larger policy debate. In part four the arguments get more specific by narrowing in on three avenues for drug policy reform: legalization, decriminalization, and harm reduction. Legalization is not an all-or-nothing proposition. There are different degrees and aspects within the legalization spectrum. Many reformers are in favor of *complete legalization*, meaning that currently illegal drugs should have the same legal status as alcohol or tobacco. Others recommend *decriminalization*; usually meaning that possession (dealing is not typically included) would not be a criminal offense but might be subject to penalties like those imposed for speeding. A final solution that reformers frequently promote is *harm reduction*. Harm reduction is a broad classification of proposals that shift the focus from prohibiting the use of drugs to dealing with the problems associated with drug use. This new direction consists of a policy of preventing the potential harms related to drug use rather than focusing on preventing the drug use itself.

One area where advocates of legalization have made progress is in the use of marijuana. According to the Drug Policy Alliance, 72 percent of Americans say that for simple marijuana possession people should be fined rather than locked up. Moreover, more Americans support legalizing marijuana for medical purposes. In fact, eleven states have approved medical marijuana initiatives. Most people regard marijuana as a much less dangerous drug than cocaine or heroin—two-thirds of the public supports the use of marijuana to ease severe pain. Yet, a solid majority still opposes general legalization of marijuana.

Part five explores the debate over marijuana prohibition—a debate that has crossed partisan borders and entered mainstream politics. Those in favor of legalizing marijuana argue that billions of taxpayer dollars are wasted each year fighting a drug that millions of Americans have tried with no negative effects—taxpayer money that is responsible for people losing their jobs, property, and freedoms for simply possessing a joint or growing a few marijuana plants. On the other hand, advocates of prohibition claim that laws against marijuana are needed because marijuana itself is harmful and that it often serves as a gateway drug to even more dangerous substances. They also suggest that a government-sanctioned program to produce and distribute drugs would likely increase the supply and therefore the use of drugs, and that the black market for drugs would still exist (along with crime).

The Netherlands and other countries in Western Europe that have experimented with legalizing drugs provide insight into the debate over drug policies in the United States. Several European countries have chosen to focus their efforts on the social welfare aspect of drug use rather than the law enforcement response. The alternative measures that have gained the most momentum in Western Europe include legalization, decriminalization, and harm reduction. The results from this experimentation have been mixed. Part six explores the pros and cons of Europe's more liberal drug policies and how they might be applied to the United States.

Closer to home, opinion polls show that the issue of drugs tends to divide Americans along political, generational, and religious lines. According to the Pew Research Center, Democrats are more likely to think of drug use as a disease rather than a crime. Republicans, on the other hand, tend to view drug abuse as a criminal behavior and not a health problem. Fifty-eight percent of those under thirty say drug use is a disease, not a crime. By comparison, just 41 percent of seniors (age 65 and older) believe drug use is a disease. There is also a significant religious divide; for example, evangelical Protestants are twice as likely to think of drug use as a criminal act than are traditional Protestants. Can the gaps between Americans over the drug war be narrowed? Although there is no panacea, the conclusion to this primer presents a few tactics for peace and a glimmer of hope for coming closer to conquering the nation's drug problem and ending the war on drugs.

An escape from the drug policy deadlock is far from obvious. The issues are complex and are filled with painful dilemmas. We are inevitably forced to accept the least bad of an array of unpleasant options. Those of us who do nothing, however, will be forced to take a stand one way or another—if we do not act, someone else will do it for us. We need to be armed with facts, a logical frame of mind, and an awareness of how these issues fit in with the big picture. Hopefully *Drug War Deadlock: The Policy Battle Continues* provides these things and enables the reader to draw his or her own conclusions concerning some of the more urgent questions of our day.

This project could not have advanced without the support and guidance of a number of individuals. First and foremost I would like to thank Hoover Institution director John Raisian for his encouragement along the way. John serves as a role model for those aiming to have a positive impact on the world. I would also like to thank Hoover fellows Gary Becker and Joseph McNamara who were most generous with their time and comments. Finally, my deepest gratitude goes to my parents, William and Kathie Bone, who equipped me with the life skills to steer clear of drugs.

Laura E. Huggins

Background

Prohibition will work great injury to the cause of temperance. It is a species of intemperance within itself, for it goes beyond the bounds of reason in that it attempts to control a man's appetite by legislation, and makes a crime out of things that are not crimes. A prohibition law strikes a blow at the very principles upon which our government was founded.

Abraham Lincoln
Speech in the Illinois House of Representatives,
December 18, 1840

Prohibition may be a disputed theory, but none can complain that it doesn't hold water.

Thomas L. Masson
Little Masterpieces of American Wit and Humor
1922

American Drug Policy: The Continuing Debate

James A. Inciardi

James A. Inciardi is director of the Center for Drug and Alcohol Studies at the University of Delaware, a professor in the Department of Sociology and Criminal Justice at Delaware, and an adjunct professor at the University of Miami School of Medicine.

This selection was excerpted from "American Drug Policy: The Continuing Debate" in *The Drug Legalization Debate* (Thousand Oaks, Calif.: Sage Publications, Inc. 1999).

Concern over the use and abuse of illegal drugs remained critical throughout the 1990s. In fact, regardless of political affiliation and ideology, socioeconomic status and ethnicity, or geographical location and occupational status, most Americans continued to rank "drugs" among the major problems facing the nation for three reasons. The first was *crack*-cocaine and its relation to crime. Although both the use of crack and rates of violent crime had declined somewhat by the middle of the decade, the linkages between "drugs and crime" had long since become fixed in the mind of America. This was exacerbated by a continuing flow of media stories about drug abuse and the escalating numbers of drug-involved offenders coming to the attention of the police, courts, and prisons.

The second issue was the movement of heroin from the inner city to mainstream culture, and in particular, the increased visibility of heroin in popular culture. A number of celebrated rock groups were linked to heroin use, through a member's overdose, arrest, or admission to treatment—Smashing Pumpkins, Red Hot Chili Peppers, and Nirvana to name but a few. Hollywood also played on heroin's popularity in *Trainspotting, Pulp Fiction,* and *Basketball Diaries.* There was the fashion industry's promotion of "heroin chic" images in magazines and on television and billboards. And then there was the death of actor River Phoenix from an overdose of heroin (in combination with cocaine and GHB).

Perhaps the most notable issue that kept drugs in the minds of the American population was the rise in drug use among the nation's youth. In 1993, data from the University of Michigan's annual *Monitoring the Future* study found significant increases in the use of certain drugs among high school seniors, 10th graders, and 8th graders. The use of marijuana in the previous year for all three groups had increased, as did the use of cigarettes in the previous 30 days. Other significant increases included inhalant use among 8th graders, LSD use among seniors, and stimulant use among seniors and 10th graders (Johnston, O'Malley, & Bachman, 1996). In the years hence, the *Monitoring the Future* study documented continuing increases in drug use among youths (Johnson et al., 1996; University of Michigan, 1997). Other national survey data reflected similar trends (Centers for Disease Control [CDC], 1998; Department of Health and Human Services [DHHS], 1998), and regional surveys of adolescent drug use tended to parallel the national trends (see Martin et al., 1997; Terry & Pellens, 1998).

Throughout the 1990s, furthermore, both politicians and the public at large examined American drug policy, pondered its problematic effectiveness, and considered alternatives. New "solutions" were advocated, ranging from mandatory treatment for *all* drug-involved offenders and massive funding for anti-drug media messages, to legalizing some or all drugs of abuse. Within the context of these concerns, assessments, and proposals, it is the intention of this opening commentary to briefly review the American drug experience and to present the backdrop for the modern drug legalization debate.

THE AMERICAN DRUG EXPERIENCE

Drug abuse in the United States evolved within the broader context of the historical relationship between people and the psychoactive organic compounds in their immediate environments. Historians and archaeologists have noted that the use of alcohol is, for the most part, a human cultural universal. The chewing of coca and other psychoactive plants has existed in many societies for millennia. Marijuana and the opium poppy are indigenous to several regions of the world and have been used as intoxicants and in rituals likely since prehistoric times. The explosion of world trade following the European discovery of America brought local psychoactive plants—from tobacco and marijuana to coca and the opium poppy, and related techniques of distillation, refining, and crossbreeding—to the attention of world consumers. The American drug experience emerged, evolved, and endured within the framework of this worldwide trafficking of what was originally local psychopharmacological plants (see Courtwright, 1982; Inciardi, 1986, pp. 1–47; Terry & Pellens, 1928, pp. 53–60).

It began with the widespread use of opium in home remedies and over-the-counter patent medicines during the latter part of the 18th century, followed by the discovery of morphine, cocaine, heroin, and hypodermic needles during the ensuing 100-year period. By 1905 there were more than 28,000 pharmaceuticals containing psychoactive drugs readily available throughout the nation, sold in an unrestricted manner by physicians, over-the-counter from apothecaries, grocers, postmasters, and printers, from the tailgates of medicine show wagons as they traveled throughout rural and urban America, and through the mail by newspaper advertisements and catalog sales (Young, 1961, pp. 19–23). Although little data are available as to the number of people dependent on opiates and cocaine during these years, estimates of the addict population at the close of the 19th century ranged as high as 3 million (Morgan, 1974; Terry & Pellens,

1928, pp. 1–20). Regardless of the accuracy of the estimates, addiction had become so visible and widespread that the medical community, the media, and the public at large called for government restrictions on the availability of drugs.

With the passage of state and local anti-drug statutes at the turn of the 20th century, the Pure Food and Drug Act in 1906, the Harrison Narcotic Act in 1914, and subsequent federal and state legislation, combined with the social and economic upheavals of the Great Depression and World War II, as the United States approached mid-century, drug abuse had significantly receded. During the postwar era of expanded world trade, economic growth, and increased urbanization, however, the drug problem grew apace. In the 1950s, heroin addiction emerged in the inner cities at epidemic levels, particularly among youths. In the 1960s, drug abuse expanded from the cities to suburbia. As part of the social revolution of the decade, adolescents and young adults began to tune in, turn on, and drop out through a whole new catalog of drugs—marijuana, hashish, and LSD, plus newly synthesized prescription analgesics, stimulants, and sedatives. By the 1970s, the psychedelic revolution of the previous decade had run its course, but the heroin epidemic had endured, marijuana consumption continued to increase, cocaine reentered the drug scene after its half-century sojourn in the netherworlds of vice and the avant-garde, and Quaaludes and PCP became prominent as the new drugs of the moment. In the 1980s, most of the old drugs remained prominent, while new entries—designer drugs, ecstasy, and crack—staked out positions. In the 1990s, as noted above, heroin reemerged as the popularity of *crack*-cocaine faltered. At the same time, the use of *powder*-cocaine and other illegal drugs endured, and marijuana and tobacco use increased among youths.

AMERICA'S "WAR ON DRUGS"

Since the passage of the Harrison Act in 1914, the federal approach to drug abuse control has included a variety of avenues for reducing both the supply of, and the demand for, illicit drugs. At first, the supply-and-demand reduction strategies were grounded in the classic deterrence model: Through legislation and criminal penalties, individuals would be discouraged from using drugs; by setting an example of traffickers, the government could force potential dealers to seek out other economic pursuits. In time, other components were added: treatment for the user, education and prevention for the would-be user, and research to determine how best to develop and implement plans for enforcement, treatment, education, and prevention.

By the early 1970s, when it appeared that the war on drugs was winning few, if any, battles, new avenues for supply and demand reduction were added. There were the federal interdiction initiatives: Coast Guard, Customs, and Drug Enforcement Administration (DEA) operatives were charged with intercepting drug shipments coming to the United States from foreign ports; in the international sector, there were attempts to eradicate drug-yielding crops at their source. The foreign assistance initiatives also included crop substitution programs and training of Latin American military groups to fight the drug war on their local soil. On the surface, however, none of these strategies seemed to have much effect, and illicit drug use continued to spread.

The problems were many. Legislation and enforcement alone were not enough, and many education programs were of the "scare" variety and quickly lost credibility. Drug abuse treatment was available but not at the level that was needed, and during the 1980s the number of existing treatment slots was drastically reduced. The federal response was, for the most part, a more concerted assault on drugs, both legislative and technological.

By 1988, it had long since been decided by numerous observers that the 74 years of federal prohibition since the passage of the Harrison Act were not only a costly and abject failure but a totally doomed effort as well. It was argued that drug laws and drug enforcement had served mainly to create enormous profits for drug dealers and traffickers, overcrowded jails, police and other government corruption, a distorted foreign policy, predatory street crime carried on by users in search of the funds necessary to purchase black market drugs, and urban areas harassed by street-level drug dealers and terrorized by violent street gangs (McBride, Burgman-Habermehl, Alpert, & Chitwood, 1986; Rosenbaum, 1987; Trebach, 1987; Wisotsky, 1986).

THE DRUG LEGALIZATION DEBATE

Discussions about legalizing drugs in the United States go back to the early decades of the 20th century. The contemporary debate over the legalization of drugs, however, emerged in 1988. It began at a meeting of the U.S. Conference of Mayors when Baltimore's Kurt L. Schmoke called for a national debate on American drug control strategies and the potential benefits of legalizing marijuana, heroin, cocaine, crack, and other illicit substances. Schmoke's argument was that for generations the United States had been pursuing policies of prosecution and repression that resulted in little more than overcrowded courts and prisons, increased profits for drug traffickers, and higher rates of addiction (Schmoke, 1989).

The drug legalization debate received considerable attention in 1988 and 1989. Media coverage was extensive, and discussions of the futility of the "drug war" became widespread in many academic circles. In the 1990s, however, the tenor of the drug debate began to change. A number of the more "hard core" legalizers softened their positions somewhat, advocating a "harm reduction" approach in favor of legalization. At the same time, many of those on the other side of the debate continued to oppose legalizing drugs but began to accept several aspects of the harm-reduction approach.

REFERENCES

Centers for Disease Control. (1998). *Tobacco use among U.S. racial/ethnic minority groups.* Available at http://www.cdc.gov/nccdphp/osh/sgr-min-fs-afr.htm.

Courtwright, D. T. (1982). *Dark paradise: Opiate addiction in America before 1940.* Cambridge, MA: Harvard University Press.

Department of Health and Human Services. (1998, August 21). *Annual national drug survey results released: Overall drug use is level, but youth drug increase persists.* Press release: http://www.health.org/pubs/nhsda/97hhs/nhs97rel.htm.

Inciardi, J. A. (1986). *The war on drugs: Heroin, cocaine, crime, and public policy.* Palo Alto, CA: Mayfield.

Inciardi, J. A., & Harrison, L. D. (in press). *Harm reduction: National and international perspectives.* Thousand Oaks, CA: Sage.

Johnston, L. D., O'Malley, P. M., & Bachman, J. G. (1996, December 19). *Monitoring the future.* News release, Ann Arbor, University of Michigan.

Martin, S. S., Enev, T. E., Peralta, R. L., Purcell, C. L., Logio, K. A., & Murphy, R. G. (1997). *Alcohol, tobacco, and other drug abuse among Delaware students.* Report to the Delaware Prevention Coalition, University of Delaware.

McBride, D. C., Burgman-Habermehl, C., Alpert, J., & Chitwood, D. D. (1986). Drugs and homicide. *Bulletin of the New York Academy of Medicine, 62,* 487–508.

Morgan, H. W. (1974). *Yesterday's addicts: American society and drug abuse.* Norman: University of Oklahoma Press.

Rosenbaum, R. (1987, February 15). Crack murder: A detective story. *New York Times Magazine,* pp. 24–33, 57, 60.

Schmoke, K. L. (1989). Foreword. *American Behavioral Scientist, 32*(3), 231–232.

Terry, C. E., & Pellens, M. (1928). *The opium problem.* New York: Bureau of Social Hygiene.

Trebach, A. S. (1987). *The great drug war.* New York: Macmillan.

University of Michigan News and Information Services. (1997, December 20). *Drug use among American teens shows some signs of leveling after a long rise.* Press release.

Wisotsky, S. (1986). *Breaking the impasse in the war on drugs.* Westport, CT: Greenwood.

Young, J. H. (1961). *The toadstool millionaires: A social history of patent medicines in America before federal regulation.* Princeton, NJ: Princeton University Press.

Drug Laws and Law Enforcement

Howard Abadinsky

Howard Abadinsky is a professor in the Department of Criminal Justice at St. John's University in New York.

This selection was excerpted from "Drug Laws and Law Enforcement" in *Drugs: An Introduction* (Belmont, Calif.: Thomson Learning, Inc. 2004).

Law enforcement in the United States operates under significant constitutional constraints, generally referred to as *due process*—literally meaning the process that is due a person before something disadvantageous can be done to him or her. Due process restrains government from arbitrarily depriving a person of life, liberty, or property. There is an inherent tension between society's desire for security and safety and the value we place on liberty [this tension will be explored throughout this volume]. . . .

The legal foundation for federal drug-law violations is Title II of the Comprehensive Drug Abuse Prevention and Control Act of 1970, as amended (usually referred to as the Controlled Substances Act [CSA]). Among the provisions of the CSA is a set of criteria for placing a substance in one of five schedules (see Box 1.1). Following the federal model, most states have established the five schedule system, but many have chosen to reclassify particular substances within those five schedules. Variation also exists in the number of schedules employed by the states (North Carolina, for example, uses six). Massachusetts categorizes drugs based on the penalty rather than the federal scheme of potential for abuse and medical use. Like federal law, state statutes refer to the drug involved (e.g., cocaine or heroin), the action involved (simple possession, possession with the intent to sell, sale, distribution, or trafficking), and the number of prior offenses. And across states there is significant variation in the penalties for cocaine, marijuana, methamphetamine, and ecstasy-related offenses.

Persons involved in the illegal drug business can be arrested and prosecuted for a number of different offenses: manufacture, importation, distribution, possession, sale; or conspiracy to manufacture, import, distribute, possess, or sell; or failure to pay the required income taxes on illegal income. Possession of drugs may be *actual*— for example, actually on the person, in pockets or in a package that he or she is holding; or *constructive*—not actually on the person, but under his or her control, directly or through other persons. Possession must be proven be a legal search, which usually requires a search warrant as per the Fourth Amendment (an important exception is at ports of entry). A search warrant requires the establishment of probable cause—providing a judge with sufficient evidence of a crime to justify a warrant. Federal trafficking penalties are shown in Box 1.2 and Box 1.3. . . .

Box 1.1 Schedule of Controlled Substances

Schedule I
  A. The drug or other substance has a high potential for abuse.
  B. The drug or other substance has no currently accepted medical use in treatment in the United States.
  C. There is a lack of accepted safety for use of the drug or other substance under medical supervision.

Schedule II
  A. The drug or other substance has a high potential for abuse.
  B. The drug or other substance has a currently accepted medical use in treatment in the United States or a currently accepted medical use with severe restrictions.
  C. Abuse of the drug or other substance may lead to severe psychological or physical dependency.

Schedule III
  A. The drug or other substance has a potential for abuse less than the drugs or other substances in Schedules I and II.
  B. The drug or other substance has a currently accepted medical use in treatment in the United States.
  C. Abuse of the drug or other substance may lead to moderate or low physical dependence or high psychological dependence.

Schedule IV
  A. The drug or other substance has a low potential for abuse relative to the drugs or other substance in schedule III.
  B. The drug or other substance has a currently accepted medical use in treatment in the United States.
  C. Abuse of the drug or other substance may lead to limited physical dependence or psychological dependence relative to the drugs or other substances in schedule III.

Schedule V
  A. The drug or other substance has a low potential for abuse relative to the drugs or other substance in schedule IV.
  B. The drug or other substance has a currently accepted medical use in treatment in the United States.
  C. Abuse of the drug or other substance may lead to limited physical dependence or psychological dependence relative to the drugs or other substances in Schedule IV.

Source: Drug Enforcement Administration, U.S. Department of Justice.

Box 1.2 Federal Trafficking Penalties

Drug/Schedule	Quantity	Penalties	Quantity	Penalties
Cocaine (Schedule II)	500–4999 g	*First Offense:* Not less than 5 yrs, and not more than 40 yrs. If death or serious injury, not less than 20 or more than life. Fine of not more than $2 million if an individual, $5 million if not an individual.	5 kg or more	*First Offense:* Not less than 10 yrs, and not more than life. If death or serious injury, not less than 20 or more than life. Fine of not more than $4 million if an individual, $10 million if not an individual.
Cocaine Base (Schedule II)	5–49 g mixture		50 g or more mixture	
Fentanyl (Schedule II)	40–399 g mixture		400 g or more mixture	
Fentanyl Analogue (Schedule I)	10–99 g mixture		100 g or more mixture	
Heroin (Schedule I)	100–999 g mixture	*Second Offense:* Not less than 10 yrs, and not more than life. If death or serious injury, life imprisonment. Fine of not more than $4 million if an individual, $10 million if not an individual.	1 kg or more mixture	*Second Offense:* Not less than 20 yrs, and not more than life. If death or serious injury, life imprisonment. Fine of not more than $8 million if an individual, $20 million if not an individual.
LSD (Schedule I)	1–9 g mixture		10 g or more mixture	
Methamphetamine (Schedule II)	5–49 g pure or 50–499 g mixture		50 g or more pure or 500 g or more mixture	
PCP (Schedule II)	10–99 g pure or 100–999 g mixture		100 g or more pure or 1 kg or more mixture	*2 or More Prior Offenses:* Life imprisonment

Drug/Schedule	Quantity	Penalties
Other Schedule I & II drugs	Any amount	*First Offense:* Not more than 20 yrs. If death or serious injury, not less than 20 yrs, or more than life. Fine $1 million if an individual, $5 million if not an individual.
Flunitrazepam (Schedule IV)	1 g or more	*Second Offense:* Not more than 30 yrs. If death or serious injury, not less than life. Fine $2 million if an individual, $10 million if not an individual.
Other Schedule III drugs	Any amount	*First Offense:* Not more than 5 years. Fine not more than $250,000 if an individual, $1 million if not an individual.
Flunitrazepam (Schedule IV)	30 to 999 mg	*Second Offense:* Not more than 10 yrs. Fine not more than $500,000 if an individual, $2 million if not an individual.
All other Schedule IV drugs	Any amount	*First Offense:* Not more than 3 years. Fine not more than $250,000 if an individual, $1 million if not an individual.
Flunitrazepam (Schedule IV)	Less than 30 mg	*Second Offense:* Not more than 6 yrs. Fine not more than $500,000 if an individual, $2 million if not an individual.
All Schedule V drugs	Any amount	*First Offense:* Not more than 1 yr. Fine not more than $100,000 if an individual, $250,000 if not an individual.
		Second Offense: Not more than 2 yrs. Fine not more than $200,000 if an individual, $500,000 if not an individual.

Source: Drug Enforcement Administration, U.S. Department of Justice.

Box 1.3 Federal Trafficking Penalties—Marijuana

Drug	Quantity	First Offense	Second Offense
Marijuana	1,000 kg or more mixture; or 1,000 or more plants	• Not less than 10 years, not more than life • If death or serious injury, not less than 20 years, not more than life • Fine not more than $4 million if an individual, $10 million if other than an individual	• Not less than 20 years, not more than life • If death or serious injury, mandatory life • Fine not more than $8 million if an individual, $20 million if other than an individual
Marijuana	100 kg to 999 kg mixture; or 100 to 999 plants	• Not less than 5 years, not more than 40 years • If death or serious injury, not less than 20 years, not more than life • Fine not more than $2 million if an individual, $5 million if other than an individual	• Not less than 10 years, not more than life • If death or serious injury, mandatory life • Fine not more than $4 million if an individual, $10 million if other than an individual
Marijuana	More than 10 kg hashish; 50 to 99 kg mixture More than 1 kg of hashish oil; 50 to 99 plants	• Not less than 20 years • If death or serious injury, not less than 20 years, not more than life • Fine $1 million if an individual, $5 million if other than an individual	• Not less than 30 years • If death or serious injury, mandatory life • Fine $2 million if an individual, $10 million if other than an individual
Marijuana Hashish Hashish Oil	1 to 49 plants; less than 50 kg mixture 10 kg or less 1 kg or less	• Not more than 5 years • Fine not more than $250,000, $1 million if other than an individual	• Not more than 10 years • Fine $500,000 if an individual, $2 million if other than an individual

Source: Drug Enforcement Administration, U.S. Department of Justice.

Thirty Years of America's Drug War: A Chronology

Frontline—Public Broadcasting Service

Available online at http://www.pbs.org/wgbh/pages/frontline/shows/drugs/cron/.

1960s *Recreational drug use rises in United States.*   In the late 1960s recreational drug use becomes fashionable among young, white, middle-class Americans. The social stigmatization previously associated with drugs lessens as their use becomes more mainstream. Drug use becomes representative of protest and social rebellion in the era's atmosphere of political unrest.

1968 *Bureau of Narcotics and Dangerous Drugs is founded.*   The Johnson administration consolidates several drug agencies into the Justice Dept.'s Bureau of Narcotics and Dangerous Drugs (BNDD). The move is intended to diminish turf wars between the various agencies, but tensions between the BNDD and Customs continue.

1969 *Study links crime and heroin addiction.*   Psychiatrist Dr. Robert DuPont conducts urinalysis of everyone entering the D.C. jail system in August of 1969. He finds 44 percent test positive for heroin. DuPont convinces the city's Mayor Walter Washington to allow him to provide methadone to heroin addicts.

1969 (Sept. 21) *Operation Intercept essentially closes the Mexican border.* In an attempt to reduce marijuana smuggling from Mexico, the Customs Dept., under Commissioner Myles Ambrose, subjects every vehicle crossing the Mexican border to a three-minute inspection. The operation lasts two weeks and wreaks economic havoc on both sides of the border. Mexico agrees to more aggressively attack marijuana trade, but the operation didn't seriously impact the flow of marijuana into the United States.

1970   *NORML is founded.*   The National Organization for the Reform of Marijuana Laws (NORML) is founded by Keith Stroup. The group lobbies for decriminalization of marijuana.

1970   *Narcotics Treatment Administration is founded.*   The Nixon administration provides funds to allow Dr. Robert DuPont to expand his methadone program in Washington, D.C. The program is controversial because some believe methadone to be nothing more than a substitute for heroin, and others feel there are racial undertones behind the effort. However, one year after the program begins, burglaries in D.C. decrease by 41 percent.

1970   (October 27) *Congress passes the Comprehensive Drug Abuse Prevention and Control Act.*   This law consolidates previous drug laws and reduces penalties for marijuana possession. It also strengthens law enforcement by allowing police to conduct "no-knock" searches. This act includes the Controlled Substances Act, which establishes five categories ("schedules") for regulating drugs based on their medicinal value and potential for addiction.

1971   (May) *Soldiers in Vietnam develop heroin addiction.*   Congressmen Robert Steele (R-CT) and Morgan Murphy (D-IL) release an explosive report on the growing heroin epidemic among U.S. servicemen in Vietnam.

1971   (June 17) *Nixon declares war on drugs.*   At a press conference Nixon names drug abuse as "public enemy number one in the United States." He announces the creation of the Special Action Office for Drug Abuse Prevention (SAODAP), to be headed by Dr. Jerome Jaffe, a leading methadone treatment specialist. During the Nixon era, for the only time in the history of the war on drugs, the majority of funding goes towards treatment, rather than law enforcement.

1971   (September) *Operation Golden Flow goes into effect in order to attack habits of U.S. servicemen.*   In June 1971, the U.S. military announces they will begin urinalysis of all returning servicemen. The program goes into effect in September and the results are favorable: only 4.5 percent of the soldiers test positive for heroin.

1972   (January) *The Office of Drug Abuse Law Enforcement is founded.* The Nixon Administration creates the Office of Drug Abuse Law Enforcement (ODALE) to establish joint federal/local task forces to fight the drug trade at the street level. Myles Ambrose is appointed director.

1972   *The French Connection is broken up.*   U.S. and French law enforcement initiate a series of successful busts of the "French Connection," a Marseilles-based heroin industry controlled by Corsican gangsters and the U.S. Mafia. The results are soon evident in a heroin shortage on the U.S. East Coast.

1973   (July) *The Drug Enforcement Administration is established.*   President Nixon sets up this "super agency" to handle all aspects of the drug problem. The DEA consolidates agents from the BNDD, Customs, the CIA and ODALE. The administrator of the new agency is John R. Bartels.

1974   (August 9) *President Nixon resigns.*   The new Ford administration is preoccupied with inflation, jobs and an energy crisis. The DEA remains the legacy of Nixon's war on drugs.

1975   (September) *Ford administration releases White Paper on Drug Abuse.* The Domestic Council Drug Abuse Task Force releases a report that recommends that "priority in Federal efforts in both supply and demand reduction be directed toward those drugs which inherently pose a greater risk to the individual and to society." The White Paper names marijuana a "low priority drug" in contrast to heroin, amphetamines and mixed barbiturates.

1975   (November 22) *Large cocaine seizure indicates significant growth of cocaine trade.*   Colombian police seize 600 kilos of cocaine from a small plane at the Cali airport—the largest cocaine seizure to date. In response, drug traffickers begin a vendetta—"Medellin Massacre." Forty people die in Medellin on one weekend. This event signals the new power of Colombia's cocaine industry, headquartered in Medellin.

1976   *Carter campaigns on the decriminalization of marijuana.*   Noting that several states had already decriminalized marijuana, Jimmy Carter campaigns in favor of relinquishing federal criminal penalties for possession of up to one ounce of marijuana. Carter's drug czar, Dr. Peter Bourne, does not view marijuana, or even cocaine, as a serious public health threat.

1976   (August) *Anti-drug parents' movement begins.*   Troubled by the presence of marijuana at her 13-year-old daughter's birthday party, Keith Schuchard and her neighbor Sue Rusche form Families in Action, the first parents' organization designed to fight teenage drug abuse. Schuchard writes a letter to Dr. Robert DuPont, then head of the National Institute of Drug Abuse, which leads DuPont to abandon his support for decriminalization.

1977   *Media glamorizes cocaine use.*   A May 30, 1977, *Newsweek* story on cocaine is later accused to have glamorized the drug's effects and underestimated its dangers. The story reports that "Among hostesses in the smart sets of Los Angeles and New York, a little cocaine, like Dom Perignon and Beluga caviar, is now de rigueur at dinners. Some partygivers pass it around along with the canapés on silver trays . . . the user experiences a feeling of potency, of confidence, of energy."

1978   *Asset forfeiture introduced.*   The Comprehensive Drug Abuse Prevention and Control Act is amended. It now allows law enforcement to seize all money and/or "other things of value furnished or intended to be furnished by any person in exchange for a controlled substance [and] all proceeds traceable to such an exchange."

1979   *Carlos Lehder purchases property on Norman's Cay.*   Carlos Lehder, a key member of the alliance that would become the Medellin cartel, revolutionizes the cocaine trade with his purchase of 165 acres on the Bahamian island of Norman's Cay. Lehder is the first to use small planes for transporting the drug. He uses the island as a hub for planes to refuel between Colombia and the United States.

1979   (July 11) *Cocaine trade becomes increasingly violent.*   A deadly shootout between Colombian traffickers in broad daylight at Miami's Dadeland Mall brings the savagery of the Colombian cocaine lords to the attention of U.S. law enforcement.

1981   *Rise of Medellin cartel.*   The alliance between the Ochoa family, Pablo Escobar, Carlos Lehder and Jose Gonzalo Rodriguez Gacha strengthens into what will become known as the "Medellin cartel."

The traffickers cooperate in the manufacturing, distribution and marketing of their cocaine. The kidnapping of Marta Ochoa by Colombian guerrillas consolidates the alliance. The traffickers form a group named MAS, a Spanish acronym for "Death to Kidnappers," announcing the imminent execution of any guerrilla kidnappers. Marta Ochoa is released without harm several months later.

1981   *U.S.-Colombia extradition treaty ratified.*   The United States and Colombia ratify a bilateral extradition treaty, which they had previously approved in 1979. When Reagan assumes office and prioritizes the war on drugs, extradition becomes the greatest fear of the Colombian traffickers.

1982   *Downfall of Norman's Cay.*   In response to U.S. pressure, the Bahamian government begins to crack down on Carlos Lehder's operation on Norman's Cay. Lehder moves his residence from the island in 1982, but operations continue for another year.

1982   *Deal between Escobar and Noriega allows cocaine transport through Panama.*   Panamanian general Manuel Noriega and Pablo Escobar cut a deal which allows Escobar to ship cocaine through Panama for $100,000 per load. The two had met in 1981 when Noriega mediated negotiations for the release of Marta Ochoa.

1982   (January 28) *South Florida Drug Task Force is formed.*   Outraged by the drug trade's increasing violence in their city, Miami citizens lobby the federal government for help. Reagan responds by creating a cabinet-level task force, the Vice President's Task Force on South Florida. Headed by George Bush, it combines agents from the DEA, Customs, FBI, ATF, IRS, Army and Navy to mobilize against drug traffickers. Reagan later creates several other regional task forces throughout the United States.

1982   (March) *Pablo Escobar is elected to the Colombian Congress.*   Escobar cultivates an image of "Robin Hood" by building low-income housing, handing out money in Medellin slums and appearing throughout the city accompanied by Catholic priests. Escobar is elected an alternate representative from Envigado, but he's driven out of Congress in 1983 by Colombia's crusading Minister of Justice, Rodrigo Lara Bonilla.

1982   (March 9) *Largest cocaine seizure ever raises U.S. awareness of Medellin cartel.*   The seizure of 3,906 pounds of cocaine, valued at over $100 million wholesale, from a Miami International Airport hangar permanently alters U.S. law enforcement's approach towards the drug trade. They realize Colombian traffickers must be working together because no single trafficker could be behind a shipment this large.

1984   *Nancy Reagan's "Just Say No" Movement begins.*   Nancy Reagan's "Just Say No" anti-drug campaign becomes a centerpiece of the Reagan administration's anti-drug campaign. The movement focuses on white, middle-class children and is funded by corporate and private donations.

1984   (March 10) *Tranquilandia bust.*   By tracking the illegal sale of massive amounts of ether to Colombia, the DEA and Colombian police discover Tranquilandia, a laboratory operation deep in the Colombian jungle. In the subsequent bust, law enforcement officials destroy 14 laboratory complexes, which contain 13.8 metric tons of cocaine, 7 airplanes, and 11,800 drums of chemicals, conservatively estimated at $1.2 billion. This bust confirms the consolidation of the Medellin cartel's manufacturing operation.

1984   (April 30) *Assassination of the Colombian attorney general fuels the extradition controversy.*   Colombian Minister of Justice Rodrigo Lara Bonilla, who had crusaded against the Medellin cartel, is assassinated by a gang of motorcycle thugs. President Belisario Betancur, who opposed extradition, announces "We will extradite Colombians." Carlos Lehder is the first to be put on the list. The crackdown forces the Ochoas, Escobar and Rodriguez Gacha to flee to Panama for several months. A few months later, Escobar is indicted for Lara Bonilla's murder and names the Ochoas and Rodriguez Gacha as material witnesses.

1984   (July 17) *The Drug War and Cold War collide.*   The *Washington Times* runs a story which details DEA informant Barry Seal's successful infiltration into the Medellin cartel's operations in Panama. The story was leaked by Oliver North to show the Nicaraguan Sandinistas' involvement in the drug trade. Ten days later, Carlos Lehder, Pablo Escobar, Jorge Ochoa and Jose Gonzalo Rodriguez Gacha are indicted by a Miami federal grand jury based on evidence obtained by Seal. In February 1986, Seal is assassinated in Baton Rouge by gunmen hired by the cartel.

1984 (Fall) *Cartel returns to Medellin.* Escobar, Gacha, Juan David and Fabio Ochoa are all spotted in Medellin, signaling the end of the government crackdown. The cartel begins to regain its command over the city.

1984 (November 6) *"Bust of the Century" in Mexico.* The DEA and Mexican officials raid a large marijuana cultivation and processing complex in the Chihuahua desert owned by kingpin Rafael Caro Quintero. Seven thousand campesinos work at the complex, where between 5000 and 10,000 tons of high-grade marijuana worth $2.5 billion is found and destroyed. *Time* magazine calls this "the bust of the century" and it reveals the existence of Mexico's sophisticated marijuana smuggling industry.

1984 (November 15) *Jorge Ochoa is arrested in Spain.* Spanish police arrest Jorge Ochoa on a U.S. warrant and both the U.S. and Colombia apply for his extradition. The Medellin cartel publicly threatens to murder 5 Americans for every Colombian extradition. The Spanish courts ultimately rule in favor of Colombia's request and Ochoa is deported. He serves a month in jail on charges of bull-smuggling before he is paroled.

1985 (January 5) *Colombia extradites first traffickers to the United States.* Colombia extradites four drug traffickers to Miami. Within days, the United States becomes aware of a Medellin cartel "hit list" which includes embassy members, their families, U.S. businessmen and journalists.

mid-1980s *Cocaine transport routes move into Mexico.* Because of the South Florida Drug Task Force's successful crackdown on drugs, traffickers turn to Mexican marijuana smugglers to move cocaine across the 2000-mile U.S.-Mexican border. By the mid-1980s it becomes the major transportation route for cocaine into the United States.

1985 (February) *DEA agent Enrique Camarena is kidnapped and murdered in Mexico.* Camarena's disappearance spotlights the pervasive drug corruption in Mexican law enforcement. The Mexicans' lack of cooperation leads Commissioner of Customs William Von Raab to order a six-day Operation Intercept–style crackdown on the Mexican border. Camarena's body is found within a week of the border closing, but evidence of a coverup by Mexican officials is clear.

1985   (July 23) *Colombian Superior Court Judge is assassinated.*   Bogota Superior Court Judge Tulio Manuel Castro Gil, who had indicted Escobar for the murder of Lara Bonilla, is assassinated as he climbs into a taxi. Throughout 1985 judicial harassment and intimidation becomes commonplace in Colombia.

1985   (November 6) *Attack on Colombian Supreme Court.*   Upping the ante in the battle against extradition, guerrillas linked to the Medellin cartel attack the Colombian Palace of Justice. At least 95 people are killed in the 26-hour siege, including 11 Supreme Court justices. Many court documents, including all pending extradition requests, are destroyed by fire.

1985   *Crack explodes in New York.*   Crack, a potent form of smokeable cocaine developed in the early 1980s, begins to flourish in the New York region. A November 1985 *New York Times* cover story brings the drug to national attention. Crack is cheap and powerfully addictive and it devastates inner-city neighborhoods.

1986   (June 19) *Death of Len Bias.*   The death of promising college basketball star Len Bias from a cocaine overdose stuns the nation. Ensuing media reports highlight the health risks of cocaine; drugs become a hot political issue.

1986   (October 27) *Reagan signs The Anti-Drug Abuse Act of 1986.*   Reagan signs an enormous omnibus drug bill, which appropriates $1.7 billion to fight the drug crisis. $97 million is allocated to build new prisons, $200 million for drug education and $241 million for treatment. The bill's most consequential action is the creation of mandatory minimum penalties for drug offenses. Possession of at least one kilogram of heroin or five kilograms of cocaine is punishable by at least ten years in prison. In response to the crack epidemic, the sale of five grams of the drug leads to a mandatory five-year sentence. Mandatory minimums become increasingly criticized over the years for promoting significant racial disparities in the prison population, because of the differences in sentencing for crack vs. powder cocaine.

1986   (November 18) *United States indicts the Medellin cartel leaders.*   A U.S. federal grand jury in Miami releases the indictment of the Ochoas, Pablo Escobar, Carlos Lehder and Jose Gonzalo Rodriguez Gacha under the RICO statute. The indictment names the Medellin cartel as the largest cocaine smuggling organization in the world.

1986   (December 17) *Murder of newspaperman outrages Colombian press.* Guillermo Cano Isaza, editor-in-chief of *El Espectador*, is assassinated while driving home from work. Cano frequently wrote in favor of stiffer penalties for drug traffickers. His murder leads to a national outrage comparable to the assassination of Lara Bonilla, and a subsequent government crackdown on traffickers.

1987   (February 3) *Carlos Lehder is captured and extradited.*   Carlos Lehder is captured by the Colombian National Police at a safe house owned by Pablo Escobar in the mountains outside of Medellin. He is extradited to the United States the next day. On May 19, 1988, Lehder is convicted of drug smuggling and sentenced to life in prison without parole, plus an additional 135 years.

1987   (June 25) *Colombia annuls extradition treaty.*   On May 28, the Colombian Supreme Court, having endured a barrage of personal threats from the traffickers, rules by a vote of 13 to 12 to annul the extradition treaty with the United States.

1987   (November 21) *Jorge Ochoa is arrested in Colombia.*   Ochoa is held in prison on the bull-smuggling charge for which he was extradited from Spain. Twenty-four hours later a gang of thugs arrive at the house of Juan Gomez Martinez, the editor of Medellin's daily newspaper *El Colombiano.* They present Martinez with a communiqué signed by "The Extraditables," which threatens execution of Colombian political leaders if Ochoa is extradited. On December 30, Ochoa is released under dubious legal circumstances. In January 1988, the murder of Colombian Attorney General Carlos Mauro Hoyos is claimed by the Extraditables.

1988   *Carlos Salinas de Gortari is elected president of Mexico.*   At a 1988 meeting, President-elect Bush tells President-elect Salinas he must prove to the U.S. Congress that he is cooperating in the drug war — a process called certification. The United States pressures Mexico to arrest Miguel Angel Felix Gallardo, the drug lord believed to have been responsible for the murder of DEA Agent Enrique Camarena.

1988   (February 5) *Noriega indicted in United States.*   A federal grand jury in Miami issues an indictment against Panamanian general Manuel Noriega for drug trafficking. Noriega had allowed the Medellin cartel to launder money and build cocaine laboratories in Panama.

1989   (Winter) *Office of National Drug Control Policy is created.*   President Bush appoints William Bennett to lead the new Office of National Drug Control Policy (ONDCP). As drug 'czar' he campaigns to make drug abuse socially unacceptable, an approach he calls denormalization. Federal spending on treatment and low enforcement increase under Bennett's tenure, but treatment remains less than one-third of the total budget.

1988   (July 2) *Murder of Mexican presidential election monitors.*   On the eve of the Mexican presidential election between Carlos Salinas and Cuahtemoc Cardenas, two key Cardenas aides are found shot to death in Mexico City. The two had been responsible for ensuring that the elections would be clean and fair. It is widely believed that Cardenas actually won the election and that vote fraud by the PRI was responsible for Salinas's election.

1989   (April 8) *Miguel Angel Felix Gallardo is arrested in Mexico.*   Guillermo Gonzalez Calderoni leads a team of federal agents who arrest the drug lord in a residential suburb of Guadalajara. Gallardo is imprisoned on charges relating to Enrique Camarena's kidnapping and murder. His nephews, the Arellano-Felix brothers, inherit part of his drug-trafficking empire.

1989   (April 14) *Kerry releases congressional report on Contra-drug connection.*   A congressional subcommittee on Narcotics, Law Enforcement and Foreign Policy, chaired by Senator John Kerry (D-MA), finds that U.S. efforts to combat drug trafficking were undermined by the Reagan administration's fear of jeopardizing its objectives in the Nicaraguan civil war. The report concludes that the administration ignored evidence of drug trafficking by the Contras and continued to provide them with aid.

1989   (August 18) *Assassination of Colombian presidential candidate.* Luis Carlos Galan, a presidential candidate who spoke in favor of extradition, is assassinated at a campaign rally near Bogota. That evening, President Virgilio Barco Vargas issues an emergency decree reestablishing the policy of extradition. In response, "the Extraditables" declare all-out war against the Colombian government, and begin bombing/murder campaign that would last until January 1991.

1989   (December 15) *Medellin cartel leader is killed.*   Jose Gonzalo Rodriguez Gacha is killed by Colombian police in a raid on his ranch in Tolu.

1989   (December 20) *United States invades Panama*   For 22 days, General Manuel Noriega eludes capture by the U.S. military. After seeking asylum in the Vatican embassy he eventually surrenders to the DEA on January 3, 1990, in Panama and is brought to Miami the next day. On July 10, 1992, Noriega is convicted on eight counts of drug trafficking, money laundering and racketeering, and sentenced to 40 years in federal prison.

1990   (January 25) *Bush proposes 50 percent increase in military spending on war on drugs.*   President Bush proposes to add an additional $1.2 billion to the budget for the war on drugs, including a 50 percent increase in military spending.

1990   (September) *Ochoa brothers surrender.*   Colombian President Cesar Gaviria Trujillo offers the traffickers reduced prison sentences to be served in Colombia, in order to entice them to surrender. All three Ochoa brothers surrender to the Colombian police by January 1991.

1991   (June 19) *New Colombian Constitution bans extradition and Escobar surrenders.*   In a secret vote, the Colombian assembly votes 51 to 13 to ban extradition in a new Constitution, to take effect July 5. The same day Pablo Escobar surrenders to Colombian police.

1991   (November) *Massacre of Mexican Federal Police.*   While attempting to stop an air shipment of Colombian cocaine, Mexican Federal Police are killed by Mexican army members, in the pay of the traffickers. Embarrassed, President Salinas orders an investigation, which results in the imprisonment of a Mexican general. He is quietly released several months later.

1992   *Carlos Salinas imposes the first written regulations on DEA officers in Mexico.*   The regulations limit the number of agents in Mexico, designate certain cities in which they must live, deny the officers diplomatic immunity, require all information to be turned over to Mexican authorities, and prohibit agents to carry weapons.

1993   (May 24) *Cardinal assassinated by the Arellano-Felix Organization.* Cardinal Juan Posadas Ocampo, the archbishop of Guadalajara, is assassinated at the Guadalajara airport by San Diego gang members hired by the Arellano-Felix Organization to kill a rival trafficker.

1993   (November 17) *NAFTA is passed and signed into law.*   President Clinton signs the North American Free Trade Agreement, which results in an enormous increase in legitimate trade across the U.S.-Mexican border. The volume of trade makes it more difficult for U.S. Customs officials to find narcotics hidden within legitimate goods.

1993   (December 2) *Pablo Escobar killed.*   Pablo Escobar is finally hunted down by the Colombian police with the aid of U.S. technology. The technology could recognize Escobar's voice on a cell phone and give police an estimated location of where he is. They find his safe house and kill Escobar as he attempts to flee with one of his bodyguards.

1995   (May) *U.S. Sentencing Commission recommends revising mandatory minimums.*   The U.S. Sentencing Commission, which administers federal sentencing guidelines, releases a report that notes the racial disparities in cocaine vs. crack sentencing. The commission proposes reducing the discrepancy, but for the first time in history, Congress overrides their recommendation.

1995   (Summer) *Top Cali cartel members arrested.*   In a series of arrests during the summer of 1995, five leaders of the Cali cartel are captured. The Cali cartel had become the most powerful drug-trafficking organization in Colombia after the dismantling of the Medellin cartel. By September 1996, all of the Cali kingpins are imprisoned.

1996   (February) *Clinton names General Barry McCaffrey as drug czar.* In his State of the Union address, President Clinton nominates Army General Barry McCaffrey, a veteran of Vietnam and Desert Storm, as director of ONDCP. Two days later, the appointment is confirmed by the Senate without debate.

1996   *Ochoas released from prison.*   Juan David and Jorge Luis Ochoa are released after serving five-year prison sentences for drug trafficking in July. Later, their younger brother Fabio Ochoa is also released.

1997   (September 24) *Ramon Arellano-Felix indicted.*   A federal grand jury in San Diego indicts Ramon Arellano-Felix on charges of drug smuggling. The same day, he is added to the FBI's 10 Most Wanted List.

1998   (May) *Operation Casablanca.*   Operation Casablanca, the largest money-laundering probe in U.S. history, leads to the indictment of 3 Mexican and 4 Venezuelan banks, and 167 individual arrests. Mexico and Venezuela are furious over the undercover operation, which they consider a threat to their national sovereignty. John Hensley oversaw the operation for the U.S. Customs Service.

1998   (July) *U.S. and Mexican Attorneys General sign Brownsville Agreement.*   As a result of Mexico's anger about U.S. actions in Operation Casablanca, Attorneys General Janet Reno and Jorge Madrazo Cuellar draft the Brownsville Agreement. Both nations pledge to inform each other about sensitive cross-border law enforcement operations.

1999   (October 13) *Fabio Ochoa rearrested in Operation Millennium.*   In a series of raids named "Operation Millennium," law enforcement agents in Mexico, Colombia and Ecuador arrest 31 for drug trafficking, including Fabio Ochoa. Ochoa is indicted in a Ft. Lauderdale court for importing cocaine into the United States. The United States requests his extradition in December 1999.

2000   (May 11) *Indictments against Benjamin and Ramon Arellano-Felix are unsealed.*   The Arellano-Felix brothers are charged with 10 counts of drug trafficking, conspiracy, money laundering and aiding and abetting violent crimes. The U.S. State Department offers a $2 million reward for information leading to their arrest and conviction.

2000   (August) *Clinton delivers $1.3 billion in aid to help Colombia combat drug traffickers.*   To assist Colombian president Andres Pastrana's $7.5 billion *Plan Colombia*, President Clinton delivers $1.3 billion in U.S. aid to fund 60 combat helicopters and training for the Colombian military, among other initiatives.

[*Ed. note:*]

Events occurring after the publication of the preceding chronology include:

2001   John P. Walters is sworn in as the Director of the White House Office of National Drug Control Policy (December 7).

2002   President Bush and Mr. Walters release the *National Drug Control Strategy*, which sets aggressive goals of a 10 percent reduction in teen and adult drug use in two years and a 25 percent reduction in teen and adult drug use in five years.

PART TWO

Foundation

Can any policy, however high-minded, be moral if it leads to widespread corruption, imprisons so many, has so racist an effect, destroys our inner cities, wreaks havoc on misguided and vulnerable individuals and brings death and destruction to foreign countries?

Milton Friedman
New York Times
January 11, 1998

Drug use degrades human character, and a purposeful, self-governing society ignores its people's character at great peril.

William J. Bennett
National Drug Control Strategy
1989

Philosophical Underpinnings

Robert J. MacCoun and Peter Reuter

Robert J. MacCoun is a professor of law and public policy at the Richard and Rhoda Goldman School of Public Policy at the University of California at Berkeley. Peter Reuter is a professor in the School of Public Policy and in the Department of Criminology at the University of Maryland.

This selection was excerpted from "Philosophical Underpinnings" in *Drug War Heresies: Learning from Other Vices, Times, and Places* (New York: Cambridge University Press, 2001).

Many of the arguments in the legalization debate involve empirical matters—either evaluative descriptions of the status quo or predictions about the likely consequences of a change in policy. But purely moral arguments also play a prominent role. Many prohibitionists assert that drugs should be banned because drug use per se is immoral. On the other side, many legalizers and decriminalizers argue that U.S. drug laws are hypocritical, or too draconian, or that they infringe on an individual's right to take drugs. Nonempirical arguments are outnumbered by empirical assertions (not necessarily accurate) in American newspapers, but quantity says nothing about the force or conviction with which the arguments were believed or felt. Nor does quantity reveal the origins of the authors' views; empirical claims may serve as a means of bolstering an essentially values-based conviction. Additionally, it may be that the kinds of people who write op-ed essays (especially those that get published) are more enamored of, or at least more fluent in, empirical argumentation. Scrolling through the messages on any of the growing number of pro-

and antidrug discussion groups on the Internet, one can find a much greater reliance on nonempirical, morals-based arguments.

The debate cannot be neatly parsed by distinguishing facts and values; philosophers and scientists have long rejected a strict fact-value dichotomy as untenable (see Cole, 1992). Values affect the selection, measurement, interpretation, and evaluation of research findings (MacCoun, 1998b). Moreover, the very belief that one might use facts to help adjudicate moral issues is itself a moral position (e.g., it is a central tenet of utilitarianism). Thus, before tackling the empirical claims, we briefly survey the underlying philosophical issues. Philosophical positions are not always explicit in the policy debate, but they nevertheless shape the politics of drug policy formation. Moreover, people's moral views (e.g., their respect for drug laws) influence the effectiveness of drug policies.

CONSEQUENTIALIST VS. DEONTOLOGICAL ARGUMENTS

The utilitarian tradition, originating in the works of Jeremy Bentham and John Stuart Mill, enjoins us to evaluate acts and rules by their consequences—specifically, by their net contribution to human utility. The term *utilitarian* carries considerable intellectual baggage and has sinister overtones for many. Most readers will have encountered thought experiments showing how chilling conclusions can follow from seemingly innocent utilitarian premises. (A surgeon has five patients facing death; each needs a different organ for transplant, but none have been donated. In walks an unwitting, healthy young flower deliveryman. . . .) Over a century of debate, the tradition has yielded many variants, each sprouting up as needed in response to utilitarianism's many critics. Utilitarian theories vary with respect to the proper objects under scrutiny (e.g., individual acts vs. rules for acting), the interpretations of utility (e.g., happiness, welfare, or the more content-free operational definitions of modern economics), and units of analysis (momentary experiences vs. individual actors vs. aggregate societies; see Parfit, 1984). We will sidestep these philosophical pot-holes by offering in place of utilitarianism a more general notion, *consequentialism*—the claim that it is appropriate to evaluate certain acts or rules by evaluating their empirical (i.e., observable) conse-quences.

Most closely associated with Immanuel Kant, *deontological* posi-tions assert that certain moral obligations hold irrespective of their empirical consequences. Most of the injunctions of the world's lead-ing religious traditions (e.g., thou shalt not kill) are deontological in nature, although as Blaise Pascal pointed out, the choice between salvation and damnation certainly offers consequentialist food for thought. Inherent sinfulness is frequently the argument against tol-eration of homosexuality and prostitution but less frequently against drug use, perhaps because though psychoactive plant use predates Biblical times by millennia, the New Testament is silent on the topic. (Drunkenness is condemned, but moderate alcohol consumption of course figures prominently in the story.) A particularly eloquent deon-tological statement against drug use comes from James Q. Wilson (1990, 1993):

> [I]f we believe—as I do—that dependency on certain mind-altering drugs *is* a moral issue and that their illegality rests in part on their immorality, then legalizing them undercuts, if it does not eliminate altogether, the moral message. That message is at the root of the distinction between nicotine and cocaine. Both are highly addictive; both have harmful physical effects. But we treat the two drugs dif-ferently, not simply because nicotine is so widely used as to be beyond the reach of effective prohibition, but because its use does not destroy the user's essential humanity. Tobacco shortens one's life, *cocaine debases it*. Nicotine alters one's habits, *cocaine alters one's soul*. The heavy use of crack, unlike the heavy use of tobacco, corrodes those natural sentiments of sympathy and duty that con-stitute our human nature and make possible our social life (Wilson, 1990, p. 26; italics added).

Deontological arguments are at least as popular on the legalization side of the debate, most prominently among libertarians (e.g., Richards, 1982; Szasz, 1974, 1987). Thomas Szasz endorses two variants of the libertarian position on drugs in the following quote:

> I believe that we also have a right to eat, drink, or inject a substance—any substance—not because we are sick and want it to cure us, nor because a government-supported medical authority claims that it will be good for us, but simply because we want to take it and because the government—as our servant rather than our master—does not have the right to meddle in our private dietary and drug affairs (Szasz, 1987, p. 349).

The affirmative argument is that we have a right to use drugs. One can readily assert a *natural* right to drug use, but it is more challenging to identify a comparable *positive* right to drug use, a right protected by the U.S. Constitution or statutory law.[1] A class of narrow exceptions involves the religious use of psychedelics by organized religious groups. The negative argument is that government has no right or standing to prohibit the ingestion of drugs (or other acts involving one's own body), so long as no one else is being harmed in the process. This latter point deserves emphasis. Few if any libertarians believe that the law must tolerate acts by drug users that cause serious and direct harm to others (see the discussion that follows); they simply assert that such acts already fall under the purview of acceptable nondrug criminal laws.

Individuals (other than philosophers) don't fit neatly into consequentialist or deontological categories. These terms refer to types of arguments, not necessarily types of people, and most of us hold a mix of both types of views. Policy analysis tends toward consequentialist positions, but most people hold many categorical deontological beliefs. It is useful to think in terms of the *psychological weights* that people place on different arguments. We give arguments zero weight

---

1. Sweet and Harris (1998) provided a detailed examination of a possible unenumerated legal right to drug use under the Ninth Amendment.

if they appear completely irrelevant, but also if they appear morally repugnant (Elster, 1992; Fiske & Tetlock, 1997). At the other extreme, arguments can be decisive and "trump" or preempt all others; in such cases, the individual's views are frozen and largely impervious to counterargument or evidence. But research on the psychology of attitudes suggests that, in practice, these trump arguments are rare.[2] We now examine the philosophical sources for many of the considerations that need to be weighed.

THE LIBERAL TRADITION

John Stuart Mill

John Stuart Mill's *On Liberty* (1859/1947) is the starting point for contemporary debates on the legislation of morals. It is the cornerstone for the liberal tradition in moral and political philosophy, not to be confused with the term *liberal* as used in contemporary U.S. debates. Early in the essay, Mill articulates what has come to be known as the *harm principle*; it is worth quoting at length:

> [T]he sole end for which mankind are warranted, individually or collectively, in interfering with the liberty of action of any of their number, is self-protection. That the only purpose for which power can be rightfully exercised over any member of a civilized community, against his will, is to prevent harm to others. His own good, either physical or moral, is not a sufficient warrant. He cannot rightfully be compelled to do or forbear because it will be better for him to do so, because it will make him happier, because, in the opinion of others, to do so would be wise or even right. These are good

---

2. Unidimensional responses to multidimensional problems are not uncommon—we'll see that offenders sometimes choose crime that way—but the explanation often involves limited motivation or cognitive capacity rather than the press of moral convictions. A psychological implication is that overall assessments will be unstable, as weights are recomputed due to situational fluctuations in the relative salience of the various dimensions.

reasons for remonstrating with him, or reasoning with him, or per-
suading him, or entreating him, but not for compelling him, or
visiting him with any evil in case he would do otherwise. . . . The
only part of the conduct of anyone, for which he is amenable to
society, is that which concerns others. In the part which merely
concerns himself, his independence is, of right, absolute. Over himself, over his own body and mind, the individual is sovereign (pp.
144–5).

Mill justified the harm principle on utilitarian grounds, stating,
"Mankind are greater gainers by suffering each other to live as seems
good to themselves, than by compelling each to live as seems good
to the rest" (p. 148).[3] But as Skolnick (1992, p. 138) noted, "the
enduring influence of *On Liberty* and its harm principle is derived
less from some exquisite utilitarian summation than from Mill's intu-
itions about the despotic potential of government."

Joel Feinberg

Joel Feinberg's (1984, 1985, 1986, 1988) four-volume analysis of "the
moral limits of the criminal law" is arguably the leading contemporary exposition of the Mill tradition. Feinberg offered what he
believed was a more defensible statement of the harm principle:

It is always a good reason in support of penal legislation that it
would be effective in preventing (eliminating, reducing) harm to
persons other than the actor (the one prohibited from acting) *and*
there is no other means that is equally effective at no greater cost
to other values (1988, p. xix).

To this, Feinberg added an *offense principle*:

It is always a good reason in support of a proposed criminal pro-

3. Mill did not assert, as is sometimes assumed, a *natural right* to freedom interfer-
ence: "I forego any advantage which could be derived to my argument from the idea of
abstract right, as a thing independent of utility" (p. 145). Nevertheless, others have derived
Mill's principle from nonconsequentialist appeals to liberty or autonomy as intrinsic rights
or goods (see George, 1993).

hibition that it is necessary to prevent serious offense to persons other than the actor and would be an effective means to that end if enacted (1988, p. xix).

For Feinberg, "the harm and offense principles, duly clarified and qualified, between them exhaust the class of good reasons for criminal prohibitions" (p. xix); together, they characterize "the liberal position." (Omitting the offense principle produces the "extreme liberal position.") Much of his four-volume work is directed toward articulating the necessary clarifications and qualifications. Two are especially important. Feinberg's harm principle applies only to *wrongful harms*, which involve "setbacks to another's interests" that violate another's rights and not to *nonwrongful harms* (setbacks that do not violate the other's rights) or *nonharmful wrongs* (violations of another's rights that do not set back another's interests). Similarly, Feinberg's offenses are "caused by wrongful (right-violating) conduct of others," but not the larger class of "disliked mental states" not caused by right-violating conduct.

Drug Laws

Feinberg's offense principle is central to debates about pornography but seems largely irrelevant to the drug law debate. Conceivably certain acts committed in a state of intoxication might meet Feinberg's offense principle, but those are readily dealt with by various nondrug criminal laws (e.g., public nuisance and public decency laws). The harm principle, on the other hand, plays a crucial role in the drug legalization debate. Because the major theoretical alternatives to the liberal tradition are generally much less restrictive about the legislation of morality, one might argue a fortiori that if drug prohibition can be justified under the harm principle, it is even more acceptable under alternative moral schemes (see Moore, 1991, p. 532).

Thus, a key question for the justification of drug laws is whether drug use causes wrongful harms to others. For decades, the term *victimless crime* was used to characterize drug use, gambling, and prostitution. But in recent years, this term has been fading from use, and to the modern ear, it already sounds quaintly naïve, or even mildly offensive. This is more of an expansion in consciousness than in conscience, reflecting not puritanism but rather an increased awareness of what economists call the "externalities" of human affairs—the many ways in which our private conduct can impose costs on others. The recent focus on the health harms of passive smoking is a prominent instance.

That claim in itself might appear to meet the Mill/Feinberg harm criterion decisively, and indeed we think it almost certainly does. But there are several complications. First, Husak (1992), in a particularly sophisticated defense of a right to use drugs, argued that most of the harms drug use poses to others are not "wrongful" or "criminal" harms subject to the Mill/Feinberg criterion, because they do not violate others' moral rights. Husak was most persuasive in arguing that any increase in drug use under legalization would not in itself violate anyone's rights; we surely have no right that others not use drugs. Husak is less convincing in his challenge to "a moral right that the drug user be an attentive parent, a good neighbor, a proficient student, a reliable employee" (p. 166). As stated, this seems compelling, but Husak's way of framing the issue set up a straw man. The roles of parent, neighbor, student, and employee are too heterogeneous to form a meaningful set; the risks and responsibilities that accompany parenthood are entirely different from (and more compelling than) those that accompany the roles of student or employee. And even though most readers will share Husak's rejection of government-mandated productivity, that isn't what prohibiters are demanding—criminalizing reckless or irresponsible role conduct is surely very different from mandating exemplary conduct. At any rate, the question isn't whether all or even most forms of disutility caused by drug use violate moral rights—some of them do; the question is whether they are sufficient to justify drug prohibition.

Second, not every incident of drug use harms others; in fact, the vast majority do not. Indeed, though this is difficult to quantify with existing data, it is likely that many if not most drug users *never* do wrongful harm to others as a result of their using careers—bearing in mind that the majority of these careers are limited in duration and intensity. Rather, each incident of drug use is accompanied by a *risk* that others will be harmed; some users, substances, settings, and modalities of use are riskier than others, but in no case is the risk zero. Drug use is not distinct in this regard; many prohibited acts are associated with harm only probabilistically—running red lights, driving under the influence, and so on. Of course, this is true to some degree of most licit human activities. Unfortunately, there is no obvious threshold probability of harm to others beyond which activities should be legally prohibited. For example, alcohol consumption poses greater risks to nonusers (through violence, accidents, and neonatal effects) than marijuana does, yet the former is legal and the latter is not.

Finally, for a Millian policy analysis, establishing that drugs harm nonusers does not settle the question. Prohibiting drugs is costly, in direct expenditures, in foregone benefits, and in the opportunity costs of diverting resources and attention from other government activities. A policy that costs society more than the harms it mitigates is difficult to justify from a consequentialist perspective. A final complication is that drug prohibition may itself be the *cause* of many of these harms to others; consider, for example, the violence associated with illicit drug markets. This raises two questions regarding Feinberg's statement of the harm principle. First, is drug prohibition "effective in preventing (eliminating, reducing) harm to persons other than the actor" (1988, p. xix)? If prohibition is itself a source of harm to others, then one must ask whether its *net* effect is to reduce such harms. Second, is there "no other means that is equally effective at no greater cost to other values"?

Table 2.1 Major philosophical positions on prohibition

	Relevant criteria for prohibition?	
	Net reduction in harm to others	Net reduction in harm to users
Legal moralism	Not relevant	Not relevant
Strict libertarianism	Not relevant	Not relevant
Millian liberalism	Necessary	Not relevant
Soft paternalism	Sufficient, but not necessary	Sufficient if legal minor or judgmentally impaired
Hard paternalism	Sufficient, but not necessary	Sufficient

ALTERNATIVES TO LIBERALISM

Legal Paternalism

Table 2.1 compares the Mill position to other major alternatives. Perhaps the major contemporary alternative is *legal paternalism*, which Feinberg defines as the belief that "[It] is always a good reason in support of a prohibition that it is necessary to prevent harm (physical, psychological, or economic) to the actor himself" (1988, p. xix).[4] That drug use is potentially harmful to the user is beyond dispute; the risks include addiction (e.g., the suffering caused by withdrawal and craving), drug overdose, disease, drug-related accidents, criminal victimization, economic hardships, and social isolation. Note that these risks are considerably greater for some drugs (cocaine, PCP) than for others (marijuana, psilocybin) (Gable, 1993; Goldstein, 1994; Julien, 1995). But a coherent paternalism must surely weight the extent to which

4. A related but distinct notion is *legal perfectionism*, the belief that laws can and should play a role in positively shaping citizens for their individual benefit. Though liberal theorists (e.g., Rawls, 1971) are generally "antiperfectionist" in this sense, and leading perfectionists are nonliberals (George, 1993), there are some notable perfectionist liberals (e.g., Raz, 1986).

prohibition and its enforcement creates, enables, or augments these harms. As with harms to others, the key policy questions are whether prohibition produces a *net* reduction in harms to users themselves, and whether alternative policy regimes would more effectively reduce harms to users. . . . [W]e attribute primary causation for each of some fifty different harms to either drug use or drug laws and their enforcement. Many of these harms are primarily borne by users, and prohibition bears the primary (but not sole) responsibility for most of these harms. Nevertheless, many of the risks drugs pose to the user are psychopharmacological effects of drug use itself—exposure to external risks produced by diminished mental capacity and psychomotor coordination during intoxication and the more direct risks of addiction and other physical and psychological harms.

Mill himself recognized a paternalistic exception to the harm principle for children and the mentally disabled:

> It is perhaps necessary to say that this doctrine is meant to apply only to human beings in the maturity of their faculties. . . . Those who are still in a state to require being taken care of by others, must be protected against their own actions as well as against external injury (1859/1947, p. 145).

This position is sometimes known as *soft paternalism*; Feinberg (1986) questioned whether it is truly an exception to the harm principle. Moore (1991) argues that Mill's paternalistic exception "offers substantial room for justifying the use of state authority to regulate drug use." Mill's notion of mature faculties can be read as requiring at least some *minimal* capacity for rational choice. This minimal requirement is clearly met for adults who contemplate drug use for the first time, except perhaps those with severe retardation or mental illness. But the threshold won't be met if judgment is impaired by either intoxication or the "weaknesses of will" caused by addiction (Kleiman, 1992a). There is a growing recognition, as well as laboratory evidence, that under the right conditions, most of us can get trapped in choices that we ourselves, if viewing the situation with no new information but a different perspective, would judge to be against our best interests (see Loewenstein & Elster, 1992; Loewenstein, 1996).[5] The argument from addiction applies with varying force across psychoactive substances; it is more compelling for drugs that produce withdrawal symptoms, obsessive craving, and/or compulsive behavior (like heroin and cocaine) than for drugs with minimal addictive potential (like psilocybin).

A vexing complication for consequentialists (e.g., Millian liberals and legal paternalists) is that a change in drug laws might have different effects at the micro level (average harm to the individual user) and the macro level (aggregate harm across drug users). Imagine, for example, that a change in drug laws reduces average harm per user (e.g., through the regulation of production, purity, and labeling) but increases total aggregate harm to users (e.g., due to substantial increases in the quantity of use and/or the number of users).[6] A "macro" consequentialist should accept whichever regime minimizes *total* harm (to others, to users, or both, depending on one's views on paternalism). On the other hand, a "micro" consequentialist might accept a regime that minimizes *average* harm (to others, to users, or both), even if some alternative regime better reduces total harm (e.g., by successfully restricting total use). For the micro consequentialist, total harm is irrelevant as long as individual acts of drug use are made safe enough. This micro consequentialist view might seem implau-

5. An alternative perspective is Gary Becker's argument that addiction can be characterized as rational behavior given appropriate external conditions (e.g., Becker & Murphy, 1988). Becker's model is an intellectual *tour de force* of unknown relevance to the phenomenon of real-world addiction.

6. Note that average and total drug harm can diverge for reasons similar to the cases where average and total utility diverge. For the latter case, philosophers usually cite examples where the population size in question changes. In a related vein, average and total drug harm can diverge when the "population" of drug incidents changes—either because each user uses more or because there are more users than before. If use remained constant, average and total harm would always move in the same direction.

sible, but note that this is in fact how many activities are implicitly treated — sports, driving, and so on. Regulation generally aims at the average safety per incident of these activities (and perhaps, the worst possible harm per incident) rather than the number of incidents or the level of total participation. Increases in participation may increase total harm enough to trigger stricter regulation, but that regulation usually targets harm levels, not participation levels.

Legal Moralism

Criminalized vices are often labeled *mala prohibita* (wrong because they are illegal), as distinct from crimes that are *mala in se* (evil in themselves). Crimes in the latter category, such as homicide, rape, and armed robbery, are generally considered evil because the offenders intentionally cause wrongful harm to others. Drug use is clearly qualitatively different from such offenses. Yet many defenders of prohibition discuss drug use in terms that suggest they find it intrinsically immoral. The label *legal moralism* characterizes the belief that "it can be morally legitimate to prohibit conduct on the ground that it is inherently immoral, even though it causes neither harm nor offense to the actor or to others" (Feinberg, 1988, pp. xix–xx).

In practice, it is difficult to distinguish legal moralism from other justifications for drug prohibition. Skolnick (1992) and Husak (1992) argued that prominent drug prohibitionists view drug use in deontological terms, as *malum in se* or morally repugnant in and of itself. The earlier quote from James Q. Wilson seems to support this thesis. But as noted at the outset, deontology is a characteristic of arguments, not people. A closer examination suggests that prominent prohibitionists ultimately define the immorality of drug use in consequentialist terms. Authors like James Q. Wilson and William Bennett described drug use as immoral, but they made their case with references to harms to self and others. For example, in the same essay,

Wilson (1990) established the consequentialist basis for his moral repugnance:

> The notion that abusing drugs such as cocaine is "a victimless crime" is not only absurd but dangerous. Even ignoring the fetal drug syndrome, crack-dependent people are, like heroin addicts, individuals who regularly victimize their children by neglect, their spouses by improvidence, their employers by lethargy, and their coworkers by carelessness.

Similarly, in his introduction to the first *National Drug Control Strategy*, William Bennett (1989) argued that "drug use degrades human character." But in the next sentence, he offered a clearly consequentialist rationale: "Drug users make inattentive parents, bad neighbors, poor students, and unreliable employees—quite apart from their common involvement in criminal activity."

Still, even though prohibitionists cite consequentialist arguments—the coin of the realm in contemporary U.S. policy debates— it does seem plausible that legal moralist sentiments run deep in American opposition to drug law reform. Legal moralism is difficult to defend from a Western (classical) liberal perspective, but it is consistent with what cognitive anthropologists (Haidt, Koller, & Dias, 1993; Shweder et al., 1997) have identified as an *ethics of community* (codes that dictate one's social roles and duties) and an *ethics of divinity* (codes that dictate physical purity). Some will endorse a legal moralist position on drugs because the escapist aspect conflicts with their ethic of community; others, because the chemical aspect conflicts with their ethic of divinity. But these reactions are likely to be vague, intuitive, and difficult to articulate.

The Benefits of Drug Use

Largely absent from this discussion has been any analysis of the benefits of drug use and their role in the moral assessment of drug prohibition. Indeed, the notion that the currently illicit drugs have benefits is almost completely ignored in the policy analytic literature on drug control (Gable, 1997). Arguing from the so-called *revealed preference* principle, many economists argue that the fact that individuals choose to use such drugs establishes de facto that they have benefit (see Becker & Murphy, 1988). Many will reflexively reject this notion. One sophisticated argument for rejecting it is Mark Kleiman's (1992a) observation that many of these drugs instigate neurological and psychological processes that motivate compulsive use, even among those who freely acknowledge they would prefer to stop using. As Kleiman would no doubt agree, this argument has more force for highly addictive drugs like nicotine, cocaine, and heroin than for cannabis or the psychedelics.

Rather than inferring the benefits of a drug by its consumption, one might explicitly identify properties of the drug experience and argue for their benefits empirically or philosophically. Interestingly, the least addictive illicit drugs—cannabis and the psychedelics—have generated the largest endorsement literature. The psychedelics in particular have been defended (subject to various caveats about safe modalities of use) by respected ethnobotanists and pharmacologists (e.g., Schultes & Hoffman, 1992), religious scholars (see Forte, 1997), literary figures (see Strausbaugh & Blaise, 1991), and psychiatrists (e.g., Bravo & Grob, 1996; Strassman, 1995). Indeed, the latter authors are conducting federally approved controlled trials to examine the safety of methylenedioxymethamphetamine (MDMA) and other psychedelics with a hope of eventually testing their psychotherapeutic potential. Many such claims may eventually fail the tests of science or cultural experience—witness Freud's notorious endorsement of cocaine—but others may well be substantiated in time.

In the end, it is no more important for consequentialists to agree on the benefits of drug use than it is to agree on the relative importance of its harms, or the harms of prohibition. Just as readers will differ in the weight they place on the freedom to use drugs, or the immorality of drug taking, it is likely that they will differ in their willingness to place positive value on the drug-taking experience.

IMPLICATIONS

This chapter has attempted to articulate the major theoretical positions on the legislation of morality. . . . The examination of these moral models is intended to identify underlying points of contention in the policy debate and places where empirical research and analysis might have leverage in shifting people's views. . . .

REFERENCES

Becker, G. S., & Murphy, K. M. (1988). A theory of rational addiction. *Journal of Political Economy*, 96, 675–701.

Bennett, W. (1989). Introduction. In Office of National Drug Control Policy, *National Drug Control Strategy* (pp. 1–10). Washington, D.C.: U.S. Government Printing Office.

Bravo, G., & Grob, C. (1996). Psychedelic psychotherapy. In B. W. Scotton, A. B. Chinen, & J. R. Battista (Eds.), *Textbook of transpersonal psychiatry and psychology* (pp. 335–43). New York: Basic Books.

Elster, J. (1992). *Local justice*. New York: Russell Sage.

Feinberg, J. (1984). *The moral limits of the criminal law, Volume 1: Harm to others*. New York: Oxford University Press.

Feinberg, J. (1985). *The moral limits of the criminal law, Volume 2: Offense to others*. New York: Oxford University Press.

Feinberg, J. (1986). *The moral limits of the criminal law, Volume 3: Harm to self*. New York: Oxford University Press.

Feinberg, J. (1988). *The moral limits of the criminal law, Volume 4: Harmless wrongdoing*. New York: Oxford University Press.

Fiske, A. J., & Tetlock, P. E. (1997). Taboo trade-offs: Reactions to transactions that transgress the spheres of justice. *Political Psychology*, 18, 255–97.

Forte, R. (Ed.) (1997). *Entheogens and the future of religion*. San Francisco: Council on Spiritual Practices.

Gable, R. S. (1993). Toward a comparative overview of dependence potential and acute toxicity of psychoactive substances used nonmedically. *American Journal of Drug & Alcohol Abuse*, 19, 263–81.

Gable, R. S. (1997). Opportunity costs of drug prohibition. *Addiction*, 92, 1179–82.

George, R. P. (1993). *Making men moral: Civil liberties and public morality*. New York: Oxford University Press.

Goldstein, A. (1994). *Addiction: From biology to drug policy*. New York: W. H. Freeman & Co.

Haidt, J., Koller, S. H., & Dias, M. G. (1993). Affect, culture, and morality, or is it wrong to eat your dog? *Journal of Personality & Social Psychology*, 65, 613–28.

Husak, D. N. (1992). *Drugs and rights*. Cambridge, England: Cambridge University Press.

Julien, R. M. (1995). *A primer of drug action: A concise, nontechnical guide to the actions, uses, and side effects of psychoactive drugs* (7th ed.). New York: W. H. Freeman & Co.

Kleiman, M. A. R. (1992a). *Against excess: Drug policy for results*. New York: Basic Books.

Loewenstein, G. (1996). Out of control: Visceral influences on behavior. *Organizational Behavior and Human Decision Processes*, 65, 272–92.

Loewenstein, G., & Elster, J. (Eds.) (1992). Choice over time. New York: Russell Sage Foundation.

MacCoun, R. (1998b). Biases in the interpretation and use of research results. *Annual Review of Psychology*, 49, 259–87.

Mill, J. S. (1859/1947). On Liberty. In S. Commins & R. N. Linscott (Eds.), *Man and the state: The political philosophers* (pp. 135–258). New York: Random House.

Moore, M. H. (1991). Drugs, the criminal law, and the administration of justice. *The Milbank Quarterly*, 69, 259–60.

Parfit, D. (1984). *Reasons and persons*. New York: Oxford University Press.

Richards, D. A. J. (1982). *Sex, drugs, death, and the law*. Totowa, NJ: Rowman and Littlefield.

Schultes, R. E., & Hofmann, A. (1992). *Plants of the gods*. Rochester, VT: Healing Arts Press.

Shweder, R. A., Much, N. C., Mahapatra, M., & Park, L. (1997). The "big three" of morality (autonomy, community, divinity) and the "big three" explanations of suffering (pp. 119–69). In A. M. Brandt & P. Rozin (Eds.), *Morality and health*. New York: Routledge.

Skolnick, J. H. (1992). Rethinking the drug problem. *Daedalus*, 121, 133–60.

Strassman, R. J. (1995). Hallucinogenic drugs in psychiatric research and treatment: Perspectives and prospects. *Journal of Nervous & Mental Disease*, 183, 127–38.

Strausbaugh, J., & Blaise, D. (Eds.). (1991). *The drug user: Documents 1840–1960*. New York: Blast Books.

Szasz, T. S. (1974). *Ceremonial chemistry: The ritual persecution of drugs, addicts, and pushers*. Garden City, NY: Doubleday.

Szasz, T. S. (1987). The morality of drug controls. In R. Harmony (Ed.), *Dealing with Drugs: Consequences of government control* (pp. 327–51). San Francisco: Pacific Research Institute for Public Policy.

Wilson, J. Q. (1990). Against the legalization of drugs. *Commentary*, 89, 21–8.

Wilson, J. Q. (1993). *The moral sense*. New York: Free Press.

The American Ambivalence: Liberty vs. Utopia

Thomas Szasz

Thomas Szasz is Professor Emeritus in Psychiatry at the State University of New York Health Science Center in Syracuse, New York.

This selection was excerpted from "The American Ambivalence: Liberty vs. Utopia" in *Our Rights to Drugs: The Case for a Free Market* (New York: Praeger Publishers, an imprint of Greenwood Publishing Group, Inc.).

> Mississippi will drink wet and vote dry so long as any citizen can stagger to the polls.
>
> —Will Rogers[1]

Ever since Colonial times, the American people have displayed two powerful but contradictory existential dispositions: They looked inward, seeking to perfect the self through a struggle for self-discipline; and outward, seeking to perfect the world through the conquest of nature and the moral reform of others. The result has been an unusually intense ambivalence about a host of pleasure-producing acts (drug use being but one) and an equally intense reluctance to confront this ambivalence, embracing simultaneously both a magical-religious and rational-scientific outlook on life. In his important work on the intellectual origins of the Constitution, Forrest McDonald notes that the colonists displayed a Puritan devotion to so-called sumptuary legislation, that is, to laws prohibiting "excessive indulgence" in frivolous pleasures, such as gambling. Yet the Framers also

1. Rogers, W., quoted in P. Yapp, ed., *The Traveller's Dictionary of Quotations* (London and New York: Routledge & Kegan Paul, 1983), p. 919.

believed "that the protection of property was a fundamental purpose for submitting to the authority of government."[2] McDonald does not acknowledge that these beliefs are mutually irreconcilable.

As the nation grew more populous and powerful, this peculiar national heritage of unresolved ambivalence became a veritable national treasure. Combined with our historically unparalleled diversity as a people, the mixture—not surprisingly—yields a uniquely vague and uncertain national identity. What makes a person an American? Or, to put it in more precise political-philosophical terms: What is the basis for our union as a people? It cannot be the English language, because too many Americans do not speak the language or speak it very badly, and because too many non-Americans speak (more or less) the same language. It cannot be the Constitution, because too many Americans do not know what it says and, if they did, would repudiate it. I submit that, lacking the usual grounds on which people congregate as a nation, we habitually fall back on the most primitive yet most enduring basis for group cohesion, namely, scapegoating.[3] Hence the American passion for moral crusades, which, thanks to the modern medicalization of morals, now appear as crusades against disease. This is why so many Americans believe there is no real difference between the effort required to combat the devastation caused by polio and that caused by heroin.[4]

In short, we must not underestimate the demagogic appeal that the prospect of stamping out evil by suitably dramatic means has always exercised, and will continue to exercise, on the minds of men

2. McDonald, F., *Novus Ordo Seclorum* (Lawrence: University Press of Kansas, 1985), pp. 10 and 16.

3. See Burke, K., "Interaction: III. Dramatism," in D. L. Sils, ed., *International Encyclopedia of the Social Sciences,* vol. 7 (New York: Macmillan and Free Press, 1968), p. 450.

4. Although the similarity between these two problems is based on nothing more than a strategic analogy, it is now commonly misunderstood as a literal equivalence; see, for example, Schrage, M., "Vaccine to fight drug addiction is needed," *Los Angeles Times,* March 1, 1990.

and women. The Romans, barbarians that they were, had circuses where they watched gladiators kill one another. Our circuses—splashed across the front pages of newspapers and magazines, and flashed unceasingly on television screens—entertain us with our own civilized, and of course scientific, spectacles. We are shown how "bad" illicit drugs injure and kill their victims, and how "good" psychiatric drugs cure them of their nonexistent mental illnesses.

MAKING THE WORLD SAFE FROM SIN

If a person prefers not to question a phenomenon, it is futile to answer his nonexistent query. Such, precisely, is our situation today with respect to drugs. Instead of pondering the so-called drug problem, people know—as Josh Billings would say—"everything that ain't so" about it.[5] Accordingly, they flit from one absurd explanation to another, without ever stopping long enough to hear what they are saying and then, appalled, stop talking and start thinking.

Former First Lady Nancy Reagan: "Any user of illicit drugs is an accomplice to murder."[6]

Former drug czar William Bennett: "It [drug abuse] is a product of the Great Deceiver. . . . We need to bring to these people in need the God who heals."[7]

New York State Governor Mario Cuomo, described while visiting a school: "Pupils and teachers waving banners gathered at the school's entrance and the band played the national anthem as Governor Cuomo walked through the door. Cuomo praised the children for taking a stand against drugs, which he called 'the devil.' . . .

5. "It is better to know nothing than to know what ain't so." Shaw, H. W. ("Josh Billings"), quoted in J. Bartlett, *Familiar Quotations*, 12th ed. (Boston: Little, Brown, 1951), p. 518.

6. Reagan, N., quoted in S. V. Roberts, "Mrs. Reagan assails drug users," *New York Times*, March 1, 1988.

7. Bennett, W., quoted in "In the news," *Syracuse Herald-Journal*, June 13, 1990.

'Thank you from the bottom of my heart,' Cuomo said. . . . 'Anybody who does not believe in the devil, think about drugs.'"[8]

These remarks can easily be multiplied. I choose them because they exemplify the nature of public discourse about drugs in the United States today. Looking at the contemporary American drug scene, it is difficult to escape the conclusion that, notwithstanding the contrary evidence of impressive scientific and technological achievements, we stand once again knee-deep in a popular delusion and crowd madness: the Great American Drugcraze. As in the persecutory movements that preceded it, harmless persons and inanimate objects are once again demonized as the enemy, invested with magically dangerous powers, and thus turned into scapegoats whose denunciation and destruction become self-evident civic duty.[9] During the Middle Ages, Nancy Reagan's "drug users" and Mario Cuomo's "devils" were witches and Jews—the former typically accused of abusing children; the latter, of poisoning wells.

America: Redeemer Nation

To understand America's protracted struggle against drugs, we must situate the current anti-drug hysteria in the context of this nation's historical penchant for waging moral crusades. Since Colonial times, the New World was perceived—by settlers and foreign observers alike—as a New Promised Land, a place where man, corrupted in the Old World, was reborn, uncorrupted. This vision inspired the colonists, informed the Founders, burned brightly in the nineteenth century, was clearly exhibited during the earlier decades of this century—first in a great war to make the world safe for democracy, then

8. Nelis, K., "Cuomo applauds students for taking on 'the devil,'" *Post Standard,* Syracuse, NY, January 28, 1988.

9. See Mackay, C., *Extraordinary Popular Delusions and the Madness of Crowds,* 1841, 1852, reprint (New York: Noonday Press, 1962); and Moore, R. I., *The Formation of a Persecuting Society* (Oxford, England: Basil Blackwell, 1987).

in an even greater war to make it safe from German and Japanese nationalism—and is now plainly manifest in the war to make the world safe from dangerous drugs.[10] Perhaps more than any recent president, George Bush embodies our self-contradictory quest for a free society *and* a utopian moral order. Giving his inaugural address in January 1989, Bush stressed two themes: the free market—and the war against it. "We know," declared the president, "how to secure a more just and prosperous life for man on earth: through free markets . . . and the exercise of free will unhampered by the state." Then, hardly pausing, he declared drugs to be the nation's chief domestic problem, and pledged, "This scourge will stop."[11]

Formerly, the conviction that America's manifest destiny was the moral reformation of the world was couched in clerical terms, as a fight against sin (drinking as "intemperance"); now, it is couched in clinical terms, as a fight against disease (drug use as "chemical dependency"). The medieval well-poisoning imagery, brought up to date, remains irresistible: General Manuel Noriega is a "narco-terrorist" who sends us cocaine to infect our children; we, in turn, launch Operation Just Cause, invade Panama, kidnap its head of state, and bring him to the United States for a fair trial. Although in his magisterial work, *Redeemer Nation*, Ernest Lee Tuveson does not mention drugs or drug controls, his book can be read as a sustained historical critique that pulls the rug of rationalizations from under the feet of the drug warriors. "To assume," Tuveson cautioned, "that what is good for America is good for the world, that saving the United States is saving mankind, is to open up a large area of temptation. . . . The danger in all this is evident."[12]

10. See Tuveson, E. L., *Redeemer Nation* (Chicago: University of Chicago Press, 1968).

11. Bush, G., "Transcript of Bush's Inaugural Address," *New York Times*, January 21, 1989.

12. Tuveson, *Redeemer Nation*, p. 132.

COMSTOCKERY: SETTING THE
STAGE FOR THE WAR ON DRUGS

There was a time, not long ago, when America was at peace with drugs—when the trade in drugs was as unregulated as the trade in diet books is today; when people did not view drugs as presenting the sort of danger that required the protection of the national government; and when, although virtually all of the drugs of which we are now deathly afraid were freely available, there was nothing even remotely resembling a "drug problem." It would be a mistake to assume, however, that in those good old days Americans minded their own business. Far from it. Then they hounded themselves and their fellows with the fear of another dangerous pollutant threatening the nation, namely, pornographic books, magazines, and pictures. Inasmuch as the turn-of-the-century war on obscenity preceded, and in part paved the way for, the twentieth-century War on Drugs, let us begin by taking a brief look at print controls or media censorship.

Censorship—that is, the prohibition of uttering or publishing "dangerous," "heretical," "subversive," or "obscene" ideas or images— is an age-old social custom. In fact, appreciation of the moral merit of the free trade in ideas and images is a very recent historical acquisition, limited to secular societies that place a high value on individual liberty and private property. In many parts of the world today, there is no press freedom and the very idea of opposing the right of the church or of the state to control information is considered to be subversive.

The reason for censorship is as obvious as the maxims celebrating the power of ideas are numerous. If the pen is mightier than the sword, we can expect sword-holders to want to sheath their adversaries' swords. As Justice Oliver Wendell Holmes, Jr., put it, censorship rests on the realization that "every idea is an incitement."[13] Perhaps

---

13. "Censorship," in the *Encyclopaedia Britannica* vol. 5 (Chicago: Encyclopaedia Britannica, 1973), p. 161.

he should have specified "every interesting idea," for a dull idea is not. By the same token, every interesting drug is an incitement. And so is everything else that people find interesting, whether it be dance, music, gambling, or sport. For a number of reasons, among them an increasing tempo of immigration and population growth, in the 1880s Americans began to feel besieged by a pitiless enemy determined to destroy the very soul of their nation. The scriptural serpent surfaced once again, put on the mask called "obscenity and pornography," and suddenly books like *Fanny Hill* and pictures of seminude women became dire threats to the welfare of the nation. So the country declared war on obscenity and soon had a censorship czar committed to stamping out smut. That czar was Anthony Comstock, whose heroic exploits so amused George Bernard Shaw that he made the czar's last name a part of the vocabulary of American English. A "comstock," according to *Webster's*, "is a ludicrous prude, esp. in matters relating to morality in art," and "comstockery [is] prudery; *specif.*: prudish concern in hunting down immorality, esp. in books, papers, and pictures."[14]

I am not going to dwell on Comstock's amazing achievements. The following episode should suffice to illustrate the power he wielded and the similarities between the war on obscenity at the beginning of this century and the War on Drugs at the end of it. As William Bennett's efforts were hampered by drug pushers, Anthony Comstock's were hampered by smut pushers, among them Margaret Sanger, the pioneer feminist and birth control advocate. Clearly, Comstock's anti-obscenity crusade and Sanger's right-to-sex-information crusade were on a collision course.

To provide women with what we now call sex education, Sanger wrote a series of articles for the socialist newspaper *Call*. The publication was stopped, however, when Comstock "announced that an

---

14. *Webster's Third New International Dictionary,* unabridged (Springfield, MA: G&C Merriam, 1961), p. 468.

article on gonorrhea violated the bounds of public taste."[15] This further inflamed Sanger, who decided to confront Comstock by publishing all the then available contraceptive information in a magazine appropriately titled *The Woman Rebel*. Comstock was ready. The magazine was banned by the Post Office and, on August 25, 1914, Sanger "was indicted by the federal government on nine counts that could bring a jail sentence of 45 years."[16] Her lawyers wanted to get her off on a technicality, but Sanger refused, preferring to flee to England. In 1915 Comstock died, and the following year the government dropped its charges against Mrs. Sanger.

Margaret Sanger had money, fame, and power, and survived the war on obscenity essentially unscathed. Others were not so lucky. In 1913, two years before his death, Comstock offered this catalog of his exploits: "In the forty-one years I have been here, I have convicted persons enough to fill a passenger train of sixty-one coaches, sixty coaches containing sixty passengers each and the sixty-first almost full. I have destroyed 160 tons of obscene literature."[17]

Deplorable though they were, the Comstockian anti-obscenity statutes were intended to protect the public only from the (ostensibly) harmful acts of others. The extension of the reach of the interventionist state from protecting people from *moral self-harm* or *vice* (by means of print censorship) to protecting them from *medical self-harm* or *illness* (by means of drug censorship) is a momentous transformation that has not received the critical scrutiny it deserves. On the contrary, academics and intellectuals now speak and write as if providing such protection has always been within the province of state intervention. Drug prohibitionists thus proudly proclaim that protecting people from themselves is just as legitimate a goal for criminal

15. Lader, L., "Margaret Sanger: Militant, pragmatist, visionary," *On the Issues* 14 (1990): 10–12, 14, 30–35; quote at p. 30.

16. Ibid.

17. Broun, H., and Leech, M., *Anthony Comstock* (New York: Literary Guild of America, 1927), pp. 15–16.

as well as civil law as protecting people from others. Accordingly, trying to save people from their own drug-using proclivities is considered to be ample warrant for depriving individuals of life, liberty, property, and any or all constitutional protections that obstruct this lofty goal. . . .

THE WAR ON DRUGS

After the turn of the century, having enjoyed the blessings of two centuries of free trade in medical care, America succumbed to the lure of European "progress," a/k/a government regulation.[21] Ever since then, the United States has waged a War on Drugs. The hostilities began with minor skirmishes before World War I, grew into guerrilla warfare after it, and now affect the daily lives of people not only in the United States but in foreign countries as well. . . .

THE MIRAGE OF A HOLY/HEALTHY UTOPIA

The War on Drugs is a moral crusade wearing a medical mask. Our previous moral crusades targeted people who were giving themselves sexual relief and pleasure (the drives against pornography and masturbation). Our current moral crusade targets people who are giving themselves pharmaceutical relief and pleasure (the drive against illicit drugs and self-medication). Although the term *drug abuse* is vague and its definition variable, by and large it is the name we give to self-medication with virtually any interesting and socially disapproved substance. Why is self-medication a problem? Because, for the reasons discussed above, we view it as both immoral and unhealthy.

And so we arrive back at our point of departure: the essentially religious, redemptive nature of the American dream of a world free from dangerous drugs. This aspiration arose, as Tuveson suggested,

---

21. See Shryock, R. H., *Medical Licensing in America, 1650–1965* (Baltimore: Johns Hopkins University Press, 1967).

from a peculiarly American mix of devotion to both religious and secular utopianism.

> The real importance of the elements of secular progress is that they have stirred up and made possible the militancy of Christianity *in this world*, which is to produce the *holy utopia*. . . . The new "benevolent and reformatory' movements [are] designed to bring human conduct and institutions into conformity with the *idea of right*.[75]

It is this longing for a holy utopia that leads to the fateful obliteration of the distinction between vice and crime, and the tragic transformation of the virtue of temperance into the vice of prohibition. In a society such as ours—religious by tradition, secular by law, and forever striving toward a free political order—this is a terrible folly, for reasons Lysander Spooner articulated perhaps better than anyone else:

> [E]verybody wishes to be protected, in his person and property, against the aggressions of other men. But nobody *wishes* to be protected, either in his person or property, against himself; because it is contrary to the fundamental laws of human nature itself, that any one should wish to harm himself. He only wishes to promote his own happiness, and to be his own judge as to what will promote, and does promote, his own happiness. This is what every one wants, and has a right to, as a human being.[76]

However, what Tuveson termed our collective striving for a "holy utopia" is the superglue that reconciles and unites in an intoxicating embrace of intolerance the diverse personalities and politics of Nancy Reagan and Jesse Jackson, George Bush and Charles Rangel, William Bennett and Ralph Nader. If our love of the Constitution and gratitude for our heritage cannot keep us united as a nation, then hatred of "dangerous drugs" must do the job.

---

75. Tuveson, *Redeemer Nation*, pp. 73–74; emphasis added.
76. Spooner, *Vices Are Not Crimes*, pp. 12–13.

Hidden Paradigms of Morality in Debates about Drugs: Historical and Policy Shifts in British and American Drug Policies

John Jay Rouse and Bruce D. Johnson

John Jay Rouse was with the New York City Department of Probation and an assistant professor of Criminal Justice at Sacred Heart University, Fairfield, Connecticut. He is now retired. Bruce D. Johnson is the director of the Institute for Special Populations Research—N. D. R. I., Inc.

This selection was excerpted from chapter nine in *The Drug Legalization Debate* edited by James A. Inciardi (Newbury Park, Calif.: Sage Publications, Inc., 1991).

A comparison of British and American drug policies over the past century-and-a-half reveals certain hidden moral paradigms that have governed public policy approaches toward drugs, either singly or jointly. These moral paradigms include commercial morality prohibition-criminalization, vice regulation, public health and rehabilitation. Both Britain and the United States were dominated by the commercial paradigm in the nineteenth century. International opium conventions (1912–1913) greatly restricted the commercial morality and developed a successful public health approach to opiates. The United States shifted toward a prohibition-criminalization approach for drug addicts, whereas Britain maintained a public health approach.

INTRODUCTION

Moral standards guide personal conduct in many spheres of behavior, particularly drug use. Moral standards adopted by society may become "invisible clothing" and an integral part of the self. Other standards of morality do not seem possible or worthy and are essentially hidden from public view and discussion. Old moral standards are forgotten; only current standards can be continuously reaffirmed. The current debate about drug legalization falls squarely in this tradition.

Imagine living in Britain or America a century ago and living within the morality of that period. In 1890 most pharmacies and/or other stores sold opium pills, pure morphine, opium for smoking, coca leaf products, pure cocaine, cocaine cigarettes (like crack today), a variety of beverages containing either alcohol plus opiates or alcohol plus cocaine, and patent medicines whose effective ingredients were opiates. A new soft drink contained coca leaf extract in its contents and name: Coca-Cola. People could purchase these commodities at a low price (even at 1890 wages) and use them with less stigma than drinking alcohol or smoking tobacco. Those who used large quantities of these substances or who overindulged might be thought of as having a bad habit, but would not likely commit crimes to obtain their drug(s) of choice. Opium smoking was a vice peculiar to the Chinese people, and perhaps a few criminals in America. A few British citizens who supported missionaries in China were proclaiming the almost absurd notion that the Indo-Chinese opium (smoking) trade was morally indefensible and should be stopped immediately. Furthermore, they proclaimed that opiates should be provided only by doctors for medical reasons, thus depriving the average citizens of their favorite patent medicines or opium pills or opiate wines. Surely such reasons were not sufficient either to restrict profits of merchants or to prevent the populace from using their favorite remedies for most maladies. Virtually no one (including the proponents of such restrictions) mentioned, much less advocated, criminal penalties and actually confining persons in jail or prison for opiate use or sales. Only in China had the barbaric practice of strangling opium smokers occurred—and that was more than 150 years ago (1830–1850).

In fact, the isolation of morphine from the poppy and cocaine from coca plants, and the invention of the hypodermic needle in the latter half of the nineteenth century, were major advances in alleviating pain and suffering from a multitude of diseases that had long plagued mankind. New professions had emerged since 1850: scientific chemists were replacing alchemists; physicians had training and skills that doctors and medicine men did not; pharmacists were replacing the friendly patent medicine salesmen. In Vienna, young Sigmund Freud had published some laudatory essays about a newly discovered drug, cocaine, to alleviate morbid depression. In short, physicians, doctors, pharmacists, entrepreneurs, and ordinary shopkeepers could sell their patients and customers the best that modern medicine had to offer which would actually alleviate (but not cure) the pain and suffering of many dreaded diseases. If a few persons overindulged and had an opium or morphine habit, this was a minor problem, not nearly as "morally wrong" as being a drunkard, or smoking pipes, or chewing snuff. Why should the average citizen either be concerned about the Chinese problem or restrict the income of doctors or businessmen? In 1890, the reasons were insufficient. But this changed rapidly in the next 40 years. . . .

PROMOTING MORALITY

Morality has its origins in religion and history and defines various behaviors as moral, or right, and immoral in various degrees (other terms include: vice, deviance, crime). Compared with definitions of normal physical health, much less agreement exists about appropriate moral behavior of citizens, and much disagreement exists within the polity about appropriate definitions for the degree and seriousness of behavior defined as immoral.

A major function of government is the promotion of moral behavior and good health practices among its citizens. So many exceptions from approved practices occur, however, that all governments have established laws. Legislators must socially construct definitions of the disapproved or questionable behaviors, define laws that provide a framework for enforcement, and establish and fund bureaucracies responsible for issuing regulations and enforcing them. The process by which such laws are passed has been well documented elsewhere (Mauss, 1975; Spector and Kitsuse, 1977). Usually, relatively small interest groups (especially business groups, and wealthy or influential persons) get their definitions passed into law, legislation, and regulations. The poor and disadvantaged have limited or little access to the legislative process, and their behaviors are frequently the object of the laws.

But generally, after several years of vigorous enforcement, most citizens come to accept legal definitions as the basis for their personal behavior. Such standards of moral behavior and good health become the "invisible clothing" that the vast majority of people in society "wear" in their personal conduct. Such "invisible clothing" (standards of appropriate behavior) may become reified into absolute right and wrong. The average conventional person can hardly conceive that anyone might engage in or enjoy such wrong behavior, or that such behavior might be defined and treated in a very different way in another society or culture. Most citizens are quite clear about their standards for right and wrong behavior, but are aware that much similar behavior by others might also be in an ambiguous zone.

Behaviors involving the consumption of drugs or nonfood psychoactive substances have always been at the crossroads where health and morality intersect, and where government efforts to promote good health and prevent practices deemed harmful by the majority collide with the rights of the minority, who enjoy and practice such behaviors. In fact, the implicit assumptions about correct behavior made by almost everyone in society consistently confound health and moral considerations, so that policy deliberations, debates, legislation, funding, and enforcement practices regarding drugs frequently contain conflicting purposes.

PARADIGMS OF MORALITY

Paradigms contain all major elements that define a theoretical model being examined. Max Weber (1947) used the term "ideal type" to provide nearly perfect definitions of the phenomena, even though such pure examples are rarely found in reality. But such ideal types or paradigms have heuristic value by making important conceptual distinctions between elements that may be otherwise confounded in reality and policy making. The following five paradigms are defined according to relatively pure ideal types; contrasts with similar paradigms are provided.

Commercial Morality

The commercial paradigm holds that the economic value and returns from a commodity are the most important criteria by which to assess a drug. Thus, if sales of a given drug can earn good profits for the seller, the drug should be made available to those who wish to buy it, and its consumption considered appropriately moral. Most persons consuming the drug are presumed to maintain normal health and to be otherwise moral persons.

Persons with a commercial interest may promote the drug as beneficial to health and as morally correct. Such proponents ignore or refute competing paradigms, which may claim that the drug is harmful or bad for health, or that consuming behavior is immoral or a vice. Proponents can be expected to advertise their product to as many potential customers as possible, and take actions which maximize profits. Historically, commercial interests have sought or used governmental laws or regulations such as patents, taxation policies, restriction of competition, lawsuits, limitations of imports, and even warfare to maximize profits. For example, coffee, tea, and several soft drinks (e.g., Coca-Cola) contain a stimulant (caffeine), but are sold without restrictions as to location, time, place, cost, labeling requirements, or advertising content. Manufacturers and sellers are not required to list the active ingredient, caffeine, nor state the amount of caffeine in a typical dosage unit.

Public Health Morality

The public health paradigm is designed to promote good (normal) health practices and to discourage or restrict practices that might harm health. Public health authorities tend to ignore morality claims and remain very skeptical of claims for product effectiveness issued by those having a commercial interest in a product. Public health practitioners are eager to restore physical health to immoral persons as well as good citizens.

Public health regulations permit purified caffeine to be legally sold in several over-the-counter drugs (e.g., No-Doz). The quantity of caffeine in a dosage unit may be listed on the label, and written directions provided about the number of pills to be taken and the frequency of consumption.

As shown below, opiates were a primary concern as public health practices and regulations were debated and institutionalized during the past two centuries. Authorities issue warnings, teach medical practitioners, and otherwise prevent users from consuming dosages that are too large or that extend for very long periods. Such authorities are also empowered to restrict the actions and profits of manufacturers and sellers of drugs in many ways: requiring labels stating contents and dosages; limiting the number of dosage units in retail packages;

regulating pricing practices, advertising content, and targets; and proving that drugs are both safe and effective.

Vice Regulation Morality

The vice regulation morality is quite unfamiliar to most Americans because prohibition-criminalization has dominated in the twentieth century. This paradigm represents an explicit recognition of conflicting moral standards of right and wrong. The vast majority of citizens have clear moral standards that define certain behaviors as immoral and unacceptable; but a sizable minority enjoy and wish to participate in and/or pay for that behavior. The vice regulation paradigm provides for laws and regulations that permit the immoral behavior to occur, but generally remain unobserved by publics whose morals would be offended.

In much of Western Europe, for example, prostitution and pornography are legal but highly regulated. In London, prostitutes cannot solicit on the streets or in bars, but may advertise in sex magazines and via discreet announcements in shop windows. Shops selling pornography are permitted no public displays that might offend the average citizen, but can sell any kind of sexually explicit material to adults who enter the premises.

Prohibition-Criminalization Morality

The prohibition-criminalization paradigm represents a collective judgment that a particular behavior is wrong and immoral and should be prohibited by law. Usually, violations of the law are punished by criminal penalties. The prohibition morality may emphasize the "symbolic crusade" (Gusfield, 1963) aspect in which a moral belief of a powerful group is enacted into law, and frequently directed against persons perceived as immoral or disreputable.

While prohibitionist sentiment enacts laws, criminalization

occurs when a specific behavior is defined as illegal by criminal law, and specific sentences in jail or prison are provided for convicted violators. Police and various enforcement agencies are created and mobilized to detect and arrest persons committing the illegal act. The types of persons targeted for enforcement of criminal laws, and the severity and certainty of detection, prosecution, and punishment, are critical.

Laws against heroin in the last half of the twentieth century in America have been based on a strongly held prohibitionist sentiment, and criminal penalties have been vigorously enforced against heroin users and user-dealers by many police and special narcotics units.

Rehabilitation Morality

The rehabilitation paradigm is concerned primarily with restoring to normal social behavior persons who are labeled by authorities or themselves as deviant, criminal, or immoral on some behavioral dimension. The major effort is to eliminate or greatly reduce the undesirable behavior as well as to teach or model appropriate behavior.

During the 1970s and 1980s, therapeutic communities have developed a strong philosophy and treatment regime that attempt to eliminate the use of all illicit drugs and alcohol, stress elimination of any negative behavior including lying and deceit, and impose activities that promote conventional behavior upon participants. In the United States, therapeutic communities have become popular and widespread because the total rehabilitation of addicts is congruent with the strong moral censure against addiction in American society.

Each of these paradigms of morality exerts considerable influence on public policies toward drugs. Each paradigm has had various constituencies promoting their morality interests to government agencies. Moreover, some of these paradigms have become the fundamental operating assumptions of government policies and laws in various historical periods and for different cultures.

Several major themes emerge in the historical record. The commercial morality dominated in the early nineteenth century and reached its zenith in the 1880s. The prohibitionist morality (against opium smoking) and public health morality (to restrict opiates for medical purposes) emerged at the end of the nineteenth century. The prohibitionist and criminalization approach toward opiates (especially heroin) was ascendant in America during the first quarter of the twentieth century and has remained dominant ever since. British policy remained firmly committed to a public health morality for the first two-thirds of the twentieth century, but has shown a shift toward prohibition-criminalization in the 1980s.

Of even greater importance is the fact that drugs, especially opiates, have had a primary role in generating political conflict among competing commercial and morality interests, which has, in turn, forced a clarification of roles among the medical, public health, and pharmaceutical professions.

The public health paradigm ascended after World War I, when the International Opium Conventions were adopted and institutionalized by almost all major nations. Opiates were legally confined to legitimated medical practices, and this worked well through the 1950s. The revival of black markets in heroin after World War II led to further restrictions on medical opiates, and vast expansion of the prohibitionist-criminalization morality (and imprisonment of addicts by the thousands) in America. But the tide of heroin abuse and cocaine/crack addiction in the last half of the 1980s was so great that prisons were not enough. The rehabilitation morality gained proponents, and funding began in the 1960s and has grown steadily ever since. . . .

CONCLUSION

A socio-historical review of drug policies in Britain and the United States shows that both countries in the nineteenth century were dominated by a commercial morality toward opiates. Strong dissatisfaction with opium cultivation, opium smoking in China and the United States, and patent medicines led to international opium conventions, which institutionalized the public health morality regarding legitimate medical uses. Starting with the Harrison Narcotic Act of 1914, the United States rapidly shifted toward a prohibitionist-criminalization paradigm toward opiate and heroin users and prevented opiate maintenance until methadone became available in the 1960s. In the 1920s, Britain rejected the criminalization approach and defined a public health morality, which worked effectively until the 1960s. This approach has remained the core of British policy to the present time. The 1980s, however, have seen the growth of a black market in heroin, a shift away from long-term maintenance of opiate addicts in Britain, and the criminalization of many heroin user-dealers.

While British policy toward opiate addicts allows them to legally obtain opiates from government clinics or their general practitioners, physicians have chosen to greatly restrict opiate maintenance. In the United States the highly moralistic prohibitionist, law enforcement approach to narcotic drugs has become increasingly stronger. . . .

"Invisible Clothing" Revisited

The "invisible clothing" of the average British and American citizen of 1890 took for granted that the commercial morality for opiates was appropriate, although heated political debate about morality toward alcohol was raging in that era. They would be astonished to learn that opiate users in the 1990s are not only routinely denied very small quantities (by 1890 measures), but routinely arrested and incarcerated for several years for possession or sale of small quantities of these drugs.

In 1990 government agencies, the press, and most people routinely reinforce the beliefs that most Americans take for granted: heroin and crack/cocaine are among the worst evils and greatest vices in the society. Persons who use these drugs become fiends who rob and steal; and society must get tough (and imprison) those who will not volunteer for rehabilitation. Indeed, average Americans in 1990 are so comfortable with prohibition-criminalization that they are surprised and unsettled to discover that not only were such drugs legal and cheap in the past, but also that very different moral standards may exist in other countries. British drug treatment personnel, operating safely within the protective public health morality of the Rolleston Committee (1926), are aware of the power of moral crusades and prohibitionist sentiment in America and its impact on British citizens. They do not want to reproduce America's drug problem.

What will be the moral standards of British and American citizens toward opiates in the future? Prognostications are not possible, but the five paradigms of morality toward opiates suggest possibilities that are not being seriously considered. Perhaps future scientists will invent drugs that are not addictive and do not have other harmful properties and which will be defined as morally correct to consume and sell, so drug users will switch away from heroin and cocaine voluntarily. Perhaps the prohibitionist-criminalization approach will succeed in stopping the growth of opiates and cocaine or their illegal import so addicts cannot get their drugs. But these optimistic scenarios appear improbable in 1990.

It is more likely that the prohibitionist-criminalization sentiment will spread, at least in the near term, thus labeling hundreds of thousands more people as criminals.

Perhaps the current, mainly academic, debate about drug legalization will achieve results as impressive as the British anti-opium movement of the 1890s (Johnson, 1975b) and bring about a willingness to discard prohibitions and criminal penalties against opiate users and sellers, as happened with alcohol in 1935 (Nadelmann, 1989). If this willingness emerges, the precise nature of any legalization will necessitate major changes in international agreements.

Each paradigm of morality offers different possibilities for legal drugs. The commercial paradigm suggests that opiates could be made available at considerably below black market costs to stop the illegal trade; subsequently, taxes could be raised to restrict use. Models borrowed from the nineteenth century and other societies could provide plausible scenarios.

The vice regulation paradigm suggests that opiates and cocaine could be provided commercially to addicts and abusers, but that the sellers would be required to maintain controls over abusers and keep them out of view and concern by straight citizens. Variations of the Dutch willingness to let users purchase and consume marijuana in coffee shops, but repress street sales and consumption in public places, appears possible.

The public health morality suggests that drug dispensing clinics and pharmacies could provide drugs legally to heroin and cocaine abusers, but attempt to constrain and lower dosages, potencies, and frequency of consumption by committed abusers. They could provide other services (counseling, rehabilitation referral, needles, etc.) in continuing efforts to contain the problem and normalize (rather than stigmatize) the user life-style, as part of a harm reduction policy. They could also engage in sustained research to develop safe drug substitutes, rehabilitation therapies, and other ways to both improve the public health and undermine the financial structures of the current black market.

The rehabilitation paradigm suggests that future improvements could be made in creating more programs and placements for drug abusers to enter treatment and attempt to normalize their lives.

In 1990 none of the above scenarios, other than an extension of the prohibitionist-criminalization morality (and many more prisoners), appears even remotely possible in the highly moralized political atmosphere of America. Changes in drug policies are most likely to emerge in Europe, where the public health and vice regulation moralities have been institutionalized for decades. Regardless of the political fate of any particular proposals for changing policies toward opiates and cocaine, policymakers and citizens must become aware of how their personal moral standards affect political life and policy choices toward heroin and cocaine abusers.

REFERENCES

Gusfield, J. (1963). *Symbolic crusade: State politics and the American temperance movement.* Urbana, IL: University of Illinois Press.

Johnson, B. D. (1975b, Fall). Righteousness before revenue: The forgotten moral crusade against the Indo-Chinese opium trade. *Journal of Drug Issues,* pp. 304–326.

Mauss, A. L. (1975). *Social problems as social movements.* Philadelphia: J. B. Lippincott Company.

Nadelmann, E. A. (1989, September 1). Drug prohibition in the United States: Costs, consequences, and alternatives. *Science, 245,* pp. 939–947.

Spector, M., & Kitsuse, J. I. (1977). *Constructing social problems.* Menlo Park, CA: Cummings.

Weber, M. (1947). *The theory of social and economic organization.* New York: Oxford University Press.

PART THREE

Perspectives

No drug, not even alcohol, causes the fundamental ills of society. If we're looking for the sources of our troubles, we shouldn't test people for drugs, we should test them for stupidity, ignorance, greed and love of power.

P. J. O'Rourke
Give War A Chance
1993

A lot of people say that we have a heavy sentence for this crime and light sentence for another crime, and what we ought to do is reduce the heavy sentence so it's more in line with the other. Wrong. In most cases we ought to increase the light sentence and make it compatible with the heavy sentence, and be serious about punishment because we are becoming too tolerant as a society.

Rush Limbaugh
Show Transcript
October 5, 1995

There's No Justice in the War on Drugs

Milton Friedman

Milton Friedman is the recipient of the 1976 Nobel Memorial Prize for economic science and a senior research fellow at the Hoover Institution.

This selection first appeared in the *New York Times*, January 11, 1998.

Twenty-five years ago, President Richard M. Nixon announced a "War on Drugs." I criticized the action on both moral and expediential grounds in my *Newsweek* column of May 1, 1972, "Prohibition and Drugs":

> On ethical grounds, do we have the right to use the machinery of government to prevent an individual from becoming an alcoholic or a drug addict? For children, almost everyone would answer at least a qualified yes. But for responsible adults, I, for one, would answer no. Reason with the potential addict, yes. Tell him the consequences, yes. Pray for and with him, yes. But I believe that we have no right to use force, directly or indirectly, to prevent a fellow man from committing suicide, let alone from drinking alcohol or taking drugs.

That basic ethical flaw has inevitably generated specific evils during the past quarter century, just as it did during our earlier attempt at alcohol prohibition.

1. *The use of informers.* Informers are not needed in crimes like robbery and murder because the victims of those crimes have a strong incentive to report the crime. In the drug trade, the crime consists of a transaction between a willing buyer and willing seller. Neither has any incentive to report a violation of law. On the contrary, it is

in the self-interest of both that the crime not be reported. That is why informers are needed. The use of informers and the immense sums of money at stake inevitably generate corruption—as they did during Prohibition. They also lead to violations of the civil rights of innocent people, to the shameful practices of forcible entry and forfeiture of property without due process.

As I wrote in 1972: ". . . addicts and pushers are not the only ones corrupted. Immense sums are at stake. It is inevitable that some relatively low-paid police and other government officials—and some high-paid ones as well—will succumb to the temptation to pick up easy money.

2. *Filling the prisons.* In 1970, 200,000 people were in prison. Today, 1.6 million people are. Eight times as many in absolute number, six times as many relative to the increased population. In addition, 2.3 million are on probation and parole. The attempt to prohibit drugs is by far the major source of the horrendous growth in the prison population.

There is no light at the end of that tunnel. How many of our citizens do we want to turn into criminals before we yell "enough"?

3. *Disproportionate imprisonment of blacks.* Sher Hosonko, at the time Connecticut's director of addiction services, stressed this effect of drug prohibition in a talk given in June 1995:

> Today in this country, we incarcerate 3,109 black men for every 100,000 of them in the population. Just to give you an idea of the drama in this number, our closest competitor for incarcerating black men is South Africa. South Africa—and this is pre–Nelson Mandela and under an overt public policy of apartheid—incarcerated 723 black men for every 100,000. Figure this out: In the land of the Bill of Rights, we jail over four times as many black men as the only country in the world that advertised a political policy of apartheid.

4. *Destruction of inner cities.* Drug prohibition is one of the most important factors that have combined to reduce our inner cities to

their present state. The crowded inner cities have a comparative advantage for selling drugs. Though most customers do not live in the inner cities, most sellers do. Young boys and girls view the swaggering, affluent drug dealers as role models. Compared with the returns from a traditional career of study and hard work, returns from dealing drugs are tempting to young and old alike. And many, especially the young, are not dissuaded by the bullets that fly so freely in disputes between competing drug dealers—bullets that fly only because dealing drugs is illegal. Al Capone epitomizes our earlier attempt at Prohibition; the Crips and Bloods epitomize this one.

5. *Compounding the harm to users.* Prohibition makes drugs exorbitantly expensive and highly uncertain in quality. A user must associate with criminals to get the drugs, and many are driven to become criminals themselves to finance the habit. Needles, which are hard to get, are often shared, with the predictable effect of spreading disease. Finally, an addict who seeks treatment must confess to being a criminal in order to qualify for a treatment program. Alternatively, professionals who treat addicts must become informers or criminals themselves.

6. *Undertreatment of chronic pain.* The Federal Department of Health and Human Services has issued reports showing that two thirds of all terminal cancer patients do not receive adequate pain medication, and the numbers are surely higher in nonterminally ill patients. Such serious undertreatment of chronic pain is a direct result of the Drug Enforcement Agency's pressures on physicians who prescribe narcotics.

7. *Harming foreign countries.* Our drug policy has led to thousands of deaths and enormous loss of wealth in countries like Colombia, Peru, and Mexico, and has undermined the stability of their governments. All because we cannot enforce our laws at home. If we did, there would be no market for imported drugs. There would be no Cali cartel. The foreign countries would not have to suffer the loss of sovereignty involved in letting our "advisers" and troops operate

on their soil, search their vessels, and encourage local militaries to shoot down their planes. They could run their own affairs, and we, in turn, could avoid the diversion of military forces from their proper function.

Can any policy, however high-minded, be moral if it leads to widespread corruption, imprisons so many, has so racist an effect, destroys our inner cities, wreaks havoc on misguided and vulnerable individuals, and brings death and destruction to foreign countries?

Don't Surrender: The drug war worked once. It can again.

William J. Bennett

William J. Bennett is a distinguished fellow at the Heritage Foundation and served as the first national drug czar in the Reagan administration.

This selection originally appeared in the *Wall Street Journal*, May 15, 2001.

George W. Bush recently announced the nomination of John P. Walters to serve as the director of the Office of National Drug Control Policy. The new "drug czar" is being asked to lead the nation's war on illegal drugs at a time when many are urging surrender.

The forms of surrender are manifold: Buzzwords like "harm reduction" are crowding out clear no-use messages. State initiatives promoting "medical marijuana" are little more than thinly veiled legalization efforts. The film *Traffic* portrayed the war on drugs as a futile effort. In a recent survey by the Pew Research Center for the People and the Press, 74% of Americans believe the war on drugs is a failure.

And yet recent history shows that, far from being a failure, drug-control programs are among the most successful public-policy efforts of the later half of the 20th century. According to a national drug survey, between 1979 and 1992, the most intense period of antidrug efforts, the rate of illegal drug use dropped by more than half, while marijuana use decreased by two-thirds. Cocaine use dropped by three-fourths between 1985 and 1992.

Why is this record described as a failure? For those who would legalize drugs, all drug-control efforts must be painted as disastrous.

But for most Americans, frustration with the drug issue stems from the fact that over the past eight years we have lost ground.

During the Clinton administration, our nation's drug policy suffered a period of malign neglect. President Clinton's two clearest statements about illegal drugs were his infamous statement "I didn't inhale" and his immediate and dramatic cut in the size of the federal antidrug staff. Morale and political leadership were both compromised, and a national cynicism about drug use resulted.

Hiring a four-star general may have fooled the public and the Washington press corps for a while, but it didn't add up to a meaningful program.

To paraphrase Arthur Miller, attention was not paid, and the problem quickly worsened: Between 1992 and 1999, rates of current drug use—defined as using once a month or more—increased by 15%. Rates of marijuana use increased 11%. The situation was far worse among our children: Lifetime use of illegal drugs increased by 37% among eighth-graders and 55% among 10th-graders. We have reached the point where more than one-quarter of all high school seniors are current users of illegal drugs; indeed, rates of monthly drug use among high school seniors increased 86% between 1992 and 1999.

We must re-engage this fight. What we were doing in the 1980s and early 1990s—vigorous law enforcement and interdiction coupled with effective prevention and treatment—worked. It can work again.

The most important component of any antidrug strategy is prevention. Children who reach the age of 21 without using illegal drugs are almost certain never to do so. The Partnership for a Drug-Free America has crafted some of the most memorable and effective advertisements in history, encouraging children to turn down illegal drugs. The message that drug use is dangerous and immoral is the essential key to prevention.

In addition, we must continue to develop effective treatment programs. Many criticisms have been leveled at America's lack of treatment capacity, but more troubling is the lack of treatment efficacy. However, 12-step programs (akin to Alcoholics Anonymous) have been shown to be both inexpensive and effective in private-sector drug treatment. Hopefully, their success can be extended to public-sector treatment as well.

Everyone agrees on the necessity of effective treatment and strong prevention efforts. Some people, however, believe that law enforcement should have no role in the process. This is an altogether simplistic model: Demand reduction cannot be effective without supply reduction.

It is true that there will always be a supply of illegal drugs as long as there is a demand. But forceful interdiction can help to increase the price and decrease the purity of drugs available, a critical means of intervening in the lives of addicts, who can only beg, borrow, and steal so much to support their habit. Government reports document that recovering addicts are more likely to relapse when faced with cheap, plentiful drugs. Aggressive interdiction efforts, then, are not supply reduction so much as the first step in demand reduction.

Some people will admit that there is a place for law enforcement, but contend we spend too much on this effort, to the detriment of demand reduction. In fact, according to Robert DuPont, who led the nation's antidrug efforts under Presidents Nixon and Ford, there has never been as much federal money spent on prevention education as is being spent today. The United States' total spending on drug-demand reduction far exceeds the amounts spent in the rest of the world combined.

A more pragmatic point: While treatment is often centered at the individual and local levels, interdiction and law enforcement must be federal responsibilities. Given the scope and complexity of drug trafficking, the federal government can and must assume the responsibility for stopping the traffic of drugs across and within our borders. The drug czar's first concerns, then, must be interdiction and law enforcement, if only because they are tasks no other agency can perform as effectively.

I believe that the position of drug czar ought to remain at the cabinet level, but more important is the president's personal support and commitment to the office. I had that backing, and I expect the new drug czar will enjoy that same support and commitment from Mr. Bush. If Mr. Walters is to have any success, he must enjoy it.

The past eight years are, once again, illustrative: Gen. Barry McCaffrey never enjoyed that support from President Clinton. In renewing the drug war, the new drug czar will not be alone. He will be able to draw on the assistance of people—parents, teachers, substance-abuse counselors, clergymen, and elected officials—who have continued to fight drug use over the past eight years. These groups are our first lines of defense; without them, the regression since 1992 would have been far worse. Their dedication gives the lie to the gospel of futility.

I look forward to America re-engaging in the war on drugs—and continuing the success that we had between 1980 and 1992.

An Open Letter to Bill Bennett

Milton Friedman

This selection first appeared in the *Wall Street Journal*, September 7, 1989.

Dear Bill: In Oliver Cromwell's eloquent words, "I beseech you, in the bowels of Christ, think it possible you may be mistaken" about the course you and President Bush urge us to adopt to fight drugs. The path you propose of more police, more jails, use of the military in foreign countries, harsh penalties for drug users, and a whole panoply of repressive measures can only make a bad situation worse. The drug war cannot be won by those tactics without undermining the human liberty and individual freedom that you and I cherish.

You are not mistaken in believing that drugs are a scourge that is devastating our society. You are not mistaken in believing that drugs are tearing asunder our social fabric, ruining the lives of many young people, and imposing heavy costs on some of the most disadvantaged among us. You are not mistaken in believing that the majority of the public share your concerns. In short, you are not mistaken in the end you seek to achieve.

Your mistake is failing to recognize that the very measures you favor are a major source of the evils you deplore. Of course the problem is demand, but it is not only demand, it is demand that must operate through repressed and illegal channels. Illegality creates obscene profits that finance the murderous tactics of the drug lords; illegality leads to the corruption of law enforcement officials; illegality monopolizes the efforts of honest law forces so that they are starved for resources to fight the simpler crimes of robbery, theft, and assault.

Drugs are a tragedy for addicts. But criminalizing their use converts that tragedy into a disaster for society, for users and non-users alike. Our experience with the prohibition of drugs is a replay of our experience with the prohibition of alcoholic beverages. I append excerpts from a column that I wrote in 1972 on "Prohibition and Drugs."

The major problem then was heroin from Marseilles; today, it is cocaine from Latin America. Today, also, the problem is far more serious than it was 17 years ago: more addicts, more innocent victims; more drug pushers, more law enforcement officials; more money spent to enforce prohibition, more money spent to circumvent prohibition.

Had drugs been decriminalized 17 years ago, "crack" would never have been invented (it was invented because the high cost of illegal drugs made it profitable to provide a cheaper version) and there would today be far fewer addicts. The lives of thousands, perhaps hundreds of thousands, of innocent victims would have been saved, and not only in the United States. The ghettos of our major cities would not be drug-and-crime-infested no-man's lands. Fewer people would be in jails, and fewer jails would have been built.

Colombia, Bolivia, and Peru would not be suffering from narco-terror, and we would not be distorting our foreign policy because of narco-terror. Hell would not, in the words with which Billy Sunday welcomed Prohibition, "be forever for rent," but it would be a lot emptier.

Decriminalizing drugs is even more urgent now than in 1972, but we must recognize that the harm done in the interim cannot be wiped out, certainly not immediately. Postponing decriminalization will only make matters worse, and make the problem appear even more intractable.

Alcohol and tobacco cause many more deaths in users than do drugs. Decriminalization would not prevent us from treating drugs as we now treat alcohol and tobacco: prohibiting sales of drugs to minors, outlawing the advertising of drugs, and similar measures. Such measures could be enforced, while outright prohibition cannot be. Moreover, if even a small fraction of the money we now spend on trying to enforce drug prohibition were devoted to treatment and rehabilitation, in an atmosphere of compassion not punishment, the reduction in drug usage and in the harm done to the users could be dramatic.

This plea comes from the bottom of my heart. Every friend of freedom, and I know you are one, must be as revolted as I am by the prospect of turning the United States into an armed camp, by the vision of jails filled with casual drug users and of an army of enforcers empowered to invade the liberty of citizens on slight evidence. A country in which shooting down unidentified planes "on suspicion" can be seriously considered as a drug-war tactic is not the kind of United States that either you or I want to hand on to future generations.

Should Drugs Be Legalized?

William J. Bennett

This selection originally appeared in the *Reader's Digest*, March 1990.

Since I took command of the war on drugs, I have learned from former Secretary of State George Shultz that our concept of fighting drugs is "flawed." The only thing to do, he says, is to "make it possible for addicts to buy drugs at some regulated place." Conservative commentator William F. Buckley Jr. suggests I should be "fatalistic" about the flood of cocaine from South America and simply "let it in." Syndicated columnist Mike Royko contends it would be easier to sweep junkies out of the gutters "than to fight a hopeless war" against the narcotics that send them there. Labeling our efforts "bankrupt," federal judge Robert W. Sweet opts for legalization, saying, "If our society can learn to stop using butter, it should be able to cut down on cocaine."

Flawed, fatalistic, hopeless, bankrupt! I never realized surrender was so fashionable until I assumed this post.

Though most Americans are overwhelmingly determined to go toe-to-toe with the foreign drug lords and neighborhood pushers, a small minority believe that enforcing drug laws imposes greater costs on society than do drugs themselves. Like addicts seeking immediate euphoria, the legalizers want peace at any price, even though it means the inevitable proliferation of a practice that degrades, impoverishes, and kills.

I am acutely aware of the burdens drug enforcement places upon us. It consumes economic resources we would like to use elsewhere. It is sometimes frustrating, thankless, and often dangerous. But the consequences of *not* enforcing drug laws would be far more costly. Those consequences involve the intrinsically destructive nature of drugs and the toll they exact from our society in hundreds of thousands of lost and broken lives . . . human potential never realized . . . time stolen from families and jobs . . . precious spiritual and economic resources squandered.

That is precisely why virtually every civilized society has found it necessary to exert some form of control over mind-altering substances and why this war is so important. Americans feel up to their hips in drugs now. They would be up to their necks under legalization.

Even limited experiments in drug legalization have shown that when drugs are more widely available, addiction skyrockets. In 1975 Italy liberalized its drug law and now has one of the highest heroin-related death rates in Western Europe. In Alaska, where marijuana was decriminalized in 1975, the easy atmosphere has increased usage of the drug, particularly among children. Nor does it stop there. Some Alaskan schoolchildren now tout "coca puffs," marijuana cigarettes laced with cocaine.

Many legalizers concede that drug legalization might increase use, but they shrug off the matter. "It may well be that there would be more addicts, and I would regret that result," says Nobel laureate economist Milton Friedman. The late Harvard Medical School psychiatry professor Norman Zinberg, a long-time proponent of "responsible" drug use, admitted that "use of now illicit drugs would certainly increase. Also, casualties probably would increase."

In fact, Dr. Herbert D. Kleber of Yale University, my deputy in charge of demand reduction, predicts legalization might cause "a five-to-sixfold increase" in cocaine use. But legalizers regard this as a necessary price for the "benefits" of legalization. What benefits?

1. *Legalization will take the profit out of drugs.* The result supposedly will be the end of criminal drug pushers and the big foreign

drug wholesalers, who will turn to other enterprises because nobody will need to make furtive and dangerous trips to his local pusher.

But what, exactly, would the brave new world of legalized drugs look like? Buckley stresses that "adults get to buy the stuff at carefully regulated stores." (Would you want one in *your* neighborhood?) Others, like Friedman, suggest we sell the drugs at "ordinary retail outlets."

Former City University of New York sociologist Georgette Bennett assures us that "brand-name competition will be prohibited" and that strict quality control and proper labeling will be overseen by the Food and Drug Administration. In a touching egalitarian note, she adds that "free drugs will be provided at government clinics" for addicts too poor to buy them.

Almost all the legalizers point out that the price of drugs will fall, even though the drugs will be heavily taxed. Buckley, for example, argues that somehow federal drugstores will keep the price "low enough to discourage a black market but high enough to accumulate a surplus to be used for drug education."

Supposedly, drug sales will generate huge amounts of revenue, which will then be used to tell the public not to use drugs and to treat those who don't listen.

In reality, this tax would only allow government to *share* the drug profits now garnered by criminals. Legalizers would have to tax drugs heavily in order to pay for drug education and treatment programs. Criminals could undercut the official price and still make huge profits. What alternative would the government have? Cut the price until it was within the lunch-money budget of the average sixth-grade student?

2. *Legalization will eliminate the black market.* Wrong. And not just because the regulated prices could be undercut. Many legalizers admit that drugs such as crack or PCP are simply too dangerous to allow the shelter of the law. Thus criminals will provide what the government will not. "As long as drugs that people very much want

remain illegal, a black market will exist," says legalization advocate David Boaz of the libertarian Cato Institute.

Look at crack. In powdered form, cocaine was an expensive indulgence. But street chemists found that a better and far less expensive — and far more dangerous — high could be achieved by mixing cocaine with baking soda and heating it. Crack was born, and "cheap" coke invaded low-income communities with furious speed.

An ounce of powdered cocaine might sell on the street for $1200. That same ounce can produce 370 vials of crack at $10 each. Ten bucks seems like a cheap hit, but crack's intense ten- to fifteen-minute high is followed by an unbearable depression. The user wants more crack, thus starting a rapid and costly descent into addiction.

If government drugstores do not stock crack, addicts will find it in the clandestine market or simply bake it themselves from their legally purchased cocaine.

Currently, crack is being laced with insecticides and animal tranquilizers to heighten its effect. Emergency rooms are now warned to expect victims of "sandwiches" and "moon rocks," life-threatening smokable mixtures of heroin and crack. Unless the government is prepared to sell these deadly variations of dangerous drugs, it will perpetuate a criminal black market by default.

And what about children and teenagers? They would obviously be barred from drug purchases, just as they are prohibited from buying beer and liquor. But pushers will continue to cater to these young customers with the old, favorite come-ons — a couple of free fixes to get them hooked, and what good will anti-drug education be when these youngsters observe their older brothers and sisters, parents and friends lighting up and shooting up with government permission?

Legalization will give us the worst of both worlds: millions of *new* drug users *and* a thriving criminal black market.

3. *Legalization will dramatically reduce crime.* "It is the high price of drugs that leads addicts to robbery, murder, and other crimes," says Ira Glasser, executive director of the American Civil

Liberties Union. A study by the Cato Institute concludes: "Most, if not all, 'drug-related murders' are the result of drug prohibition."

But researchers tell us that many drug-related felonies are committed by people involved in crime *before* they started taking drugs. The drugs, so routinely available in criminal circles, make the criminals more violent and unpredictable.

Certainly there are some kill-for-a-fix crimes, but does any rational person believe that a cut-rate price for drugs at a government outlet will stop such psychopathic behavior? The fact is that under the influence of drugs, normal people do not act normally, and abnormal people behave in chilling and horrible ways. DEA agents told me about a teenage addict in Manhattan who was smoking crack when he sexually abused and caused permanent internal injuries to his one-month-old daughter.

Children are among the most frequent victims of violent, drug-related crimes that have nothing to do with the cost of acquiring the drugs. In Philadelphia in 1987 more than half the child-abuse fatalities involved at least one parent who was a heavy drug user. Seventy-three percent of the child-abuse deaths in New York City in 1987 involved parental drug use.

In my travels to the ramparts of the drug war, I have seen nothing to support the legalizers' argument that lower drug prices would reduce crime. Virtually everywhere I have gone, police and DEA agents have told me that crime rates are highest where crack is cheapest.

4. *Drug use should be legal since users only harm themselves.* Those who believe this should stand beside the medical examiner as he counts the thirty-six bullet wounds in the shattered corpse of a three-year-old who happened to get in the way of his mother's drug-crazed boyfriend. They should visit the babies abandoned by cocaine-addicted mothers—infants who already carry the ravages of addiction in their own tiny bodies. They should console the devastated relatives of the nun who worked in a homeless shelter and was stabbed to

death by a crack addict enraged that she would not stake him to a fix.

Do drug addicts only harm themselves? Here is a former cocaine addict describing the compulsion that quickly draws even the most "responsible" user into irresponsible behavior: "Everything is about getting high, and any means necessary to get there becomes rational. If it means stealing something from somebody close to you, lying to your family, borrowing money from people you know you can't pay back, writing checks you know you can't cover, you do all those things—things that are totally against everything you have ever believed in."

Society pays for this behavior, and not just in bigger insurance premiums, losses from accidents, and poor job performance. We pay in the loss of a priceless social currency as families are destroyed, trust between friends is betrayed, and promising careers are never fulfilled. I cannot imagine sanctioning behavior that would increase that toll.

I find no merit in the legalizers' case. The simple fact is that drug use is wrong. And the moral argument, in the end, is the most compelling argument. A citizen in a drug-induced haze, whether on his backyard deck or on a mattress in a ghetto crack house, is not what the founding fathers meant by the "pursuit of happiness." Despite the legalizers' argument that drug use is a matter of "personal freedom," our nation's notion of liberty is rooted in the ideal of a self-reliant citizenry. Helpless wrecks in treatment centers, men chained by their noses to cocaine—these people are slaves.

Imagine if, in the darkest days of 1940, Winston Churchill had rallied the West by saying, "This war looks hopeless, and besides, it will cost too much. Hitler can't be *that* bad. Let's surrender and see what happens." That is essentially what we hear from the legalizers.

This war *can* be won. I am heartened by indications that education and public revulsion are having an effect on drug use. The National Institute on Drug Abuse's latest survey of current users shows a 37 percent *decrease* in drug consumption since 1985. Cocaine is down 50 percent; marijuana use among young people is at its lowest rate since 1972. In my travels I've been encouraged by signs that Americans are fighting back.

I am under no illusion that such developments, however hopeful, mean the war is over. We need to involve more citizens in the fight, increase pressure on drug criminals and build on antidrug programs that have proved to work. This will not be easy. But the moral and social costs of surrender are simply too great to contemplate.

Just Say No: Government's War on Drugs Fails

John Stossel

John Stossel is co-anchor of ABC News's 20/20.

This selection first appeared on an ABCNEWS.com original report (July 30, 2002, available online at http://abcnews.go.com/onair/2020/stossel_drugs _020730.html).

July 30—Have you ever used illegal drugs? The government says a third of Americans have at some point—and about 5 percent use them regularly.

The number may be higher, because how many people honestly answer the question, "Have you used an illicit drug in the past month?"

What should America do about this? So far, our approach has been to go to war—a war that police departments fight every day. A war that U.S. politicians tackle in a different way than their European counterparts. And a war that is not going away.

Asa Hutchinson, President Bush's choice to run the Drug Enforcement Administration, travels the world telling Americans that we're winning the drug war. "Overall drug use in the United States has been reduced by 50 percent over the last 20 years," he says.

But it's questionable whether the fall is attributable to the government's policies, or whether it was just people getting smarter after the binges of the 1970s. In the last 10 years drug use hasn't dropped— despite federal spending on the drug war rising 50 percent. And despite all the seizures, drugs are still as available as they ever were.

Hutchinson agrees that there are problems with the government's efforts. "We have flat-lined. I believe we lost our focus to a certain extent," he says. "I don't believe that we had the same type of energy devoted to it as we have in certain times in the past."

Detroit Police Chief Jerry Oliver is not convinced that expending more energy—and making more drug arrests—will help America win the crusade. "We will never arrest our way out of this problem," he says. "All you have to do is go to almost any corner in any city. It will tell you that . . ."

"Clearly, we're losing the war on drugs in this country [and] it's insanity to keep doing the same thing over and over again."

SEDUCED BY MONEY

We know the terrible things drugs can do. We've seen the despair, the sunken face of the junkie. No wonder those in government say that we have to fight drugs. And polls show most Americans agree. Drug use should be illegal. Or as former "drug czar" Bill Bennett put it: "It's a matter of right and wrong."

But when "right and wrong" conflict with supply and demand, nasty things happen. The government declaring drugs illegal doesn't mean people can't get them, it just means they get them on the black market, where they pay much more for them.

"The only reason that coke is worth that much money is that it's illegal," argues Father Joseph Kane, a priest in a drug-ravaged Bronx neighborhood in New York City. "Pure cocaine is three times the cost of gold. Now if that's the case, how are you gonna stop people from selling cocaine?"

Kane has come to believe that while drug abuse is bad, drug prohibition is worse—because the black market does horrible things to his community. "There's so much money in it, it's staggering," he says.

Orange County, Calif., Superior Court Judge James Gray agrees with Kane. He spent years locking drug dealers up, but concluded it's pointless, because drug prohibition makes the drugs so absurdly valuable. "We are recruiting children in the Bronx, in the barrios, and all over the nation, because of drug money," he says.

Besides luring kids into the underworld, drug money is also corrupting law enforcement officers, he argues.

Cops are seduced by drug money. They have been for years. "With all the money, with all the cash, it's easy for [dealers] to purchase police officers, to purchase prosecutors, to purchase judges," says Oliver, the Detroit police chief.

The worst unintended consequence of the drug war is drug crime. Films like *Reefer Madness* told us that people take drugs and just go crazy. But, in reality people rarely go crazy or become violent because they're high.

The violence happens because dealers arm themselves and have shootouts over turf. Most of the drug-related violence comes from the fact that it's illegal, argues Kane. Violence also happens because addicts steal to pay the high prices for drugs.

AN ALTERNATIVE TO PROHIBITION

There's no question that drugs often wreck lives. But the drug war wrecks lives too, creates crime, and costs billions of dollars.

Is there an alternative? Much of Europe now says there is.

In Amsterdam, using marijuana is legal. Holland now has hundreds of "coffee shops" where marijuana is officially tolerated. Clients pick up small amounts of marijuana the same way they would pick up a bottle of wine at the store.

The police regulate marijuana sales—shops may sell no more than about five joints worth per person, they're not allowed to sell to minors, and no hard drugs are allowed.

What has been the result of legalizing marijuana? Is everyone getting stoned? No. In America today 38 percent of adolescents have smoked pot—in Holland, it's only 20 percent.

What Amsterdam police did was take the glamour out of drug use, explains Judge Gray. The Dutch minister of health has said, "We've succeeded in making pot boring."

The DEA has said legalizing cannabis and hash in the Netherlands was a failure—an unmitigated disaster. Not so, say people in Amsterdam. And Rotterdam Police Superintendent Jur Verbeek says selling the drug in coffee shops may deter young, curious people who will try marijuana one way or another, from further experimentation with harder drugs.

"When there are no coffee shops, they will go to the illegal houses, where the dealer says, 'OK, you want to have marijuana. Good. But we have cocaine as well. And we have heroin for you,'" Verbeek argues.

DON'T ASK, DON'T TELL

Still, in America, there's little interest in legalizing any drug. President Bush says "drug use threatens everything." And officials talk about fighting a stronger war. Some say it shouldn't be even talked about.

In 1991, Joycelyn Elders, who would become President Clinton's surgeon general, dared to suggest legalization might reduce crime. Critics almost immediately called for her resignation. "How can you ever fix anything if you can't even talk about it?" Elders says.

What the Dutch are doing makes sense to Gray. "They're addressing it as managers," he says. "We address it as moralizers. We address it as a character issue, and if you fail that test, we put you in prison."

Experiments with being more permissive of drugs have spread beyond the Netherlands. Today, police in most of Europe ignore marijuana use. Spain, Italy, and Luxembourg have decriminalized most drug use.

That's not to say that all the experiments succeed everywhere. Switzerland once tried what became known as Needle Park, a place where anyone could use any drug. It attracted crime because it became a magnet for junkies from all over Europe.

Critics say the Netherlands has become an island of drug use. But while illegal selling still happens, the use of drugs in the Netherlands and all Europe is still far lower than in the United States, and European countries are proposing even more liberalization.

American politicians have shown little interest in that.

"We in America should have a different approach," explains Hutchinson. "You do not win in these efforts by giving in."

HOPELESS FIGHT?

Still, how many wars can America fight? Now that we're at war against terrorism, can we also afford to fight a drug war against millions of our own people? Is it wise to fight on two fronts?

The last time America engaged in a war of this length was Vietnam, and then, too, government put a positive spin on success of the war.

But today more people have doubts. Judge Gray questions the government's ability to protect us from ourselves. "It makes as much sense to me to put actor Robert Downey Jr. in jail for his drug abuse as it would have Betty Ford in jail for her alcohol abuse. It's really no different."

Gray advocates holding people accountable for what they do—not for what they put into their bodies.

Why not sell drugs like we do alcohol, he says, though maybe with more restrictions. "Let's make it available to adults. Brown packaging, no glamour, take the illegal money out of it and then furnish it, holding people accountable for what they do," he suggests. "These drugs are too dangerous not to control."

Legal drugs—that's a frightening thought. Maybe more people would try them.

Gray says even if they did, that would do less harm than the war we've been fighting for the past thirty years.

"What we're doing now has failed. In fact it's hopeless," he argues. "This is a failed system that we simply must change."

A War Worth Fighting

Lou Dobbs

Lou Dobbs is the anchor and managing editor of CNN's "Lou Dobbs Tonight."

This selection originally appeared in the *Washington Times*, August 16, 2003.

We've spent hundreds of billions of dollars on law enforcement, prevention, and treatment since President Richard Nixon declared the war on drugs in 1971. Yet the use of illicit drugs continues to plague our country. The federal government spends nearly $1 billion a month to fight the war on drugs, but users spend more than 5 times that much a month to buy drugs.

Beyond the horrific human toll of 20,000 drug-induced deaths each year, illegal drugs cost our economy more than $280 billion annually, according to the Substance Abuse and Mental Health Services Administration.

Incredibly, there are those who choose to ignore the human devastation and the economic cost of the drug plague. Many of them are pseudo-sophisticated Baby Boomers who consider themselves superior and hip in their wry, reckless disregard of the facts. They may also smoke marijuana, advocate its legalization, and rationalize cocaine by calling it a recreational drug.

And there is a surprising list of libertarians and conservatives, including William F. Buckley and Nobel laureate economist Milton Friedman, who advocate the legalization or decriminalization of drugs.

Another Nobel laureate, Gary S. Becker, professor of economics

at the University of Chicago, told me: "It [legalization] would certainly save a lot of resources for society. We could tax drug use so it
could even lead to government revenue. . . . We would be able to
greatly cut the number of people in prison, which would save
resources for state and local government."

But the cost of drug abuse goes well beyond the expense to control supply and demand. Drug users cost the country $160 billion
each year in lost productivity. Parental substance abuse is responsible
for $10 billion of the $14 billion spent nationally each year on child
welfare costs. And drugs are involved in 7 out of every 10 cases of
child abuse and neglect.

Pete Wilson, the former governor of California, is a strong opponent of drug legalization. Mr. Wilson says the problem that advocates
of legalization fail to acknowledge is that drugs are addictive in
nature, and are therefore not just another commodity.

"Drugs did not become viewed as bad because they are illegal,"
Mr. Wilson says. "Rather, they became illegal because they are clearly
bad."

Although the war on drugs certainly has not captured the American public's attention to the extent that it should, there has been
success in efforts to curb drug use and supply. According to the University of Michigan's "Monitoring the Future" study, the percentage
of high-school seniors who reported using any drug within the past
month decreased from 39 percent in 1978 to 26 percent in 2001.
There are a total of 9 million fewer drug users in America now than
there were in 1979. And coca cultivation was 15 percent lower in
Colombia in 2002, due to the combined efforts of the United States
and Colombian governments.

Drug czar John Walters, director of the Office of National Drug
Control Policy, is optimistic about the war on drugs.

"We have to remember that, since we got serious in the '80s,
overall drug use is half of what it was—and that's progress," Mr. Walters told me last week.

I would say that is quite a lot of progress. But the job is only half
done.

The Drug War: The American Junkie

Joseph D. McNamara

Joseph D. McNamara is a research fellow at the Hoover Institution and the former police chief of San Jose, California.

This selection originally appeared in the *Hoover Digest*—2004 No. 2 (Stanford, Calif: Hoover Institution Press, 2004).

The average white American's image of drug users is that of dangerous young people of color—males who will rob them to obtain money to buy drugs or youthful black female prostitutes spreading disease and delivering crack babies as a result of enslavement to drugs. These cherished misconceptions are the enduring and erroneous foundations of the ill-conceived "war on drugs."

Actually, the overwhelming majority of American drug users have historically been Caucasians. The fact that minorities are arrested and incarcerated at vastly disproportionate rates for drug offenses contributes to false stereotypes and permits the continuation of one of the most irrational public policies in the history of the United States. Blacks make up approximately 15 percent of America's drug users, but more than one-third of adults arrested for drug violations are black. Similar distortions in drug arrests and incarcerations apply to Hispanics.

Relatively few of America's estimated 90 million illegal drug users go on to commit non-drug crimes. In fact, the majority of police I hired during my 18 years as police chief in two of the largest cities in America admitted prior use of illegal drugs. They did not commit other crimes and grew out of their early drug use. As one candidate put it to me, "Of course, I smoked pot. I was in the Army. I went to college."

And I can remember, some forty years ago, as a young policeman in Harlem, gathering with my colleagues in a tavern after work, listening to them complain vigorously about the junkies who made our work so difficult. During our discussions, we drank prodigious amounts of beer without the slightest awareness that we were consuming a drug that could be as lethal as heroin. Indeed, far more of my fellow police died in driving accidents after these drinking sessions than were slain in the line of duty.

Even today, ninety years after the federal government first outlawed narcotics with the Harrison Narcotic Act, December 17, 1914, public and police attitudes toward the dangerousness of drugs are shaped by ignorance of their impact and by mistaken prejudices regarding their users. Stereotypes created more than a century ago by nativist American elites targeting blacks, immigrant Irish, German, Italian, and Jewish populations and their "strange" religions, languages, and cultures led to anti-drug legislation.

President Theodore Roosevelt, who held many of the same racial, ethnic, and class biases, greatly encouraged the anti-drug groups. Roosevelt, who was not an alcohol prohibitionist, was motivated by an anti-opium attitude, as well as by a desire to develop America into one of the great world powers. He hoped that stopping England, France, Holland, and Spain from compelling the unwilling China to accept highly profitable (for the exporting nations) opium shipments would win Chinese goodwill and allow Americans to compete with the colonial trading nations in opening the vast China market to other goods.

Despite revelations from Rush Limbaugh, Bill Clinton, Al Gore, John Kerry, Newt Gingrich, and George W. Bush (when questioned about prior drug use he didn't deny it, simply said that he did young and foolish things), our government continues to paint users of certain chemicals as evil and immoral, when in fact they often are successful people from across the political spectrum. Luckily for most of them, they didn't get busted under today's draconian laws and were able to mature into careers that most of us can admire.

A DRUG-FREE AMERICA?

For the first 140 years of this republic, the right to life, liberty, and the pursuit of happiness included the right to consume whatever substance one pleased. In fact, Thomas Jefferson criticized France for passing laws regulating diet and drugs on the basis that "a government that tries to control what kind of food you eat and medicine that you take will soon try to control how you think."

The idea that pleasure could be derived from sex, gambling, dancing, consumption of alcohol, or other drugs struck many influential groups as sinful and immoral. In *The Symbolic Crusade*, the sociologist Joseph Gusfield described how these same biased irrationalities led to passage of the failed Eighteenth Amendment, the criminal prohibition of alcohol.

This odd tendency to impose the heavy hand of criminal law to "sinful" and "immoral" behavior leads to numerous anomalies. For one thing, it diverts scarce resources from pursuing de facto crimes such as murder, assault, rape, theft, and the increasing threat of terrorism. In addition, individuals taking Prozac, Valium, or other psychoactive prescription drugs are regarded as patients. Yet millions of our own citizens using heroin, cocaine, or marijuana have been, and are still, regarded as dangerous enough to be caged in brutal prisons, frequently under mandatory sentences more characteristic of a totalitarian society than a democracy. State and local police alone average around 1,600,000 drug arrests a year. All except a couple of hundred thousand are for possession of small amounts of drugs but nevertheless frequently trigger long mandatory prison sentences.

The impetus for the passage of the Harrison Narcotic Act of 1914 came from the lobbying efforts of American missionary societies in

China. These groups enlisted the aid of other alcohol temperance organizations and religious groups in the United States to get their version of sin written into the penal code. The anti-drug arguments advocating the Harrison Act were replete with statements claiming that it was the duty of whites to save the inferior races. Those moving to criminalize drugs made references to Negroes under the influence of drugs murdering whites, degenerate Mexicans smoking marijuana, and "Chinamen" seducing white women with drugs. This racist nonsense would be laughed at today, but it was quite influential in the passage of anti-drug legislation.

Dr. David Musto, the renowned drug historian and professor of child psychiatry and the history of medicine at the Yale University School of Medicine, wrote in *The American Disease: Origins of Narcotics Control*, "Consequently, the story of the Harrison Act's passage contains many examples of the South's fear of the Negro as a ground for permitting a deviation from the strict interpretation of the Constitution." Musto also noted that opium use in the United States had been declining for about 16 years before the federal government saw fit to outlaw it.

The Harrison Narcotic Act of 1914 represented a gross departure from past federal practice of not interfering with state police powers. The racist arguments convinced southern representatives, who were reluctant to acknowledge federal power over states' rights, to vote for the act. Uneasiness regarding the law's constitutionality caused Congress to label the act a revenue measure, but in 1925, the U.S. Supreme Court correctly interpreted it as a penal statute, making it the cornerstone of laws leading to the present "war on drugs." Similarly, queasiness over constitutionality led Congress to label the 1937 law prohibiting marijuana, the Marijuana Tax Act.

It is one of the ironies of history that national black political leadership today paradoxically seems to accept the racist implications of white southern politicians in 1914: that Negroes were especially susceptible to the negative impact of drug use. With the notable exception of Kurt Schmoke, former mayor of Baltimore, who called for the medicalization of drug use, many African-American politicians describe decriminalization of drugs as racial genocide, thus subliminally reinforcing fears that people of color are more susceptible to drug use and the harm it can cause.

GOVERNMENT THOUGHT CONTROL

The Harrison Act was a remarkably radical change in public policy. Racism, religious pressure, and an elitist concern to ensure that the lower classes were protected from temptations to lead "immoral" lives prevailed over the promises of the Declaration of Independence. Jefferson's fears of government thought control have come to fruition in the drug war.

That may sound far-fetched, but the Clinton White House was embarrassed when a journalist disclosed that the government had been secretly paying television entertainment and news programs, magazines, and newspapers to covertly insert "correct" material on drug use for our education. Now the government openly spends millions of dollars on simplistic anti-drug ads during the television Super Bowl extravaganza, right alongside commercial ads pushing beer, drugs to cure erectile dysfunction and other real or imagined illnesses, and food that the government itself has labeled as dangerously unhealthy.

WHAT PRICE GLORY?

Since 1914, American drug control efforts have ebbed and peaked. However, a sea change occurred in 1972 when Richard Nixon saw political advantage in telling the citizenry that a war against drugs was necessary. The federal budget for the war was roughly $101 million that year. Presently, it is around $20 *billion* a year. By comparison, the average monthly Social Security retirement check in 1972 was $177. Presently, the payment averages slightly more than $900 a month. If, however, Social Security benefits had increased at the same rate as drug war spending, today's check would be around $30,000 a month. The annual cost of the drug war exceeds $40 billion a year when state and local costs are added to federal costs.

The magnitude of increase and paucity of positive results have recently begun to cause concern among some of the leading academic supporters of the drug war. A major focus of government strategy has been to reduce foreign production of illegal drugs. Yet a dozen years after the U.S. Congress proclaimed that we would have a drug-free America by 1995 (the United Nations has made an even more grandiose claim for a drug-free world), opium production has doubled in Southeast Asia and cocaine crops have increased by a third in Central and South America. Opium production has also greatly increased in liberated Afghanistan.

Periodic government announcements of epidemic increases in the use of "designer drugs" such as methamphetamines and ecstasy are intended to mobilize more public support for the drug war. What the anti-drug propaganda really illustrates, however, is the futility of attempts by the United States to reduce world drug production since domestically produced drugs are quickly substituted. The government has been forced to concede that, despite intensive efforts at interdiction, around 90 percent of the illegal drugs that arrive in this country are undetected.

The United States, as well as most of the world, is awash in illegal drugs, the violence of the illegal drug black market, and unprecedented police and political corruption resulting from the extreme markup caused by the prohibition of cheaply produced chemical substances.

AN UNCONSCIONABLE WAR

Reasonable people agree that all drugs—including aspirin and others sold over the counter or those prescribed by physicians—present potential danger to users, especially to children, and should be approached with caution. However, the sheer irrationality of continuing to expand a policy doomed to failure begs an explanation. A jihad comes to mind—a holy war that must be fought regardless of the resulting human horrors. A subcommittee of the National Academy of Sciences, in response to a request from the Clinton administration to analyze the effectiveness of the nation's efforts to control drugs, concluded last year that it was "unconscionable" for the government to implement a program of this "magnitude" without measuring its impact. Predictably, this group of researchers recommended more research on the drug war's impact, not a cease-fire.

Nonetheless, some scholars, bureaucrats, prosecutors, judges, and politicians who can no longer ignore the injustices of long mandatory drug sentences for minor offenders, and the inevitable failure of past practices, now proclaim a new more "humane" solution. The government is eagerly expanding "coerced abstinence" as a compassionate alternative. Coerced abstinence is the practice of continuously drug-testing convicted criminals (and eventually, in all probability, many others), by special drug courts, to detect the presence of illegal drugs in their bodies. In March 2004, a physician who prescribed OxyContin (oxycodone HCl controlled-release) for pain relief reported that a blood test indicated the patient had *not* been taking the medicine. The patient was arrested in the doctor's office.

PRESUMPTION OF INNOCENCE?

Many judges, who traditionally functioned as impartial legal experts to guarantee due process of law, have now become shamans taking on the responsibilities of judging who is falling under evil spells. We

have legions of real-life "Judge Judys" routinely operating with religious fervor, denouncing and incarcerating people not on the basis of
crimes they committed but because certain chemicals are present in
their urine. Of course, it's for their own "good," but some critics call
it life on the installment plan.

Scholars who know well the difference between correlation and
causation have causally disregarded two axioms of behavioral science
by advancing coerced abstinence as new when, in fact, it is the same
old demonization of certain drugs present in our culture and the
same dehumanization of their users.

It is true that many individuals convicted of crime do have a
history of previous use of illegal drugs. But high correlations of ille-
gitimacy, illiteracy, extreme poverty, lack of health care, child abuse,
failure in school, smoking, gambling, unhealthy diets, poor employment history, and a host of other variables are also present in criminal
populations. Drug use as the sole explanation for criminal behavior
is no more persuasive than these other characteristics. In truth, if we
foolishly outlawed the conduct mentioned above, we would create
the same criminal identities presently imposed on users of illegal
drugs. Experts know that past behavior, including the use of certain
chemicals, cannot be used to predict the future criminal behavior of
a particular individual to the extent that it scientifically or morally
justifies imprisonment.

America's drug war has always trifled with science. But the
assumption that the presence of a particular chemical in a person's
bloodstream is sufficient cause for incarceration replaces the fundamental American right of presumption of innocence with the police-
state mentality of assumed guilt. Yet, like many repressive
governments, advocates of coerced abstinence say that we should not
worry. Our children, friends, and relatives in jail cells for minor drug
violations are not prisoners. They are simply patients undergoing the
new therapy of coerced abstinence, "tough love."

One advocate of present drug policies argued that certain drugs are not bad because they are illegal, they are illegal because they are bad. History, however, indicates that a century ago the groups that successfully lobbied to criminalize some drugs were equally motivated by their mistaken impression of which and why certain groups used specific chemical substances.

If you're under the misimpression that such bias has changed, conduct your own experiment. Watch television and count the number of drug commercials. The messages are certainly not that we need a "drug-free America." Instead, omniscient ads convey the idea that drugs are "cool" depending mostly on who uses them.

Our nation's drug policy has squandered hundreds of billions of dollars, locked up millions of Americans, destroyed countless families and neighborhoods, and created immeasurable violence and corruption. It is untenable to continue such policies by contending that conditions would be even worse without the drug war.

Congressional Testimony in Opposition to Drug Legalization

Bruce D. Glasscock

Bruce D. Glasscock serves as the chief of the Plano, Texas, police department and second vice president of the International Association of Chiefs of Police.

The following selection is congressional testimony by Bruce D. Glasscock before the House Committee on Government Reform, Subcommittee on Criminal Justice, Drug Policy, and Human Resources, Washington, DC, on July 13, 1999.

My name is Bruce Glasscock; I am the chief of the Plano, Texas, police department and also serve as second vice president of the International Association of Chiefs of Police. I am pleased to be here this morning to share my experience in combating drug abuse and my views on the question of drug legalization. The issue of drug legalization is of great concern to those of us in the law enforcement community. It is my belief the nature of our profession provides law enforcement officials with a unique insight into the ravages caused by the abuse of narcotics and other dangerous drugs. These experiences have clearly demonstrated to me that this nation should not be considering legalizing drugs, but rather we should increase our efforts to combat drug traffickers and assisting those individuals who have become addicted on drugs to break the cycle of addiction.

Over the last few years, my position as chief of the Plano Police Department has provided me with a firsthand look at the problems and dangers that accompany drug abuse. The recent heroin overdose death of former Dallas Cowboy Mark Tuinci received extensive national media coverage; unfortunately, it was not the first such occurrence in Plano. Our community was faced with a series of events involving heroin overdoses that resulted in our taking an aggressive plan of action in dealing with drug abuse. In June 1995 the city of Plano experienced its first heroin-related death. Additionally, between 1995 and 1996, our detectives noted an increase in burglaries being committed by heroin addicts to support their addictions. During this same time period local hospitals reported they were seeing about 6 overdoses a week, some of which resulted in death. Between 1995 and YTD 1999, there were 18 heroin overdose deaths related to Plano in some fashion—1 in 1995; 3 in 1996; 9 in 1997; 3 in 1998; and 2 deaths so far in 1999. The victims of these deaths were not your stereotypical drug addicts. The average age was 20 years old (range 14—36); most were young adolescent white males; most considered your average "All American Kid." Because of the rise in incidences of heroin overdoses, in early 1997 the Plano Police Department adopted a multifaceted strategy to attack the heroin crisis. First, we undertook aggressive enforcement action to identify and prosecute those responsible for supplying the heroin. The police department joined with the DEA, FBI, Texas Department of Public Safety, and other local law enforcement agencies in a coordinated effort.

Because of this effort, 29 individuals were indicted on federal charges of conspiring to distribute heroin and cocaine, as well as charges of contributing to heroin overdose deaths. Another of our enforcement actions involved an undercover operation in our senior high schools, which resulted in the arrest of 37 individuals on 84 cases of narcotics violations. We believe our enforcement actions have greatly reduced the amount of heroin being sold in the Plano community and the number of heroin overdoses.

The second part of this strategy involved using education as a means to reduce the demand for heroin. The DEA's Demand Reduction Specialist, who provided us with guidance in demand reduction, spoke at community meetings, helped utilize the media effectively, and assisted us in this effort. During this time our department hosted several community meetings, the largest occurring in November of 1997. This meeting was attended by more than 1,800 citizens and was televised and covered by the national and local media as well as the city cable television network. Our education efforts would not have been successful if it were not for the cooperation of the Plano Community Task Force, Plano's Promise, and many other community organizations not affiliated with the police department. These community organizations provided education programs to high school groups, PTAs, neighborhood associations, and church and parent groups. In addition to the above-mentioned strategies, our department is involved with several organizations that are working to continue the fight against drug abuse. These organizations strive to prevent drug usage through education, as well as intervention. The department is currently involved with the Kick Drugs Out of America Program, which is a school-based program designed to teach children the skills needed to resist drug and gang-related pressure. This program is in addition to the police department–run D.A.R.E. program, which also teaches elementary school children the risks of drugs and how to resist peer pressure.

We are currently working with a nonprofit organization in Florida that offers home drug-testing kits to families. This organization, Drug Free America, offers a free and anonymous way for parents to find out if their children are using drugs. If the child tests positive for drugs, Drug Free America provides the family with support organizations in or near the community to help with intervention efforts.

Our statistics show a clear reduction in the number of heroin overdose deaths, as well as hospitals reporting a reduction in overdose cases, which leads to the conclusion our strategy is working. Our continuing investigations also show a reduced availability of heroin on the streets in our community. Unfortunately, the battle is not over. Our drug risk assessment continues to show the North Texas area is a major hub for shipment and distribution of a variety of illegal drugs by Mexican drug traffickers. These drugs include methamphetamine, heroin, cocaine, and marijuana.

The porous Texas/Mexico border has 1,241 miles of frontier that challenges all our local, state, and federal resources. Since the enactment of the North American Free Trade Agreement (NAFTA) the major ports of entry have experienced approximately a 30 percent increase in legitimate commercial and passenger traffic. The number of vehicles inspected has increased, but the overall inspection rate has decreased, affording new opportunities for smuggling. Our statistics show, since passage of NAFTA in 1992, Texas had the highest volume of drug trafficking in the nation. All of this directly impacts local communities located along the NAFTA transportation corridors and will continue to do so.

This massive effort represents what just one city faces and has gone through to combat the flow of drugs into its community in order to protect its citizens. Plano is not unique; similar scenarios are being repeated in communities throughout the nation. Combined strategies like the ones I have just described to you are expensive, complex to manage, and sometimes controversial. However, they are working. Unfortunately, if those who favor legalization have their way, our efforts to reduce crime and protect our children from the horrors of drug abuse will be wasted. It is a simple fact: increased drug abuse and increased crime go hand in hand. It makes no difference whether users can purchase their drugs legally or not, they must still find a way to pay for them. And the way most drug addicts finance their habits is through crime. Eventually they will do one of two things— "they will either steal or deal." This is not just speculation on my part; in 1996 a study conducted by the National Institute of Justice clearly demonstrated drug users are more likely to be involved in criminal activities.

The findings in this study indicated that a median 68 percent of arrestees test positive for at least one drug at arrest, and the same study conducted in 1995 revealed that 31 percent of both male and female arrestees reported that they were under the influence of drugs or alcohol at the time they committed crimes. That year's report also indicated that 28 percent of inmates arrested for homicides were under the influence of drugs when they committed that crime.

In 1986, during the midst of the crack epidemic, violent crime reached a level of 617 violent crimes per 100,000 citizens. As we experienced a continuing escalation of drug-related violence, this figure rose in 1993 to 746 violent crimes for every 100,000 citizens. In response, an outraged public joined together with government leaders to challenge the escalating violent crime. As a result of these efforts vigorous new enforcement programs were implemented in the 1990s that have begun to reverse this trend. In recent years, we have seen a decrease in the violent crime rate in many communities—such as New York City, Boston, and Houston—attributable to aggressive law enforcement efforts and the incarceration of criminals. We know vigorous law enforcement actions aimed at criminal activity, including illegal drug use, can have a material effect on reducing violent crime in our communities. After making progress against violent crime during the past several years, we should not erode these gains by instituting policies such as the legalization of drugs, which we know will increase drug use and drug-related crime.

In addition, aside from the fact that legalization will lead to an increase in the level of crime and violence in our communities, increased drug use has terrible consequences for our citizens in other ways. Drug-related illness, death, and crime are estimated to cost Americans almost $67 billion a year. That translates into every American having to pay $1,000 per year to carry the costs of health care, extra law enforcement, car crashes, crime, and lost productivity due to drug use.

Drug use also impacts on the productivity of America's workers. Seventy-one percent of all illicit drug users are 18 or older and employed. In a study conducted by the U.S. Postal Service, the data collected shows that among drug users, absenteeism is 66 percent higher and health benefits utilization is 84 percent greater in dollar terms when compared against other workers. Disciplinary actions are 90 percent higher for employees who are drug users, as compared to non–drug users.

Public safety is another critical area that is impacted by drug abuse. A 1993 National Highway Traffic Safety Administration study reported that 18 percent of 2,000 fatally injured drivers from seven states had drugs other than alcohol in their systems when they died.

I trust it is clear by now why other law enforcement officials and I believe the legalization of drugs is the wrong course for our nation to take. Drug legalization will lead to increased crime; a decline in economic productivity; significantly increase the burden on an already strained health care system; endanger those traveling on our roadways; and, perhaps most tragically, sends a message to our children that drug use is acceptable.

The Partnership for a Drug Free America reported the results of a recent survey showing that as young Americans perceive that drugs are dangerous, drug use drops proportionately. Conversely, as young Americans get the message that social disapproval drops, as they hear the legalization debate, drug use increases. Drug use in America was reduced significantly between the years 1985 and 1992. Since 1992, and until recently, the amount of antidrug messages has decreased. As recently retired DEA Administrator Tom Constantine once said, ". . . as a nation we took our eye off the ball and began to get complacent about drugs—drug use among young people began to rise again in 1992." The legalization movement and the growing destigmatization of drugs, along with the confusing message we are giving our young people, will result in further decreases in the perceptions of risk, and I believe a concurrent increase in drug use among our youth.

Within this atmosphere it is very difficult—if not impossible—to reach children and convince them that doing drugs is bad. We must not make it easier or more acceptable for today's young people to start down the slippery slope from drug experimentation to drug addiction. We, as a nation, must continue to clearly, and unequivocally, state that drug use is dangerous, drug use is unhealthy, and drug use is illegal.

PART FOUR

Getting Specific

We're not really going to get anywhere until we take the criminality out of drugs.

> George P. Shultz
> *McNeil-Lehrer News Hour*
> December 18, 1989

Drugs are not dangerous because they are illegal; drugs are illegal because drugs are dangerous.

> David Griffin
> Canadian Police Association spokesman
> 2001

Current Controversies: Drug Legalization

Scott Barbour

Scott Barbour is the managing editor of Greenhaven Press.

The following selection first appeared in *Current Controversies—Drug Legalization* edited by Scott Barbour (San Diego, CA: Greenhaven Press, Inc. 2000).

In August 1999, federal agents announced that they had broken up one of America's twenty largest drug rings in a yearlong operation dubbed "Operation Southwest Express." In all, agents indicted 100 suspects, arrested 77, and seized 5,622 pounds of cocaine, two tons of marijuana, $1 million in cash, two Ferraris, a Land Rover, and seven weapons. In the process, they disrupted a network of smugglers and dealers that were bringing drugs into the country from Mexico through El Paso and supplying several major cities in the eastern and Midwestern United States, including Chicago, New York, and Boston.

While officials consider drug busts like Operation Southwest Express crucial to America's antidrug efforts, critics of the nation's drug war contend that breaking up one drug ring will have virtually no impact on the availability of drugs. Due to the great demand for illegal drugs in America—and the astronomical profits to be made by supplying them—another drug operation will quickly replace every one dismantled by the federal government. As David D. Boaz, vice president of the Cato Institute, states, "As long as Americans want to use drugs, and are willing to defy the law and pay high prices to do so, drug busts are futile. Other profit-seeking smugglers and dealers will always be ready to step in and take the place of those arrested."

The debate over law-enforcement tactics like Operation Southwest Express reflects the larger debate over drug legalization. Critics of the war on drugs, such as Boaz, contend that drug prohibition is a futile, costly effort that has failed to reduce drug use. They point out that the drug war costs the federal government more than $16 billion a year and that billions more are spent at the state and local levels. As a result of this massive antidrug campaign, four hundred thousand Americans are imprisoned for drug law violations. Sixty percent of federal prisoners and 25 percent of state and local inmates are held on drug charges—mostly for the relatively minor offenses of possession or low-level dealing to fund their personal use.

Despite this enormous effort, drug war opponents argue, drugs remain readily available and their use is increasing. In 1998, the Monitoring the Future Survey conducted by the University of Michigan reported that 90.4 percent of high school seniors say marijuana is "fairly easy" or "very easy" to obtain. The National Household Survey on Drug Abuse (NHSDA), conducted annually by the U.S. Department of Health and Human Services, found that the number of drug users in America has increased from 12 million in 1992 to 13.6 million in 1998. The number of teens reporting drug use within the prior month increased from 5.3 percent in 1992 to 11.4 percent in 1997. Although that number dropped slightly to 9.9 percent in 1998, it still remains well above the 1992 level. Among young adults age eighteen to twenty-four, drug use has risen from 13.3 percent in 1994 to 16.1 percent in 1998. According to opponents of drug prohibition, these numbers are proof that the war on drugs is failing.

Rather than continuing to wage this disastrous war, critics assert, America should legalize drugs. Supporters of legalization contend that easing the nation's drug laws would have numerous benefits. Perhaps most importantly, they say, it would destroy the black market for drugs and the criminality that surrounds it. If drugs were legal and available in the legitimate marketplace, drug smugglers and their networks of dealers would be put out of business. Drug gangs would no longer engage in violent battles for turf. Inner-city children would no longer be lured into drug-dealing gangs. As the American Civil Liberties Union (ACLU) puts it, drug legalization "would sever the connection between drugs and crime that today blights so many lives and communities."

Specific proposals for how to implement legalization vary widely. Libertarians advocate eliminating all federal drug laws. Others call for more modest reforms. Some focus exclusively on legalizing marijuana—either for medical purposes or more general use—while others want laws against all drugs relaxed. Some call for outright legalization, whereas others promote decriminalization—keeping laws on the books but reducing them to misdemeanor offenses or enforcing them selectively. Some favor legalizing all drugs but under a system of strict governmental regulation. Despite their differences, all advocates of legalization share the conviction that the current prohibitionist drug policies are not working—that they are in fact making drug-related problems worse—and that liberalization of the nation's drug laws is the only solution.

Opponents of legalization acknowledge that the war on drugs has not succeeded in eliminating drugs from society, but they reject the charge that the effort has been a total failure. While drug use has risen in many categories since the early 1990s, they concede, it is still much lower than it was in the 1970s, prior to the launching of the drug war. In 1979, according to the NHSDA, 14.1 percent of Americans surveyed reported having used an illegal drug during the previous month. That number declined to a low of 5.8 percent in 1992, and although it has since risen to 6.4 percent in 1997, it still remains well below the 1979 level. Drug use among teens shows a similar pattern, dropping from 16.3 percent in 1979 to 5.3 percent in 1992, then rising and falling and eventually hitting 9.9 percent in 1998.

Thus, while the drug war has not wiped drugs off the American scene, supporters maintain, it has clearly impacted drug use.

Legalization opponents also reject the argument that liberalizing drug laws would benefit society. They insist that legalizing drugs would inevitably lead to an increase in the use of newly legalized drugs such as marijuana, cocaine, heroin, and amphetamines. As Barry R. McCaffrey, the director of the Office of National Drug Control Policy, states, "Studies show that the more a product is available and legalized, the greater will be its use." This increased drug use would cause a variety of problems, including a decrease in workplace productivity and a rise in automobile and on-the-job accidents, health problems, addiction, and crime. Joseph A. Califano Jr., the president of the National Center on Addiction and Substance Abuse at Columbia University (CASA), explains that although legalization may result in a short-term decrease in drug arrests, the long-term consequences would be devastating: "Any short-term reduction in arrests from repealing drug laws would evaporate quickly as use increased and the criminal conduct—assault, murder, rape, child molestation, and other violence—that drugs like cocaine and methamphetamine spawn exploded."

Opponents of legalization insist that America must continue its antidrug campaign. Some support efforts to reduce the supply of drugs by disrupting international drug cartels and arresting smugglers and dealers. Others favor reducing the demand for drugs through treatment and education. Still others call for a comprehensive approach combining both supply and demand control elements. Despite these differences, all agree that relaxing the drug laws is not the answer to the nation's drug problem. As stated by Charles B. Rangel, a Democratic Congressman from New York, "Rather than holding up the white flag and allowing drugs to take over our country, we must continue to focus on drug demand as well as supply if we are to remain a free and productive society."

The debate over drug legalization, while rooted in real-world concerns over crime, violence, and public health, is also about values. Often a person's position on the issue is based less on the practicality of maintaining or dismantling the nation's drug laws than on underlying beliefs about the morality of drug use. This moral dimension of the drug legalization debate adds another layer of complexity to an already difficult issue.

The Case for Legalisation: Time for a Puff of Sanity

The Economist

A series of articles entitled "High Time" appeared in the *Economist* on July 28, 2001, presenting the case for drug legalization in the United States. The following selection is the editorial expressing this position.

It is every parent's nightmare. A youngster slithers inexorably from a few puffs on a joint, to a snort of cocaine, to the needle and addiction. It was the flesh-creeping heart of *Traffic*, a film about the descent into heroin hell of a pretty young middle-class girl, and it is the terror that keeps drug laws in place. It explains why even those politicians who puffed at a joint or two in their youth hesitate to put the case for legalising drugs.

The terror is not irrational. For the first thing that must be said about legalising drugs, a cause the *Economist* long advocated and returns to this week, is that it would lead to a rise in their use, and therefore to a rise in the number of people dependent on them. Some argue that drug laws have no impact, because drugs are widely available. Untrue: drugs are expensive—a kilo of heroin sells in America for as much as a new Rolls-Royce—partly because their price reflects the dangers involved in distributing and buying them. It is much harder and riskier to pick up a dose of cocaine than it is to buy a bottle of whisky. Remove such constraints, make drugs accessible and very much cheaper, and more people will experiment with them.

A rise in drug-taking will inevitably mean that more people will become dependent—inevitably, because drugs offer a pleasurable experience that people seek to repeat. In the case of most drugs, that dependency may be no more than a psychological craving and affect fewer than one in five users; in the case of heroin, it is physical and affects maybe one in three. Even a psychological craving can be debilitating. Addicted gamblers and drinkers bring misery to themselves and their families. In addition, drugs have lasting physical effects and some, taken incompetently, can kill. This is true both for some "hard" drugs and for some that people think of as "soft": too much heroin can trigger a strong adverse reaction, but so can ecstasy. The same goes for gin or aspirin, of course; but many voters reasonably wonder whether it would be right to add to the list of harmful substances that are legally available.

OF MILL AND MORALITY

The case for doing so rests on two arguments: one of principle, one practical. The principles were set out, a century and a half ago, by John Stuart Mill, a British liberal philosopher, who urged that the state had no right to intervene to prevent individuals from doing something that harmed them, if no harm was thereby done to the rest of society. "Over himself, over his own body and mind, the individual is sovereign," Mill famously proclaimed. This is a view that the *Economist* has always espoused, and one to which most democratic governments adhere, up to a point. They allow the individual to undertake all manner of dangerous activities unchallenged, from mountaineering to smoking to riding bicycles through city streets. Such pursuits alarm insurance companies and mothers, but are rightly tolerated by the state.

True, Mill argued that some social groups, especially children, required extra protection. And some argue that drug-takers are also a special class: once addicted, they can no longer make rational choices about whether to continue to harm themselves. Yet not only are dependent users a minority of all users; in addition, society has rejected this argument in the case of alcohol—and of nicotine (whose addictive power is greater than that of heroin). The important thing here is for governments to spend adequately on health education.

The practical case for a liberal approach rests on the harms that spring from drug bans, and the benefits that would accompany legalisation. At present, the harms fall disproportionately on poor countries and on poor people in rich countries. In producer and entrepot countries, the drugs trade finances powerful gangs who threaten the state and corrupt political institutions. Colombia is the most egregious example, but Mexico too wrestles with the threat to the police and political honesty. The attempt to kill illicit crops poisons land and people. Drug money helps to prop up vile regimes in Myanmar and Afghanistan. And drug production encourages local drug-taking, which (in the case of heroin) gives a helping hand to the spread of HIV/AIDS.

In the rich world, it is the poor who are most likely to become involved in the drugs trade (the risks may be high, but drug-dealers tend to be equal-opportunity employers), and therefore end up in jail. Nowhere is this more shamefully true than in the United States, where roughly one in four prisoners is locked up for a (mainly non-violent) drugs offence. America's imprisonment rate for drugs offences now exceeds that for all crimes in most West European countries. Moreover, although whites take drugs almost as freely as blacks and Hispanics, a vastly disproportionate number of those arrested, sentenced and imprisoned are non-white. Drugs policy in the United States is thus breeding a generation of men and women from disadvantaged backgrounds whose main training for life has been in the violence of prison.

LEGALISE TO REGULATE

Removing these harms would bring with it another benefit. Precisely because the drugs market is illegal, it cannot be regulated. Laws cannot discriminate between availability to children and adults. Governments cannot insist on minimum quality standards for cocaine; or warn asthma sufferers to avoid ecstasy; or demand that distributors take responsibility for the way their products are sold. With alcohol and tobacco, such restrictions are possible; with drugs, not. This increases the dangers to users, and especially to young or incompetent users. Illegality also puts a premium on selling strength: if each purchase is risky, then it makes sense to buy drugs in concentrated form. In the same way, Prohibition in the United States in the 1920s led to a fall in beer consumption but a rise in the drinking of hard liquor.

How, if governments accepted the case for legalisation, to get from here to there? When, in the 18th century, a powerful new intoxicant became available, the impact was disastrous: it took years of education for gin to cease to be a social threat. That is a strong reason to proceed gradually: it will take time for conventions governing sensible drug-taking to develop. Meanwhile, a century of illegality has deprived governments of much information that good policy requires. Impartial academic research is difficult. As a result, nobody knows how demand may respond to lower prices, and understanding of the physical effects of most drugs is hazy.

And how, if drugs were legal, might they be distributed? The thought of heroin on supermarket shelves understandably adds to the terror of the prospect. Just as legal drugs are available through different channels—caffeine from any café, alcohol only with proof of age, Prozac only on prescription—so the drugs that are now illegal might one day be distributed in different ways, based on knowledge about their potential for harm. Moreover, different countries should experiment with different solutions: at present, many are bound by a United Nations convention that hampers even the most modest moves towards liberalisation, and that clearly needs amendment.

To legalise will not be easy. Drug-taking entails risks, and societies are increasingly risk-averse. But the role of government should be to prevent the most chaotic drug-users from harming others—by robbing or by driving while drugged, for instance—and to regulate drug markets to ensure minimum quality and safe distribution. The first task is hard if law enforcers are preoccupied with stopping all drug use; the second, impossible as long as drugs are illegal. A legal market is the best guarantee that drug-taking will be no more dangerous than drinking alcohol or smoking tobacco. And, just as countries rightly tolerate those two vices, so they should tolerate those who sell and take drugs.

Against the Legalization of Drugs

James Q. Wilson

James Q. Wilson is the James A. Collins Professor of Management and Public Policy Emeritus at the University of California, Los Angeles, and a lecturer at Pepperdine University.

This selection originally appeared in *Commentary*, February 1990.

In 1972, the president appointed me chairman of the National Advisory Council for Drug Abuse Prevention. Created by Congress, the Council was charged with providing guidance on how best to coordinate the national war on drugs. (Yes, we called it a war then, too.) In those days, the drug we were chiefly concerned with was heroin. When I took office, heroin use had been increasing dramatically. Everybody was worried that this increase would continue. Such phrases as "heroin epidemic" were commonplace.

That same year, the eminent economist Milton Friedman published an essay in *Newsweek* in which he called for legalizing heroin. His argument was on two grounds: As a matter of ethics, the government has no right to tell people not to use heroin (or to drink or to commit suicide); as a matter of economics, the prohibition of drug use imposes costs on society that far exceed the benefits. Others, such as the psychoanalyst Thomas Szasz, made the same argument.

We did not take Friedman's advice. I do not recall that we even discussed legalizing heroin, though we did discuss (but did not take action on) legalizing a drug, cocaine, that many people then argued was benign. Our marching orders were to figure out how to win the war on heroin, not to run up the white flag of surrender.

That was 1972. Today, we have the same number of heroin addicts that we had then—half a million, give or take a few thousand. Having that many heroin addicts is no trivial matter; these people deserve our attention. But not having had an increase in that number for over fifteen years is also something that deserves our attention. What happened to the "heroin epidemic" that many people once thought would overwhelm us?

The facts are clear: A more or less stable pool of heroin addicts has been getting older, with relatively few new recruits. In 1976 the average age of heroin users who appeared in hospital emergency rooms was about twenty-seven; ten years later it was thirty-two. More than two-thirds of all heroin users appearing in emergency rooms are now over the age of thirty. Back in the early 1970s, when heroin got onto the national political agenda, the typical heroin addict was much younger, often a teenager. Household surveys show the same thing— the rate of opiate use (which includes heroin) has been flat for the better part of two decades. More fine-grained studies of inner-city neighborhoods confirm this. John Boyle and Ann Brunswick found that the percentage of young blacks in Harlem who used heroin fell from 8 percent in 1970–71 to about 3 percent in 1975–76.

Why did heroin lose its appeal for young people? When the young blacks in Harlem were asked why they stopped, more than half mentioned "trouble with the law" or "high cost" (and high cost is, of course, directly the result of law enforcement). Two-thirds said that heroin hurt their health; nearly all said they had had a bad experience with it. We need not rely, however, simply on what they said. In New York City in 1973–75, the street price of heroin rose dramatically and its purity sharply declined, probably as a result of the heroin shortage caused by the success of the Turkish government in reducing the supply of opium base and of the French government in closing down heroin-processing laboratories located in and around Marseilles. These were short-lived gains for, just as Friedman predicted, alternative sources of supply—mostly in Mexico—quickly emerged. But the three-year heroin shortage interrupted the easy recruitment of new users.

Health and related problems were no doubt part of the reason for the reduced flow of recruits. Over the preceding years, Harlem youth had watched as more and more heroin users died of overdoses, were poisoned by adulterated doses, or acquired hepatitis from dirty needles. The word got around: heroin can kill you. By 1974 new hepatitis cases and drug-overdose deaths had dropped to a fraction of what they had been in 1970.

Alas, treatment did not seem to explain much of the cessations in drug use. Treatment programs can and do help heroin addicts, but treatment did not explain the drop in the number of *new* users (who by definition had never been in treatment) nor even much of the reduction in the number of experienced users.

No one knows how much of the decline to attribute to personal observation as opposed to high prices or reduced supply. But other evidence suggests strongly that price and supply played a large role. In 1972 the National Advisory Council was especially worried by the prospect that U.S. servicemen returning to this country from Vietnam would bring their heroin habits with them. Fortunately, a brilliant study by Lee Robins of Washington University in St. Louis put that fear to rest. She measured drug use of Vietnam veterans shortly after they had returned home. Though many had used heroin regularly while in Southeast Asia, most gave up the habit when back in the United States. The reason: Here, heroin was less available and sanctions on its use were more pronounced. Of course, if a veteran had been willing to pay enough—which might have meant traveling to another city and would certainly have meant making an illegal contact with a disreputable dealer in a threatening neighborhood in order to acquire a (possibly) dangerous dose—he could have sustained his drug habit. Most veterans were unwilling to pay this price, and so their drug use declined or disappeared.

RELIVING THE PAST

Suppose we had taken Friedman's advice in 1972. What would have happened? We cannot be entirely certain, but at a minimum we would have placed the young heroin addicts (and, above all, the prospective addicts) in a very different position from the one in which they actually found themselves. Heroin would have been legal. Its price would have been reduced by 95 percent (minus whatever we chose to recover in taxes). Now that it could be sold by the same people who make aspirin, its quality would have been ensured—no poisons, no adulterants. Sterile hypodermic needles would have been readily available at the neighborhood drugstore, probably at the same counter where the heroin was sold. No need to travel to big cities or unfamiliar neighborhoods—heroin could have been purchased anywhere, perhaps by mail order.

There would no longer have been any financial or medical reason to avoid heroin use. Anybody could have afforded it. We might have tried to prevent children from buying it, but as we have learned from our efforts to prevent minors from buying alcohol and tobacco, young people have a way of penetrating markets theoretically reserved for adults. Returning Vietnam veterans would have discovered that Omaha and Raleigh had been converted into the pharmaceutical equivalent of Saigon.

Under these circumstance, can we doubt for a moment that heroin use would have grown exponentially? Or that a vastly larger supply of new users would have been recruited? Professor Friedman is a Nobel Prize–winning economist whose understanding of market forces is profound. What did he think would happen to consumption under his legalized regime? Here are his words: "Legalizing drugs might increase the number of addicts but it is not clear that it would. Forbidden fruit is attractive, particularly to the young."

Really? I suppose that we should expect no increase in Porsche sales if we cut the price by 95 percent, no increase in whiskey sales if we cut the price by a comparable amount—because young people only want fast cars and strong liquor when they are "forbidden." Perhaps Friedman's uncharacteristic lapse from the obvious implications of price theory can be explained by a misunderstanding of how drug users are recruited. In his 1972 essay he said that "drug addicts are deliberately made by pushers, who give likely prospects their first few doses free." If drugs were legal it would not pay anybody to produce addicts, because everybody would buy from the cheapest source. But as every drug expert knows, pushers do not produce addicts. Friends or acquaintances do. In fact, pushers are usually reluctant to deal with nonusers because a nonuser could be an undercover cop. Drug use spreads in the same way any fad or fashion spreads: Somebody who is already a user urges his friends to try, or simply shows already eager friends how to do it.

But we need not rely on speculation, however plausible, that lowered prices and more abundant supplies would have increased heroin usage. Great Britain once followed such a policy and with almost exactly those results. Until the mid-1960s, British physicians were allowed to prescribe heroin to certain classes of addicts. (Possessing these drugs without a doctor's prescription remained a criminal offense.) For many years this policy worked well enough because the addict patients were typically middle-class people who had become dependent on opiate painkillers while undergoing hospital treatment. There was no drug culture. The British system worked for many years, not because it prevented drug abuse, but because there was no problem of drug abuse that would test the system.

All that changed in the 1960s. A few unscrupulous doctors began passing out heroin in wholesale amounts. One doctor prescribed almost 600,000 heroin tablets—that is, over thirteen pounds—in just one year. A youthful drug culture emerged with a demand for drugs far different from that of the older addicts. As a result, the British government required doctors to refer users to government-run clinics to receive their heroin.

But the shift to clinics did not curtail the growth in heroin use. Throughout the 1960s the number of addicts increased—the late John Kaplan of Stanford estimated by fivefold—in part as a result of the diversion of heroin from clinic patients to new users on the streets. An addict would bargain with the clinic doctor over how big a dose he would receive. The patient wanted as much as he could get, the doctor wanted to give as little as was needed. The patient had an advantage in this conflict because the doctor could not be certain how much was really needed. Many patients would use some of their "maintenance" dose and sell the remaining part to friends, thereby recruiting new addicts. As the clinics learned of this, they began to shift their treatment away from heroin and toward methadone, an addictive drug that, when taken orally, does not produce a "high" but will block the withdrawal pains associated with heroin abstinence.

Whether what happened in England in the 1960s was a mini-epidemic or an epidemic depends on whether one looks at numbers or at rates of change. Compared to the United States, the numbers were small. In 1960 there were sixty-eight heroin addicts known to the British government; by 1968 there were two thousand in treatment and many more who refused treatment. (They would refuse in part because they did not want to get methadone at a clinic if they could get heroin on the street.) Richard Hartnoll estimates that the actual number of addicts in England is five times the number officially registered. At a minimum, the number of British addicts increased by thirty-fold in ten years; the actual increase may have been much larger.

In the early 1980s the numbers began to rise again, and this time nobody doubted that a real epidemic was at hand. The increase was estimated to be 40 percent a year. By 1982 there were thought to be 20,000 heroin users in London alone. Geoffrey Pearson reports that many cities—Glasgow, Liverpool, Manchester, and Sheffield among them—were now experiencing a drug problem that once had been largely confined to London. The problem, again, was supply. The country was being flooded with cheap, high-quality heroin, first from Iran and then from Southeast Asia.

The United States began the 1960s with a much larger number of heroin addicts and probably a bigger at-risk population than was the case in Great Britain. Even though it would be foolhardy to suppose that the British system, if installed here, would have worked the same way or with the same results, it would be equally foolhardy to suppose that a combination of heroin available from leaky clinics and from street dealers who faced only minimal law-enforcement risks would not have produced a much greater increase in heroin use than we actually experienced. My guess is that if we had allowed either doctors or clinics to prescribe heroin, we would have had far worse results than were produced in Britain, if for no other reason than the vastly larger number of addicts with which we began. We would have had to find some way to police thousands (not scores) of physicians and hundreds (not dozens) of clinics. If the British civil service found it difficult to keep heroin in the hands of addicts and out of the hands of recruits when it was dealing with a few hundred people, how well would the American civil service have accomplished the same tasks when dealing with tens of thousands of people?

BACK TO THE FUTURE

Now cocaine, especially in its potent form, crack, is the focus of attention. Now as in 1972 the government is trying to reduce its use. Now as then some people are advocating legalization. Is there any more reason to yield to those arguments today than there was almost two decades ago?[1]

I think not. If we had yielded in 1972 we almost certainly would

---

1. I do not here take up the question of marijuana. For a variety of reasons—its widespread use and its lesser tendency to addict—it presents a different problem from cocaine or heroin. For a penetrating analysis, see Mark Kleiman, *Marijuana: Costs of Abuse, Costs of Control* (Westport, Conn.: Greenwood Press, 1989).

have had today a permanent population of several million, not several hundred thousand, heroin addicts. If we yield now we will have a far more serious problem with cocaine.

Crack is worse than heroin by almost any measure. Heroin produces a pleasant drowsiness and, if hygienically administered, has only the physical side effects of constipation and sexual impotence. Regular heroin use incapacitates many users, especially poor ones, for any productive work or social responsibility. They will sit nodding on a street corner, helpless but at least harmless. By contrast, regular cocaine use leaves the user neither helpless nor harmless. When smoked (as with crack) or injected, cocaine produces instant, intense, and short-lived euphoria. The experience generates a powerful desire to repeat it. If the drug is readily available, repeat use will occur. Those people who progress to "bingeing" on cocaine become devoted to the drug and its effects to the exclusion of almost all other considerations—job, family, children, sleep, food, even sex. Dr. Frank Gawin at Yale and Dr. Everett Ellinwood at Duke report that a substantial percentage of all high-dose, binge users become uninhibited, impulsive, hypersexual, compulsive, irritable, and hyperactive. Their moods vacillate dramatically, leading at times to violence and homicide.

Women are much more likely to use crack than heroin, and if they are pregnant, the effects on their babies are tragic. Douglas Besharov, who has been following the effects of drugs on infants for twenty years, writes that nothing he learned about heroin prepared him for the devastation of cocaine. Cocaine harms the fetus and can lead to physical deformities or neurological damage. Some crack babies have for all practical purposes suffered a disabling stroke while still in the womb. The long-term consequences of this brain damage are lowered cognitive ability and the onset of mood disorders. Besharov estimates that about 30,000 to 50,000 such babies are born every year, about 7,000 in New York City alone. There may be ways to treat such infants, but from everything we now know the treatment will be long, difficult, and expensive. Worse, the mothers who are most likely to produce crack babies are precisely the ones who, because of poverty or temperament, are least able and willing to obtain such treatment. In fact, anecdotal evidence suggests that crack mothers are likely to abuse their infants.

The notion that abusing drugs such as cocaine is a "victimless crime" is not only absurd but dangerous. Even ignoring the fetal drug syndrome, crack-dependent people are, like heroin addicts, individuals who regularly victimize their children by neglect, their spouses by improvidence, their employers by lethargy, and their coworkers by carelessness. Society is not and could never be a collection of autonomous individuals. We all have a stake in ensuring that each of us displays a minimal level of dignity, responsibility, and empathy. We cannot, of course, coerce people into goodness, but we can and should insist that some standards must be met if society itself—on which the very existence of the human personality depends—is to persist. Drawing the line that defines those standards is difficult and contentious, but if crack and heroin use do not fall below it, what does?

The advocates of legalization will respond by suggesting that my picture is overdrawn. Ethan Nadelmann of Princeton argues that the risk of legalization is less than most people suppose. Over 20 million Americans between the ages of eighteen and twenty-five have tried cocaine (according to a government survey), but only a quarter million use it daily. From this Nadelmann concludes that at most 3 percent of all young people who try cocaine develop a problem with it. The implication is clear: Make the drug legal and we only have to worry about 3 percent of our youth.

The implication rests on a logical fallacy and a factual error. The fallacy is this: The percentage of occasional cocaine users who become binge users *when the drug is illegal* (and thus expensive and hard to find) tells us nothing about the percentage who will become dependent when the drug is legal (and thus cheap and abundant).

Drs. Gawin and Ellinwood report, in common with several other researchers, that controlled or occasional use of cocaine changes to compulsive and frequent use "when access to the drug increases" or when the user switches from snorting to smoking. More cocaine more potently administered alters, perhaps sharply, the proportion of "controlled" users who become heavy users.

The factual error is this: The federal survey Nadelmann quotes was done in 1985, before crack had become common. Thus the probability of becoming dependent on cocaine was derived from the responses of users who snorted the drug. The speed and potency of cocaine's action increases dramatically when it is smoked. We do not yet know how greatly the advent of crack increases the risk of dependency, but all the clinical evidence suggests that the increase is likely to be large.

It is possible that some people will not become heavy users even when the drug is readily available in its most potent form. So far there are no scientific grounds for predicting who will and who will not become dependent. Neither socioeconomic background nor personality traits differentiate between casual and intensive users. Thus, the only way to settle the question of who is correct about the effect of easy availability on drug use, Nadelmann or Gawin and Ellinwood, is to try it and see. But that social experiment is so risky as to be no experiment at all, for if cocaine is legalized and if the rate of its abusive use increases dramatically, there is no way to put the genie back in the bottle, and it is not a kindly genie.

HAVE WE LOST?

Many people who agree that there are risks in legalizing cocaine or heroin still favor it because, they think, we have lost the war on drugs. "Nothing we have done has worked" and the current federal policy is just "more of the same." Whatever the costs of greater drug use, surely they would be less than the costs of our present, failed efforts.

That is exactly what I was told in 1972—and heroin is not quite as bad a drug as cocaine. We did not surrender and we did not lose. We did not win, either. What the nation accomplished then was what most efforts to save people from themselves accomplish: The problem was contained and the number of victims minimized, all at a considerable cost in law enforcement and increased crime. Was the cost worth it? I think so, but others may disagree. What are the lives of would-be addicts worth? I recall some people saying to me then, "Let them kill themselves." I was appalled. Happily, such views did not prevail.

Have we lost today? Not at all. High-rate cocaine use is not commonplace. The National Institute of Drug Abuse (NIDA) reports that less than 5 percent of high school seniors used cocaine within the last thirty days. Of course this survey misses young people who have dropped out of school and miscounts those who lie on the questionnaire, but even if we inflate the NIDA estimate by some plausible percentage, it is still not much above 5 percent. Medical examiners reported in 1987 that about 1,500 died from cocaine use; hospital emergency rooms reported about 30,000 admissions related to cocaine abuse.

These are not small numbers, but neither are they evidence of a nationwide plague that threatens to engulf us all. Moreover, cities vary greatly in the proportion of people who are involved with cocaine. To get city-level data we need to turn to drug tests carried out on arrested persons, who obviously are more likely to be drug users than the average citizen. The National Institute of Justice, through its Drug Use Forecasting (DUF) project, collects urinalysis data on arrestees in twenty-two cities. As we have already seen, opiate (chiefly heroin) use has been net or declining in most of these cities over the last decade. Cocaine use has gone up sharply, but with great variation among cities. New York, Philadelphia, and Washington, D.C., all report that two-thirds or more of their arrestees tested positive for cocaine, but in Portland, San Antonio, and Indianapolis the percentage was one-third or less.

In some neighborhoods, of course, matters have reached crisis proportions. Gangs control the streets, shootings terrorize residents, and drug dealing occurs in plain view. The police seem barely able to contain matters. But in these neighborhoods—unlike at Palo Alto cocktail parties—the people are not calling for legalization, they are calling for help. And often not much help has come. Many cities are willing to do almost anything about the drug problem except spend more money on it. The federal government cannot change that; only local voters and politicians can. It is not clear that they will.

It took about ten years to contain heroin. We have had experience with crack for only about three or four years. Each year we spend perhaps $11 billion on law enforcement (and some of that goes to deal with marijuana) and perhaps $2 billion on treatment. Large sums, but not sums that should lead anyone to say, "We just can't afford this anymore."

The illegality of drugs increases crime, partly because some users turn to crime to pay for their habits, partly because some users are stimulated by certain drugs (such as crack or PCP) to act more violently or ruthlessly than they otherwise would, and partly because criminal organizations seeking to control drug supplies use force to manage their markets. These also are serious costs, but no one knows how much they would be reduced if drugs were legalized. Addicts would no longer steal to pay black-market prices for drugs, a real gain. But some, perhaps a great deal, of that gain would be offset by the great increase in the number of addicts. These people, nodding on heroin or living in the delusion-ridden high of cocaine, would hardly be ideal employees. Many would steal simply to support themselves, since snatch-and-grab, opportunistic crime can be managed even by people unable to hold a regular job or plan an elaborate crime. Those British addicts who get their supplies from government clinics are not models of law-abiding decency. Most are in crime, and though their per capita rate of criminality may be lower thanks to the cheapness of their drugs, the total volume of crime they produce may be quite large. Of course, society could decide to support all unemployable addicts on welfare, but that would mean that gains from lowered rates of crime would have to be offset by large increases in welfare budgets.

Proponents of legalization claim that the costs of having more addicts around would be largely if not entirely offset by having more money available with which to treat and care for them. The money would come from taxes levied on the sale of heroin and cocaine.

To obtain this fiscal dividend, however, legalization's supporters must first solve an economic dilemma. If they want to raise a lot of money to pay for welfare and treatment, the tax rate on the drugs will have to be quite high. Even if they themselves do not want a high rate, the politicians' love of "sin taxes" would probably guarantee that it would be high anyway. But the higher the tax, the higher the price of the drug, and the higher the price the greater the likelihood that addicts will turn to crime to find the money for it and that criminal organizations will be formed to sell tax-free drugs at below-market rates. If we managed to keep taxes (and thus prices) low, we would get that much less money to pay for welfare and treatment and more people could afford to become addicts. There may be an optimal tax rate for drugs that maximizes revenue while minimizing crime, bootlegging, and the recruitment of new addicts, but our experience with alcohol does not suggest that we know how to find it.

THE BENEFITS OF ILLEGALITY

The advocates of legalization find nothing to be said in favor of the current system except, possibly, that it keeps the number of addicts smaller than it would otherwise be. In fact, the benefits are more substantial than that.

First, treatment. All the talk about providing "treatment on demand" implies that there is a demand for treatment. That is not quite right. There are some drug-dependent people who genuinely want treatment and will remain in it if offered; they should receive it. But there are far more who want only short-term help after a bad crash; once stabilized and bathed, they are back on the street again, hustling. And even many of the addicts who enroll in a program honestly wanting help drop out after a short while when they discover that help takes time and commitment. Drug-dependent people have very short time horizons and a weak capacity for commitment. These two groups—those looking for a quick fix and those unable to stick with a long-term fix—are not easily helped. Even if we increase the number of treatment slots—as we should—we would have to do something to make treatment more effective.

One thing that can often make it more effective is compulsion. Douglas Anglin of UCLA, in common with many other researchers, has found that the longer one stays in a treatment program, the better the chances of a reduction in drug dependency. But he, again like most other researchers, has found that drop-out rates are high. He has also found, however, that patients who enter treatment under legal compulsion stay in the program longer than those not subject to such pressure. His research on the California civil commitment program, for example, found that heroin users involved with its required drug-testing program had over the long term a lower rate of heroin use than similar addicts who were free of such constraints. If for many addicts compulsion is a useful component of treatment, it is not clear how compulsion could be achieved in a society in which purchasing, possessing, and using the drug were legal. It could be managed, I suppose, but I would not want to have to answer the challenge from the American Civil Liberties Union that it is wrong to compel a person to undergo treatment for consuming a legal commodity.

Next, education. We are now investing substantially in drug-education programs in the schools. Though we do not yet know for certain what will work, there are some promising leads. But I wonder how credible such programs would be if they were aimed at dissuading children from doing something perfectly legal. We could, of course, treat drug education like smoking education: Inhaling crack and inhaling tobacco are both legal, but you should not do it because it is bad for you. That tobacco is bad for you is easily shown; the Surgeon General has seen to that. But what do we say about crack? It is pleasurable, but devoting yourself to so much pleasure is not a good idea (though perfectly legal)? Unlike tobacco, cocaine will not give you cancer or emphysema, but it will lead you to neglect your duties to family, job, and neighborhood? Everybody is doing cocaine, but you should not?

Again, it might be possible under a legalized regime to have effective drug-prevention programs, but their effectiveness would depend heavily, I think, on first having decided that cocaine use, like tobacco use, is purely a matter of practical consequences; no fundamental moral significance attaches to either. But if we believe—as I do—that dependency on certain mind-altering drugs is a moral issue and that their illegality rests in part on their immorality, then legalizing them undercuts, if it does not eliminate altogether, the moral message.

That message is at the root of the distinction we now make between nicotine and cocaine. Both are highly addictive; both have harmful physical effects. But we treat the two drugs differently, not simply because nicotine is so widely used as to be beyond the reach of effective prohibition, but because its use does not destroy the user's essential humanity. Tobacco shortens one's life, cocaine debases it. Nicotine alters one's habits, cocaine alters one's soul. The heavy use of crack, unlike the heavy use of tobacco, corrodes those natural sentiments of sympathy and duty that constitute our human nature and make possible our social life. To say, as does Nadelmann, that distinguishing morally between tobacco and cocaine is "little more than a transient prejudice" is close to saying that morality itself is but a prejudice.

THE ALCOHOL PROBLEM

Now we have arrived where many arguments about legalizing drugs begin: Is there any reason to treat heroin and cocaine differently from the way we treat alcohol?

There is no easy answer to that question because, as with so many human problems, one cannot decide simply on the basis either of moral principles or of individual consequences; one has to temper any policy by a commonsense judgment of what is possible. Alcohol, like heroin, cocaine, PCP, and marijuana, is a drug—that is, a mood-altering substance—and consumed to excess it certainly has harmful consequences: auto accidents, barroom fights, bedroom shootings. It is also, for some people, addictive. We cannot confidently compare the addictive powers of these drugs, but the best evidence suggests that crack and heroin are much more addictive than alcohol.

Many people, Nadelmann included, argue that since the health and financial costs of alcohol abuse are so much higher than those of cocaine or heroin abuse, it is hypocritical folly to devote our efforts to preventing cocaine or drug use. But as Mark Kleiman of Harvard has pointed out, this comparison is quite misleading. What Nadelmann is doing is showing that a *legalized* drug (alcohol) produces greater social harm than *illegal* ones (cocaine and heroin). But of course. Suppose that in the 1920s we had made heroin and cocaine legal and alcohol illegal. Can anyone doubt that Nadelmann would now be writing that it is folly to continue our ban on alcohol because cocaine and heroin are so much more harmful?

And let there be no doubt about it—widespread heroin and cocaine use are associated with all manner of ills. Thomas Bewley found that the mortality rate of British heroin addicts in 1968 was 28 times as high as the death rate of the same age group of nonaddicts, even though in England at the time an addict could obtain free or low-cost heroin and clean needles from British clinics. Perform the following mental experiment: Suppose we legalized heroin and cocaine in this country. In what proportion of auto fatalities would the state police report that the driver was nodding off on heroin or recklessly driving on a coke high? In what proportion of spouse-assault and child-abuse cases would the local police report that crack was involved? In what proportion of industrial accidents would safety investigators report that the forklift or drill-press operator was in a drug-induced stupor or frenzy? We do not know exactly what the proportion would be, but anyone who asserts that it would not be much higher than it is now would have to believe that these drugs have little appeal except when they are illegal. And that is nonsense.

An advocate of legalization might concede that social harm— perhaps harm equivalent to that already produced by alcohol—would follow from making cocaine and heroin generally available. But at least, he might add, we would have the problem "out in the open" where it could be treated as a matter of "public health." That is well and good, *if* we knew how to treat—that is, cure—heroin and cocaine abuse. But we do not know how to do it for all the people who would need such help. We are having only limited success in coping with chronic alcoholics. Addictive behavior is immensely difficult to change, and the best methods for changing it—living in drug-free therapeutic communities, becoming faithful members of Alcoholics Anonymous or Narcotics Anonymous—require great personal commitment, a quality that is, alas, in short supply among the very persons—young people, disadvantaged people—who are often most at risk for addiction.

Suppose that today we had, not 15 million alcohol abusers, but half a million. Suppose that we already knew what we have learned from our long experience with the widespread use of alcohol. Would we make whiskey legal? I do not know, but I suspect there would be a lively debate. The Surgeon General would remind us of the risks alcohol poses to pregnant women. The National Highway Traffic Safety Administration would point to the likelihood of more highway fatalities caused by drunk drivers. The Food and Drug Administration might find that there is a nontrivial increase in cancer associated with alcohol consumption. At the same time the police would report great difficulty in keeping illegal whiskey out of our cities, officers being corrupted by bootleggers, and alcohol addicts often resorting to crime to feed their habit. Libertarians, for their part, would argue that every citizen has a right to drink anything he wishes and that drinking is, in any event, a "victimless crime."

However the debate might turn out, the central fact would be that the problem was still, at that point, a small one. The government cannot legislate away the addictive tendencies in all of us, nor can it remove completely even the most dangerous addictive substances. But it can cope with harms when the harms are still manageable.

One advantage of containing a problem while it is still containable is that it buys time for science to learn more about it and perhaps to discover a cure. Almost unnoticed in the current debate over legalizing drugs is that basic science has made rapid strides in identifying the underlying neurological processes involved in some forms of addiction. Stimulants such as cocaine and amphetamines alter the way certain brain cells communicate with one another. That alteration is complex and not entirely understood, but in simplified form it involves modifying the way in which a neurotransmitter called dopamine sends signals from one cell to another.

When dopamine crosses the synapse between two cells, it is in effect carrying a message from the first cell to activate the second one. In certain parts of the brain that message is experienced as pleasure. After the message is delivered, the dopamine returns to the first cell. Cocaine apparently blocks the return, or "reuptake," so that the excited cell and others nearby continue to send pleasure messages. When the exaggerated high produced by cocaine-influenced dopamine finally ends, the brain cells may (in ways that are still a matter of dispute) suffer from an extreme lack of dopamine, thereby making the individual unable to experience any pleasure at all. This would explain why cocaine users often feel so depressed after enjoying the drug. Stimulants may also affect the way in which other neurotransmitters, such as serotonin and noradrenaline, operate.

Whatever the exact mechanism may be, once it is identified it becomes possible to use drugs to block either the effect of cocaine or its tendency to produce dependency. There have been experiments using desipramine, imipramine, bromocriptine, carbamazepine, and other chemicals. There are some promising results.

Tragically, we spend very little on such research, and the agencies funding it have not in the past occupied very influential or visible posts in the federal bureaucracy. If there is one aspect of the "war on drugs" metaphor that I dislike, it is the tendency to focus attention almost exclusively on the troops in the trenches, whether engaged in enforcement or treatment, and away from the research-and-development efforts back on the home front where the war may ultimately be decided.

I believe that the prospects of scientists in controlling addiction will be strongly influenced by the size and character of the problem they face. If the problem is a few hundred thousand chronic high-dose users of an illegal product, the chances of making a difference at a reasonable cost will be much greater than if the problem is a few million chronic users of legal substance. Once a drug is legal, not only will its use increase but many of those who then use it will prefer the drug to the treatment: They will want the pleasure. Whatever the cost to themselves or their families, they will resist—probably successfully—any effort to wean them away from experiencing the high that comes from inhaling a legal substance.

IF I AM WRONG . . .

No one can know what our society would be like if we changed the law to make access to cocaine, heroin, and PCP easier. I believe, for reasons given, that the result would be a sharp increase in use, a more widespread degradation of the human personality, and a greater rate of accidents and violence.

I may be wrong. If I am, then we will needlessly have incurred heavy costs in law enforcement and some forms of criminality. But if I am right, and the legalizers prevail anyway, then we will have consigned millions of people, hundreds of thousands of infants, and hundreds of neighborhoods to a life of oblivion and disease. To the lives and families destroyed by alcohol we will have added countless more destroyed by cocaine, heroin, PCP, and whatever else a basement scientist can invent.

Human character is formed by society; indeed, human character is inconceivable without society, and good character is less likely in a bad society. Will we, in the name of an abstract doctrine of radical individualism, and with the false comfort of suspect predictions, decide to take the chance that somehow individual decency can survive amid a more general level of degradation?

I think not. The American people are too wise for that, whatever the academic essayists and cocktail-party pundits may say. But if Americans today are less wise than I suppose, then Americans at some future time will look back on us now and wonder, what kind of people were they that they could have done such a thing?

Alternative Perspectives on the Drug Policy Debate

Duane McBride, Yvonne M. Terry-McElrath, and James A. Inciardi

Duane McBride is chair of the Behavioral Sciences Department at Andrews University and director of the university's Institute for the Prevention of Addictions. Yvonne M. Terry-McElrath is a research fellow at the Institute for Social Research, University of Michigan. And James A. Inciardi is the director of the Center for Drug and Alcohol Studies and a professor in the Department of Sociology and Criminal Justice at the University of Delaware.

The selection was excerpted from "Alternative Perspectives on the Drug Policy Debate" in *The Drug Legalization Debate* (Thousand Oaks, Calif.: Sage Publications, Inc. 1999).

The decriminalization position emerged most clearly during the past decade. Supporters forcefully argued that current national drug policy has failed to prevent recent increases in youth drug use while succeeding in eroding basic civil rights, overwhelming the criminal justice system, and eroding public support for law enforcement. Many of those who today advocate for decriminalization previously supported medicalization or some type of mild regulation. However, they have become much more radical: They believe that almost any type of government prohibition or regulation is doomed to failure and will bring about enormously negative civil and moral consequences. As Arnold Trebach has said, "I have come to believe that the urban situation in America is so desperate as to demand the nearly immediate dismantling of drug prohibition" (in Trebach & Inciardi, 1993, p. 13).

Decriminalization has many similarities to other "reform" positions: It consistently calls for more humane treatment of drug addicts, including physician treatment. The position also seems to advocate elements of harm reduction: Supporters want accurate, scientifically based information about drugs and their real effects available to the public. Most also urge distribution of paraphernalia as the avenue of the safest possible use. Decriminalization also resembles the legalization/regulation perspective in that supporters wish to immediately remove criminal penalties from drug use. However, one crucial difference divides the two positions. That difference rests on John Stuart Mill's philosophy as presented in his book *On Liberty* (1921). Mill concluded that the government has no business prohibiting or even regulating the personal choice of free citizens (for further presentation of the decriminalization perspective, see Trebach in Trebach & Inciardi, 1993, as well as the bimonthly journal *Drug Policy Letter*).

Unlike other perspectives along the drug policy continuum, the decriminalization approach does not attempt to develop complex alternatives that involve using government-mandated harm reduction, public health education, prevention, or intervention. It does not necessarily advocate utilizing the medical community to manage addiction. It certainly does not want the increased complexity of governmental regulation. The decriminalization perspective seems to imply that all other alternatives have many of the same inherent weaknesses that bedevil current prohibition policy: namely, that any attempt by government to regulate drugs has an inherent potential for abuse.

The decriminalization perspective simply wants to eliminate laws that prohibit or regulate the manufacture or distribution of current illegal drugs. While there are partial and full decriminalizers, the basic position is that of libertarianism. As such, government should not be involved in either prohibition or regulation of the private behavioral or property choices of its citizens—even if such policies may be deemed to be in the interest of the citizens. Perhaps this is most clearly stated by Thomas Szasz (Friedman & Szasz, 1992): "I favor free trade in drugs . . . in a free society it is none of the government's business what ideas a man puts into his mind, likewise, it should be none of its business what drugs he puts into his body." Friedman and Szasz (1992) essentially argue for a return to the consumerism policy of the 19th century with use levels determined by intelligent, educated consumers.

Another leading proponent of decriminalization, Arnold Trebach, also argues for giving back to people a right taken away from them by government early in this century—the right to freely choose to use drugs: "My preferred plan of legalization [decriminalization] seeks essentially to turn the clock back to the last century" (Trebach & Inciardi, 1993, p. 79). In a book entitled *Our Right to Drugs*, Szasz (1996) argues that drugs are a form of property and, as such, the government has no right to interfere with how free citizens use their private property.

This position has some attractive strengths. It is rooted in the basic assumptions of a free and democratic society. These include the assumption that citizens are self-governing and capable of exercising self-control and good citizenship without the paternalistic intrusiveness of government as overseer. Within this tradition, there is also the belief that a free society must accept as the price of freedom that a proportion of its citizens will make decisions that may be harmful to the health, happiness, or longevity of those citizens. This position seems to be, to an extent, in touch with the political trends of the era. There is currently little interest in a large intrusive government; indeed, there has been a devolution of authority from national government to local government to individual responsibility. Distrust of government is very high. Adoption of decriminalization-based policy would involve minimal government intrusion or regulation. This perspective further points toward the enormous amounts of money that would be saved as inappropriate governmental intrusion into private citizen choices is eliminated. A decriminalization policy would allow the police to focus on behavior that clearly harms other citizens while preventing the justice system from interfering with individual behavior that harms no one but the user (see Stares, 1996a, 1996b).

CRITICISMS OF DECRIMINALIZATION

Each of the other drug policy positions has implicit or explicit criticisms of decriminalization (see Inciardi in Trebach & Inciardi, 1993, for a comprehensive critique of decriminalization). Basic criticisms of decriminalization focus on a significant underestimation of the social and economic harm of increased drug use, a misunderstanding of the nature of addiction and initiation processes, and a naive confidence in the free market. Critics of decriminalization argue that harm resulting from drug abuse is not individual but systemic. It thereby fulfills the criteria elucidated by Mill (1921) to warrant societal concern. Harms arising from drug abuse include psychopharmacological effects related to violence as well as significant health care costs. Substance use plays a significant role in accidents that also injure nonusers. In addition, the nostalgic view of 19th-century America may not be reflected in the reality of those who experienced that century. It was a century without access to health care and without any type of welfare safety net. There was minimal recognition of governmental or societal responsibility for those who needed health or human services. Although government is reducing its sense of responsibility for many of these services, there still seems to be an expectation of some responsibility for its citizens. We are no longer in a society of isolated nonintegrated parts. It may be difficult to separate what is only harmful to the individual from what is also costly to society. If there is an expectation of societal aid, then there may be an expectation of societal regulations. Indeed, Szasz (1996) argues that as long as society makes others pay for the health care costs of drug users society will have the incentive to regulate drug use. Szasz appears to advocate dismantling publicly funded health care and placing the responsibility of payment on those who make the choice to use drugs (Szasz in Buckley & Nadelmann, 1996).

It also seems that the decriminalization position may not recognize the complexity or implications of addictive substances in a free market treatment. The very nature of addiction limits free choice. One can perhaps construct a notion that free choice occurs the first few times an individual uses an addictive substance, but that choice disappears as addiction becomes an experienced reality. This position further fails to recognize the role that advertising can be allowed to play in a free market economy. The logical culmination of a true policy of decriminalization whereby there is only minimal if any governmental regulation or penalties would be an equally free environment for advertising drugs. In turn, this onslaught of publicity would have serious ramifications on youth populations.

Serious questions should be raised about the ability of youths, some as young as 13, to have the information, critical capacity, and wisdom to make a free choice about a substance that is highly addictive. A truly unregulated free market would have few if any barriers to prevent drug use by youths. It is self-evident that decriminalizers do not advocate drug use by youths nor see youths as necessarily having the capacity to make informed decisions about drug use. Rather, decriminalizers focus on drug use as an adult choice. However, as noted by Califano (1997), initiation of drug use usually occurs prior to age 21. The data simply do not support the assumption that drug use is an adult choice. Increasingly, it is the choice of youths aged 12 to 17 both for initiation and continuing use. Recently released data from the National Household Survey show that about 11% of youths aged 12 to 17 used an illegal drug in the past month. About 30% reported use in the past year. Further, youths aged 12 to 17 were more likely to use an illegal drug in the past month than individuals aged 26 and over (CESAR, 1998). These data indicate that it is not adults who are choosing to use drugs; rather, it is the very population that decriminalizers say they specifically do not wish to see using drugs—America's youths. Decriminalization policies would seem to be particularly weak in preventing youth drug use.

A focus on decriminalization for a national drug policy also raises serious questions about our current national expectations of a free market. Our society and the world in general seem to be enamored with the concept. The free market is seen as providing the best chance for economic strength, political freedom, civil rights, and, it appears, even human happiness. This era seems to have extraordinary faith in the free market to solve everything, even drug abuse. The free market may be the best producer of high-quality, cost-effective products and services, but it may not be the best policy for dealing with addictive substances. Issues of marketing, target marketing, and the human cost of increased drug abuse seem to be naively ignored by advocates of decriminalization. The effective critical capacity that is applied by decriminalizers to the current prohibition position seems strangely absent in the examination of their own assumptions and the very real consequences that might result from the adoption of this position.

REFERENCES

Buckley, W. F., Jr., and Nadelmann, E. A. (1996). The war on drugs is lost. *National Review*, 48 (2), 34–48.

Califano, J. A. (1997). Addiction isn't freedom. *USA Today*, 125, 46–47.

CESAR. (1998). *Preliminary results from the 1997 National Household Survey on Drug Abuse: Illicit drug use continues to rise among youth, stable among other groups*. Adapted by CESAR from data of the Substance Abuse and Mental Health Services Administration (SAMHSA).

Friedman, M., and Szasz, T. (1992). *On liberty and drugs*. Washington, DC: Drug Policy Foundation.

Mill, J. S. (1921). *On liberty*. Boston: Atlantic Monthly Press.

Stares, P. B. (1996a, June). Drug legalization. *Current*, pp. 383–390.

Stares, P. B. (1996b). Drug legalization? Time for a real debate. *Brookings Review*, 14 (2), 18–21.

Szasz, T. (1996). *Our right to drugs: The case for a free market*. Syracuse, NY: Syracuse University Press.

Trebach, A. S., and Inciardi, J. A. (1993). *Legalize it? Debating American drug policy*. Washington, DC: American University Press.

The Decriminalization Alternative

Sam Staley

Sam Staley directs the Urban Futures Program for the Reason Public Policy Institute.

The following excerpt first appeared in "The Decriminalization Alternative" in *Drug Policy and the Decline of American Cities* (New Brunswick, NJ: Transaction Publishers).

Despite billions of dollars spent in reducing the supply of drugs and incarcerating millions of drug users, public policy has been unable to reduce accessibility to drugs over the long run.

In the meantime, the illicit drug industry has become a growth industry in American cities. High profits, induced by a supply-side oriented drug policy, have attracted tens of thousands of low-skilled, undereducated youth into a violent industry that threatens to rip apart the social fabric of inner-city neighborhoods. The widespread use of force and rejection of the rule of law is undermining the very institutions necessary to sustain long-term economic growth.

Moreover, trends in contemporary urban policy reinforce this breakdown of institutions by encouraging the breakdown of the rule of law in the legitimate economy. While the aboveground economy lacks the violent characteristics of the drug trade, personal politics is becoming more important than the adherence to basic rules that protect people and businesses from the arbitrary will of politics. The rising authority of the local state is contributing to a parallel degeneration of the institutions necessary for promoting economic growth.

Public policy plays a vital role in providing an environment capable of nurturing economic development. Current drug policy is inconsistent with obtaining more far-reaching goals such as establishing a framework that allows cities to prosper. Rather than reduce the threat of the drug economy to America's central cities, current drug policy enhances it. Ultimately, the only solution will be to significantly reduce the influence of a violent drug trade in the social and economic environment of the city.

TOWARD A DEMAND-ORIENTED DRUG POLICY

While the United States is far from a "nation of addicts," it has certainly become a nation of drug users. Over 100 million people use alcohol and over 50 million use tobacco. In addition, almost 30 million use marijuana, 6 million use cocaine, and almost 1 million use heroin. These categories, of course, are not strictly additive. Almost all of those who use illicit substances also drink and smoke. These numbers, then, may actually overstate drug use since they ignore the proportion of multiple drug users (people who smoke and drink, or use cocaine and drink, etc.). Moreover drug use does not imply drug addiction, nor drug abuse.

American drug policy has concentrated almost completely on the supply-side, focusing on interdiction, crop reduction strategies in foreign countries, and the incarceration of drug traffickers. On the local level law enforcement agencies have emphasized drug trafficking and intra-state interdiction.

Demand-side strategies have almost exclusively been directed at incarcerating users for possession. In the early days of the drug war, these efforts relied on a "buy and bust" strategy. More recently, private and public agency drug testing programs have been implemented to increase the personal risks of drug use. Testing positive for drug use can lead to unemployment or, in some cases, jail.

Virtually every observer of the drug war acknowledges that an exclusively supply-side strategy will not work. In fact, most contemporary observers acknowledge current drug control strategies are largely ineffective.

In this chapter, the data and arguments of previous sections will be marshaled to propose an alternative strategy: decriminalization. Decriminalization is not advanced as a panacea for the drug problem, nor as analogy for drug addicts. On the contrary, decriminalization is proposed as a fundamental shift in strategy from a supply-side approach to a demand-side approach more consistent with the political, economic, and cultural traditions of the United States. The shift will provide a better foundation for public policy as a first step toward a solution. . . .

DECRIMINALIZATION AS A POLICY OPTION

The prospects for significant decriminalization appear slim in the early 1990s. Yet, a "legalization debate" sprouted during the late 1980s that has legitimized serious discussion of the topic. The effects of drug trafficking emerged as one of the preeminent concerns in public opinion and public policy. As the War on Drugs failed to produce significant results (e.g., decreases in crime rates, supplies of drugs, etc.), dissenters from the current prohibitionist strategy emerged in the public debate.

Conservative icon William F. Buckley endorsed legalization in 1985, beginning what seems to be a steadily rising tide in favor of the movement. By the 1990s, "thinking the unthinkable" became standard fare in drug policy debates.[1] Other "legalizers" include former San Jose police chief Joseph McNamara, Baltimore mayor Kurt Schmoke, former secretary of state George Shultz, Arnold Trebach of the Drug Policy Foundation, and federal judge Robert Sweet.

The legalization movement is distinctive, gaining notoriety

1. For a popular review of the pros and cons of legalization, see George J. Church, "Thinking the Unthinkable," *Time*, 20 May 1988, pp. 12–19.

through support from nonliberal sectors of the political landscape. Political conservatives have joined with civil libertarians in the growing call for decriminalization of major drugs. Buckley, for example, switched his original position favoring drug prohibition (for heroin in the 1970s) to comprehensive legalization in the 1980s. Economists Milton Friedman, Thomas Sowell, and the influential *Economist* magazine have also taken public positions in favor of legalization. The Cato Institute has also developed an active policy research agenda exploring the decriminalization of drugs.

Of course, legalization advocates have been around for decades. Milton Friedman has been advocating drug legalization since the early 1970s, when a widespread movement surfaced to decriminalize marijuana. In 1975, the state of Alaska effectively legalized small amounts of marijuana by interpreting the state's constitutional protection of privacy to include the cultivation and use of marijuana for personal use. Currently, eleven states have decriminalized the possession and use of marijuana by reducing punishment and sentencing. Even predating this movement, however, libertarians have argued that the decision to use drugs was personal and should not be a concern of government.

The biggest boost for the legalization movement may have come in 1988, when Baltimore mayor Kurt Schmoke advocated decriminalization. A former prosecutor, Schmoke argued that decriminalization should at least be part of a national debate on the future of drug policy. The weight of a big-city mayor, grappling with the drug problems in the "trenches" of America's inner cities, placed enough pressure on Congress that hearings were held on drug legalization in 1988.

Intellectually, legalization received a boost from a young academic at Princeton University. Ethan Nadelmann wrote several influential articles in the periodicals *Foreign Policy, Science, The Public Interest,* and the *New Republic* that significantly improved the respectability of prolegalization advocates. As the legalization movement gained grudging popular acceptance, early advocates of decriminalization such as Arnold Trebach (a moderate by contemporary standards) found an increasingly receptive audience.

Despite its high media profile, decriminalization represents an ad hoc collection of proposals. Some proponents intend to legalize only the use and sale of marijuana. Others advocate the comprehensive legalization of all psychoactive substances. Still other variations of decriminalization argue for the legalization of use and possession, but not trafficking in large amounts of drugs. Indeed, a significant weakness of the "legalization movement" according to its opponents, has been its lack of consensus concerning a practical policy position.

None of the advocates of drug decriminalization suggest that their approach will "solve" the drug problem. Rather, they advocate legalization as a first step toward a better and more effective public policy. In addition, few advocates propose legalization in desperation. On the contrary, most proponents have arrived at their position after careful reflection on the problem and the role of public policy. Decriminalization represents an approach to looking at the drug problem rather than a schedule of specific policy recommendations. As Ethan Nadelmann observes,

> In its broadest sense . . . legalization incorporates the many arguments and growing sentiment for de-emphasizing our traditional reliance on criminal justice resources to deal with drug abuse and for emphasizing instead drug abuse, prevention, treatment, and education, as well as noncriminal restrictions on the availability and use of psychoactive substances and positive inducements to abstain from drug abuse.[2]

Thus, decriminalization represents a *strategic shift* in drug policy away from treating drug abuse as a law enforcement problem to treating drug abuse as a behavioral problem. In this sense, decriminali-

---

2. Ethan A. Nadelmann, "Drug Prohibition in the United States: Costs, Consequences, and Alternatives," *Science* 245, no. 4921 (1 September 1989): 939.

zation represents a *policy shift* from the supply-side strategy dominating the War on Drugs to a demand-side strategy emphasizing the human and social consequences of drug abuse.

Ultimately, use becomes a social problem when drugs are abused, becoming privately and socially disruptive. Like alcohol, the major drugs—marijuana, cocaine, and heroin—can be used without this use inevitably leading to addiction or socially disruptive behavior. Ultimately, the causes of drug abuse are far more complex than the legal system is capable of addressing. Decriminalization proposes a more realistic foundation and informed attitude toward drug use, focusing on the harms of abuse (rather than mere use) and addiction.

A move toward decriminalization requires that public policy toward illicit drugs be reconstituted on a fundamentally different foundation. Rather than focusing on which drugs would be legalized and how they would be regulated, the decriminalization alternative focuses on how drug abuse is viewed and interpreted through the legal system and public policy. Drug decriminalization acknowledges that addicts cannot be cured by throwing them in jail. The current law enforcement system virtually ignores the complexities of addiction and other behavioral aspects of drug use, such as the psychological and social profile of the individual and the family context.

On the supply side, the decriminalization alternative acknowledges that the "drug trade" is an economic development issue and problem. The drug trade, like much black-market activity, flourishes in poverty and economic deprivation. By removing the profits from the drug trade, American cities can more effectively address inner-city development problems, particularly in minority communities.

ARGUMENTS FOR DECRIMINALIZATION

Arguments for the decriminalization of drug use in the United States claim several origins. This, in part, reflects the diversity of backgrounds from which legalizers and decriminalizers have emerged.

Some, such as Arnold Trebach, have extensive clinical and academic experience in drug treatment and policy analysis. Others, such as Ira Glasser of the American Civil Liberties Union and Steven Wisotsky of the NOVA Law School in Florida, approach the subject from a civil libertarian and legal background. Still others, such as Mayor Kurt Schmoke, Judge Robert Sweet, and Police Chief Joseph McNamara, have come to their position after a long, bitter experience fighting the War on Drugs in the streets and courts. Although the individuals cannot be lumped together as if they have the same interests and backgrounds, decriminalization arguments can be broken down into at least four broad categories: libertarian, cost-benefit, public health, and economic development. . . .

The Libertarian Position

One of the oldest arguments favoring decriminalization has come from civil libertarians such as psychiatrist Thomas Szasz[3] who focus on the role government plays in the lives of individual citizens. Constitutionally, every citizen has a right to privacy and the absence of the arbitrary intrusion of government into their personal lives. The War on Drugs directly intervenes into personal life by attempting to control voluntary, noncoercive behavior among citizens even when their behavior does not injure others. Indeed drug enforcement is especially difficult precisely because drug trafficking is a voluntary activity and drug use occurs in private.

Despite the perceived harmfulness by prohibitionists, drug use is a voluntary activity and unlikely to inflict injury on an uninvolved third party. For libertarians, the only time a role for the state can be justified is when drug use jeopardizes the health and welfare of others

---

3. For a brief discussion of Szasz's perspective and a thoroughly libertarian argument, see Thomas Szasz, "The War Against Drugs," *Journal of Drug Issues* 12, no. 2 (Winter 1982): 115–22; and the path-breaking work *Ceremonial Chemistry: The Ritual Persecution of Drugs, Addicts, and Pushers*, rev. ed. (Holmes Beach, Fl.: Learning Publications, 1985).

(e.g., driving under the influence, assault under the influence, drug use during pregnancy, etc.).

Broadly interpreted, the libertarian argument often parallels more traditional objections to the separation of Church and state embedded in the First Amendment. Issues of morality and religion should not be a concern of the government. As long as drug use is considered a moral issue, the government does not have standing in regulating its use.

Government agencies are liberalizing statutes regulating the power of law enforcement personnel to seize private property, even when the property cannot be directly linked to the commission of a crime. In some cases, the requirement that criminal punishment can be imposed only after someone is proven guilty "beyond reasonable doubt" is retreating to "probable cause." Libertarians further argue that the War on Drugs threatens the civil liberties that provide a stable foundation for democratic government. In the long run, democratic societies cannot afford to wage such a socially destructive (and ultimately divisive) war.

In an open letter to Drug Czar William Bennett, economist and Nobel Laureate Milton Friedman may have summarized the libertarian's worst fears of the end result of the War on Drugs. Writing in the *Wall Street Journal*, Friedman implores,

> Every friend of freedom . . . must be as revolted as I am by the prospect of turning the United States into an armed camp, by the vision of jails filled with casual drug users and of an army of enforcers empowered to invade the liberty of citizens on slight evidence. A country in which shooting down unidentified planes "on suspicion" can be seriously considered as a drug-war tactic is not the kind of United States that either you [Bill Bennett] or I want to hand on to future generations.[6]

6. Milton Friedman, "An Open Letter to Bill Bennett," *Wall Street Journal*, 7 September 1989, reprinted in *The Crisis in Drug Prohibition*, ed. David Boaz (Washington, D.C.: Cato Institute, 1990), 114–16.

Given the risks to democratic government, in practice the War on Drugs is a counterproductive exercise of government coercion.

To maintain consistency, libertarians argue, all psychoactive substances would have to be banned, not just politically unpopular drugs. The prohibition on marijuana, cocaine, and heroin is hypocritical given the widespread acceptance of alcohol and tobacco in American culture. Indeed, the health consequences of alcohol and tobacco loom far larger than currently illicit substances. Since the cultural restrictions on the use of marijuana, cocaine, and heroin are much more severe than for tobacco and alcohol, many libertarians perceive drug prohibition as an attempt to enforce a narrow set of values rather than serious concern over the harms of drug use.

One of the most significant obstacles faced by libertarians is their small numbers. As a voting bloc, libertarians remain a smaller proportion of the American electorate than conservatives (who agree with state intervention on moral issues) and populists (who agree with state intervention on both moral and economic issues) according to recent estimates by pollsters and political scientists. A study of the California public found that only 14 percent of the voting public could be classified as libertarian.[8]

Cost-Benefit Analysis

Although the libertarian argument is the oldest argument in favor of decriminalization, the argument that may have had the most impact on current public opinion is the cost-benefit perspective. Many of the most visible advocates of drug decriminalization fall (publicly) into this category. In essence, the cost-benefit argument claims that the costs of waging a drug war are simply too high to continue. While these costs may include the abridgement of civil liberties, they also include the crime and violence associated with drug prohibition, the

8. Mervin Field, "Trends in American Politics," in *Left, Right, and Babyboom: America's New Politics*, ed. David Boaz (Washington, D.C.: Cato Institute, 1986), 15–21.

health-care crisis resulting from contaminated drugs (as a result of poor quality control), the effects on U.S. foreign policy, and the vast sums of money expended on law enforcement.

Among the most prominent cost-benefit decriminalizers might be David Boaz, the executive vice president of the Cato Institute in Washington, D.C.; James Ostrowski, a lawyer in Buffalo, New York; Ethan Nadelmann, a professor of public policy at Princeton University; William F. Buckley, Jr., conservative columnist and prominent author; and federal judge Robert Sweet of New York.

Buckley, writing in 1985, may have summed up the attitudes of most legalizers when he noted,

> It is hardly a novel suggestion to legalize dope. Shrewd observers of the scene have recommended it for years. I am on record as having opposed it in the matter of heroin. The accumulated evidence draws me away from my own opposition, on the purely empirical grounds that what we have now is a drug problem plus a crime problem plus a problem of huge export of capital to the dope-producing countries.[9]

Cost-benefit arguments emphasize the impracticalities of a drug prohibition policy given the physical limitations on jails, prisons, and courts and the geographic limitations on successfully controlling the supply of drugs. Decriminalizers conclude that, ultimately, public expenditures on drug prohibition strategies are a "black hole" for government spending. The only people who gain are employees of law enforcement agencies and the drug traffickers. Richard Cowan, a frequent writer for the conservative political magazine *National Review*, argues that the "narcocracy" is the primary reason drug prohibition persists despite widespread empirical evidence that the policy is a failure.[10]

9. William F. Buckley, Jr., "Legalize Dope," *Washington Post*, 1 April 1985, sec. A, p. 11.

10. Richard C. Cowan, "How the Narcs Created Crack," *National Review* 38, no. 23 (December 1986): 28–29.

Ultimately, the costs to society do not warrant the continuation of drug prohibition given the potential benefits of a legalization strategy. David Boaz of the Cato Institute enlists the cost-benefit position as an important supplement to a more general libertarian argument:

> We can either escalate the war on drugs, which would have dire implications for civil liberties and the right to privacy, or find a way to gracefully withdraw. Withdrawal should not be viewed as an endorsement of drug use; it would simply be an acknowledgement that the cost of this war—billions of dollars, runaway crime rates and restrictions on personal freedom—is too high.[11]

While decriminalizers do not argue that legalizing drugs would solve the problems of drug abuse, they do argue society would reap important benefits by reducing crime and black-market profits and avoiding the wholesale scrapping of the Bill of Rights.

Public Health

A third general category of arguments among the decriminalizers involves public health. The most vocal advocates of this position may be Kurt Schmoke and Arnold Trebach. Trebach favors effective decriminalization for drug use and possession. Rather than consider users of illicit drugs "enemies of the state," a more rational approach is to treat addicts and drug abusers.[13] Education and treatment, Trebach believes, is far more effective than making the "drug problem" a "criminal problem" where resources are squandered on ineffective and inhumane supply-side strategies (e.g., interdiction, crop eradication, and arresting small-time dealers).

---

11. David Boaz, "Let's Quit the Drug War," *New York Times*, 17 March 1988.

13. Arnold S. Trebach, *The Great Drug War: And Radical Proposals That Could Make America Safe Again* (New York: Macmillan, 1987). Trebach does not believe in the legalization of all drugs. Publicly, he favors the legalization of marijuana although he thinks it should be taxed heavily and the proceeds used to fund drug treatment (see pp. 368–69).

Kurt Schmoke also criticizes the current drug prohibition strategy for treating drug abuse as a criminal problem rather than a health problem. Calling for a drug war led by the surgeon general rather than the attorney general, Schmoke argues that drug abuse will be curtailed only when drug users recognize the dangers of the substances they ingest. Further, throwing addicts in jail will not provide the treatment they need to "kick" their habit. In fact, based on some of the evidence presented in the previous chapter, prison may increase exposure to major drugs.

The most compelling public health argument, however, may be associated with the reduction in crime that would result from decriminalization.[15] Drug prohibition feeds a criminal element that fears itself more than the criminal justice system. The profits gleaned from illicit drug trafficking spark violence and crime that could be largely eliminated by adopting a comprehensive decriminalization policy.

At its core, the public health approach calls for a comprehensive reorientation of drug policy away from treating abuse and addiction as a legal problem to an education and treatment problem. The current policy, through its focus on criminal justice solutions, ignores the human dimensions of addiction, abuse, and crime.

Economic Development

The final argument for decriminalization emphasizes the economic development consequences of the current drug strategy. This approach to the drug problem has received little systematic attention. Newspapers, television, and some economists have focused on the economics of the drug trade, detailing its multifaceted distribution system, but few have delved deeply into the potential consequences for economic development in cities. The implications of drug prohibition extend far beyond their impact on users and the narrow

15. Kurt Schmoke, "Drugs: A Problem of Health and Economics," *Washington Post*, 15 May 1988; reprinted in Boaz, *The Crisis in Drug Prohibition*, 9–12.

world of the drug trafficker. They influence the way of life in American inner cities.

Through drug prohibition, public policy has created a vast black market for illicit substances, fueling violence and disrespect for law and human life. These values become an essential element of survival in economically devastated urban areas that offer few legitimate opportunities for employment. When those opportunities exist, as the case of Washington, D.C., clearly illustrates, they are far less attractive (financially) than the potential gains from drug trafficking.

The economic development perspective focuses on the implications for a system that trains young workers in an industry marked by violence and deceit, and transfers them into the legitimate economy. While many have learned some skills (e.g., counting, inventory control, supervision), the values are less consistent with the requirements of normal business activity in the legitimate economy.

Drug prohibition works against the best interests of the community by dampening the incentives for its citizens to pursue economically productive and prosperous employment in the legitimate sector. Drug prohibition encourages new entrants into the labor force to emphasize short-term gains through drug trafficking rather than the long-term gains from legitimate employment and occupational training. Ultimately, the current policy is pushing the inner city even further toward economic destruction by weakening the institutional foundations necessary for a productive and prosperous society.

ARGUMENTS OPPOSING LEGALIZATION

The decriminalization alternative remains unpopular among most leading scholars and policymakers. Former drug czar William Bennett publicly called the idea "stupid" and suggested that many of its advocates are racist.[16] Others, such as Congresswoman Patricia

---

16. William Bennett's remarks occurred after federal judge Robert Sweet in New York announced he was in favor of legalization in December 1989.

Schroeder (D-Colorado), oppose decriminalization because they fear the United States will become a "nation of addicts."[17] Others, basing their recommendations on more scholarly assessments of the drug problem, oppose legalization because they feel the increase in the number of addicts would not justify the benefits of legalized use.[18]

Like the arguments for decriminalization, general themes are detectable in their opposition. Prohibition proponents argue that the decriminalizers ignore the public health consequences of increased drug use, that legalization will feed the criminal element, and, perhaps most important, society cannot appear to condone or encourage drug use.

Public Health Consequences of Legalization

Most prohibition proponents emphasize that prohibition works from a public health perspective. Any reduction in the price, either through criminal sanctions or the price system, will increase the number of drug users. The higher levels of drug use inevitably place more burdens on the health care system. Moreover, prohibition proponents note that during alcohol prohibition, diseases associated with alcohol consumption actually declined.

A decriminalization strategy will doom society as the number of addicts increases dramatically. Senator Alfonse D'Amato (R-New York), for example, is quoted as saying legalization would lead to "a society of drug-related zombies."[19] A. M. Rosenthal, a columnist for the *New York Times*, claims that advocating the legalization of drugs

17. This claim was made by Representative Schroeder during a debate on drug legalization sponsored by *Firing Line*.

18. See John Kaplan, *The Hardest Drug: Heroin and Public Policy* (Chicago: University of Chicago Press, 1983); Mark A. R. Kleiman, *Marijuana: Costs of Abuse, Costs of Control* (New York: Greenwood Press, 1989).

19. Quoted in "Bennett: Legalized Drug Idea 'Stupid,'" *USA Today*, 18 December 1989, sec. A, p. 3.

is the same as advocating slavery.[20] By reducing the price of drugs, legalization would induce millions into a life of addiction which, according to Rosenthal, is a virtual state of bondage. Charles Kraut- hammer, an editor for the *New Republic*, summarized the argument when he wrote, "In order to undercut the black market, legalization must radically reduce the price of drugs. And the price of drugs is the surest predictor of use. Drugs are like any other commodity, the lower the price, the higher the consumption."[21] Ultimately, prohi- bitionists say, the drug problem would become much worse if legal- ization were effective. Moreover, even though alcohol and tobacco are legalized, their legal status does not support legalizing another harmful substance.

James A. Inciardi, director of the Division of Criminal Justice at the University of Delaware and a leading opponent of legalization, suggests that the very mechanism legalizers rely on to reduce the harms of drug use will exacerbate them. One of the most "powerful aspects of American tradition," Inciardi notes, is "the ability of an entrepreneurial market system to create, expand, and maintain high levels of demand."[22]

The prohibitionists assume, of course, that the primary determi- nant of drug use is the drug's legal status or the price. In essence, they buy the strict economic argument that price and quantity demanded are inversely related. Indeed, even decriminalizers agree that lower prices will probably increase overall consumption. The point of disagreement revolves around the magnitude. Decriminal- izers believe that other factors intervene irrespective of legal status and even price. Data does not exist capable of deciding this issue

20. A. M. Rosenthal, "Legalize Drugs: A Good Case for Slavery," *Dayton Daily News*, 7 January 1990, sec. B, p. 7. Reprinted from the *New York Times*.

21. Charles Krauthammer, "Mistakes of the Legalizers," *Washington Post*, 13 April 1990, sec. A, p. 25.

22. James A. Inciardi, "The Case Against Legalization," in *The Drug Legalization Debate*, ed. James A. Inciardi (Newbury Park, Calif.: Sage Publications, 1991), 56.

once and for all. The evidence presented [here], however, strongly suggests that the costs of addiction will increase only modestly.

Historically, consumers have reacted to information about drugs in dramatic ways. David F. Musto, a historian of drug laws, notes that the Pure Food and Drug Act of 1906 substantially altered the consumption of patent medicines when they were required to list narcotics as ingredients. Within a few years after the Act was passed, "it was estimated that patent medicines containing such drugs dropped in sale by about a third."[26] More recently, consumers have moved steadily toward less potent legal drugs such as light beer, wine coolers, and low-tar cigarettes.

Potential increases in drug use must also be compared to the costs of prohibition. A death resulting from an overdose may have substantially different consequences than a death resulting from a drug-related drive-by shooting. For example, if the government sends a soldier to war and he dies, few claim that the government is a murderer. If, on the other hand, the government kills civilians for reasons unrelated to national security or protecting its citizens, the action is considered murder and the perpetrators tried in criminal proceedings. The standard for evaluating death varies with the circumstances.

Similarly, an addict who dies from an overdose of drugs should not be compared to the gunning down of a nine-year-old child as a consequence of a drug market turf battle. The first case, while tragic, is at least controllable by the addict. The addict can choose when he or she will take drugs and from whom the drugs will be bought. To the extent that the drug overdose is due to imperfect information (e.g., there may be no way to test for drug quality), the death may also be a result of a prohibitionist policy that undermines competition aimed at ensuring quality products are placed on the market.

The latter death, however, is a symbol of how the rules of the

---

26. David F. Musto, *The American Disease: Origins of Narcotic Control*, exp. ed. (New York: Oxford University Press, 1987), 22.

game have changed and reflects the full force of the current prohibitionist policy. Prohibition engenders violent solutions to solving disputes. The result is a genuine breakdown of law and order and the significant discounting of human life. The death of a nine-year-old child is symptomatic of a shift in how individuals are relating to each other. Even if the child's death is a mistake, it becomes an accepted part of the trade and the risks of living in a drug neighborhood.

In the end, the legalization opponent is not willing to take the risk that the number of addicts will increase. "True, there is a large segment of people who won't find drugs attractive," economist Peter Reuter observes, "but who wants to take the risk of seeing whether the number of those who want drugs is 500 percent greater than now, rather than only 50 percent greater."

Feeding the Criminal Element

A second argument advanced by decriminalization opponents is that legalizing the distribution of drugs would actually feed criminals and drug cartels. "What seems at least as likely," writes *Washington Post* columnist William Raspberry, "is the development of drug cartels with an interest both in increasing the number of drug users and in maintaining prices at levels that would ensure their profitability."[28] Existing organizations have proven extremely efficient in distributing drugs to consumers and they will likely continue. If drugs are decriminalized, the argument continues, the same people selling drugs now will be selling them later.

The drug cartels and the institutionalized violence seem an indelible characteristic of the drug market. Comprehensive decriminalization will not eliminate the criminals. After all, alcohol prohibition did not create the Mafia. Similarly, the Mafia remains even after Prohibition ended.

---

28. William Raspberry, "Don't Legalize Drugs," *Washington Post*, 26 May 1989.

Strong empirical and theoretical reasons exist suggesting that this is an unlikely consequence.[29] First, the argument assumes that the behavior tolerated and encouraged in the illegal drug market would persist in a legal drug market. This argument also ignores the importance of public policy in defining the environment, or rules of the game, for economic market activity. Although Prohibition did not create the Mafia, it provided the environment conducive to its growth and the consolidation of a large underworld of violence, corruption and arbitrary personal power. Similarly, prohibition has provided the incentive and fuel for the growth and consolidation of violent drug cartels. The characteristics of the illegal drug market suggest that it is an inferior system of distribution and production. A decriminalized drug environment would radically alter the character of drug markets. The ability to solve disputes peacefully through the court system would substantially reduce violence in the drug markets. Liquor stores are rarely fortresses. Alcohol is rarely bought or sold in open-air markets on street corners or in school-yards.

More important, drug-distribution systems that operate as legitimate businesses would grow and become even more efficient, competing for business by offering better service and better quality products. Accountability exists in illicit drug markets only at the end of a gun. In legitimate economic markets, accountability is more efficiently implemented through the profit and loss system. Stable and permanent locations are essential to ensure a stable and peaceful clientele and have proven time and time again to be superior to street peddling.

---

29. Inciardi, however, has argued that violence will escalate with legalization. While the violence associated with the drug trade might decrease, violence associated with the pharmacological effects of drug use would increase. Although the present author believes Inciardi's point is important, his conclusion that "in all likelihood *any declines in systemic violence would be accompanied by corresponding increases in psychopharmacologic violence*" (emphasis in original) seems much too strong given the evidence he presents. See Inciardi, "The Case Against Legalization," 58–59.

Society Cannot Condone Drug Use

Perhaps the most common argument invoked against decriminalization centers on morality and socially acceptable behavior. Drugs are bad and therefore society should not condone drug use. Anything short of comprehensive prohibition would send the "wrong signals" to children and adults concerning drug use. Government is viewed as a direct representative of the collective will of society.

This argument assumes that citizens take their cues concerning right and wrong from government policy or the legal system. If this were true, the fundamental principles of representative government have been turned on their head. While laws are reflections of culture, democratic governments are established to protect the rights of their citizens. Oftentimes, these rights conflict with broader social concerns. The law, for example, protects the right of the Ku Klux Klan to hold public rallies and demonstrations. This is not interpreted as public support for the goals, objectives, and beliefs of the Klan.

In contemporary democratic societies, moral values are not imposed by the state. More important, democratic governments are responsible for protecting individual rights rather than the collective rights of specific interest groups. While the government enforces the law, it cannot pass judgment on the correctness of the law.

A compelling argument can also be made that prohibition has supported the behavior prohibitionists want to discourage. Richard Cowan has noted that prohibition has created "accidental perversities" in drug consumption.[30] By making drug distribution a risky and expensive undertaking, the unintended consequences of government control have been to encourage the production, marketing, and consumption of more potent drugs that can be distributed more easily.

Intensified interdiction efforts encouraged drug traffickers to switch from marijuana, which is bulky and easily detectable, to

30. Cowan, "How the Narcs Created Crack," 28.

cocaine, which can be transported in small quantities. The reduction in imported marijuana has resulted in domestic cultivation of more potent strains. Similarly, the army's crackdown on marijuana in Vietnam led to a heroin epidemic. More recently, crack was developed (a technical innovation) as a potent, but cheap, alternative to cocaine capable of being marketed in poor sections of America's inner cities. In principle, every naturally grown drug could be substituted for by more potent designer drugs capable of being developed in the crudest chemistry labs. Thus, while consumers are opting for less potent legal drugs, public policy is encouraging the development and distribution of more potent illicit drugs. . . .

CONCLUSION

A substantial philosophical schism exists between decriminalizers and prohibitionists that significantly undermines the prospects for developing a "third way." Decriminalization and prohibition advocates operate from different sets of principles. On the one hand, those proposing decriminalization emphasize individual accountability and responsibility. The role of public policy centers on the protectionist state where personal rights and freedoms are defended.

On the other side, prohibition advocates emphasize the importance of collectivism. "Society" has an obligation to impose certain standards on individual behavior even when the behavior is voluntary and rational. Prohibitionists, unlike many decriminalizers, view the state as a unified expression of a collective will that supersedes voluntary and peaceful actions of individual citizens.

Prohibition proponents have criticized decriminalization advocates for not proposing specific policy recommendations. This criticism, however, is a red herring. A detailed policy recommendation presumes that a consensus exists that America's drug policy should be reconstituted on the principles of decriminalization. Any recommended strategy will not satisfy prohibition proponents because they remain unconvinced that decriminalization is a legitimate or viable policy option.

The War on Drugs has created observable effects, many of them negative. Drug prohibition has not limited the accessibility of drugs for most potential users. On the contrary, drug accessibility has increased over the years. Yet, drug prohibition has resulted in huge drug profits that have facilitated the emergence of violent drug cartels. More peaceful, small-time traffickers have been excluded from legitimate economic markets, retreating to the violence of black-market operations. The black-market trade is an artifact of the legal system.

In the process, the War on Drugs is undermining the values that are essential components of the institutions favorable to economic development. By encouraging and sustaining an environment that reinforces violence and the arbitrary decisions of people instead of abstract principles embodied in the legal system, the respect for law and private property is weakened. Without these institutions, urban communities will continue to stagnate economically, further entrenching the underground economy as the foundation of the inner-city economic and social system.

Decriminalization will eliminate most (but not all) of the law enforcement problem that has emerged. It will also move public policy more in line with the principles necessary to promote economic and community development. As earlier chapters have attempted to outline, the "drug problem" today is largely a crime problem, manifesting itself in overcrowded jails, attenuation of civil liberties, and the expansion of the power of law enforcement agencies at the expense of freedom.

Decriminalization is offered as a first step toward refocusing drug policy on the human dimension. From a social perspective, the "drug problem" should encompass social controls over drug abuse and the consequences of addiction. Prohibiting any use of illicit drugs ignores the complexities of drug use and addiction. Decriminalization admits that not all drug use, like not all alcohol use, is drug abuse.

The argument for decriminalization rests on an understanding that America's current "drug problem" is not a "drug addiction" or a "drug abuse" problem. The harms associated with drug use and abuse revolve around the violence and apparent chaos in the inner cities, which, in turn, is an unintended consequence of public policy. Decriminalization would allow policymakers and policy analysts to focus on the consequences of drug use. The current regime concerns itself almost exclusively with the legal dimensions.

Broadly speaking, the decriminalization argument acknowledges that economics figures prominently in any solution to the drug problem. The foot soldiers of the drug industry are taken from the ranks of the unemployed with few realistic options in the legitimate economy. In addition, as long as a demand for illicit drugs exists, profits will persist. Eventually, as long as the industry remains underground, the effects will become violent and destructive. Only by acknowledging the limits of public policy in a free society and the fundamentally economic character of the drug problem in the United States can the problem be addressed substantively. Ultimately, decriminalization of heroin, cocaine, and marijuana provides the most realistic and progressive alternative.

The Great Drug Policy Debate— What Means This Thing Called Decriminalization?

Ronald Bayer is Professor of Public Health at the Columbia University Mailman School of Public Health.

This selection was excerpted from "The Great Drug Policy Debate—What Means This Thing Called Decriminalization?" in *Confronting Drug Policy: Illicit Drugs in a Free Society* edited by Ronald Bayer and Gerald M. Oppenheimer (New York, NY: Cambridge University Press, 1993).

A profound sense of dissatisfaction characterizes the contemporary American discussion of drug policy. From across the political spectrum a chorus of critical voices is heard, linking those who most typically see each other as ideological antagonists. Their common platform asserts that prohibitionist policies that are given force by the criminal law have failed to prevent the use of drugs, and that efforts to restrict drug use have created a plethora of social evils far worse than the problem of drug use itself. Enormous resources are expended on the effort to interdict the international and domestic commerce in drugs. The courts are clogged with defendants arrested for violating the drug laws and the jails and prisons are filled with inmates convicted of violating those laws, whether by property crimes designed to pay the inflated black-market prices of illicit drugs or by acts of violence spawned by the struggles that pervade the underground economy. The streets of the urban ghettos have become wastelands dominated by the often armed sellers, buyers, and users of drugs. HIV infection spreads among drug injectors under legal conditions that encourage the sharing of syringes and needles. Civil liberties are routinely violated as government agents prosecute the war on drugs. Only a radical change in policy, it is argued, will provide a remedy to this situation. Criminalization is a failure. Decriminalization must then be the answer.

BUT WHAT MEANS THIS THING
CALLED DECRIMINALIZATION?

Beyond the common commitment to a break with the use of the criminal law as the primary social weapon in the struggle against drug use, there is little agreement. For the minimalists among the advocates of reform, what is necessary is an end to the prosecution of people who have drugs in their possession, or who are engaged in small-scale, street-level trade. For yet others decriminalization implies the need to medicalize the problem, replacing policemen with physicians, punishment with treatment. Finally, increasingly, some have come to believe that only a maximalist conception of decriminalization can meet the challenge created by the disaster that the enforcement of prohibition has produced. Legalization of drugs and creation of a regulated market like that now prevailing for alcohol would be, from this perspective, the only effective remedy to the crisis we are facing. Each of these conceptions of decriminalization entails very different adjustments in the dominant policy perspective, carries with it very different implications for the risks of increased drug use, implies very different standards of tolerance for drug use, and suggests very different roles for the functions of medicine and the criminal law.

It is a remarkable feature of the contemporary debate over the future of drug policy that it takes place with only the dimmest recognition of the extended and perspicuous discussion that centered on drug policy in the period following World War II and that all but ended in the mid-1970s. This historical amnesia is the more striking because in virtually all respects the contemporary debate mimics what occurred in the earlier period. It is my purpose in this introduction to recall the earlier debate in order to place the current discussion into some perspective.

THE RISE AND DECLINE OF THE DECRIMINALIZATION DEBATE: POST–WORLD WAR II ERA

For much of this century the United States has sought to confront the challenge of drug use with policies derived from a prohibitionist perspective (Musto 1973). The sale, possession, and use of controlled substances was deemed an appropriate subject of the criminal law. Punishing violators of such restrictive statutes was to serve the ends of both specific and general deterrence. Physicians were restricted from prescribing a broad range of substances that were deemed to have no legitimate clinical purpose. Therapeutic options were virtually unknown, a reflection of both profound pessimism about the ability of medicine to help the drug user and the ideological dominance of those committed to law enforcement. In the face of periodic rises in drug use, public panic ensued. At such moments the severity of the punishment of drug law violators was intensified, the latitude available to judges to impose sentences restricted.

The Liberal Challenge

In the period following World War II, when an increase in heroin addiction provoked great consternation, American liberals took up the challenge of the broad critique of American narcotics policies (Bayer 1975a). Above all else, the liberal position was an exculpatory one, eschewing notions of blameworthiness and guilt that are central to the criminalization of drug use.

The perception of the addict as a victim of blocked opportunity was derived from the sociologists, to whom liberals turned for explanations of troubling behavior and who provided so much of the academic justification for the social policies with which liberalism came to be identified (Cloward and Ohlen 1960). Like the problem of juvenile delinquency to which it was so intimately linked in the public mind, addiction suggested to liberals the need to "finish the work of the New Deal" (*Nation* 1970, 228). This theme ran like a powerful leitmotif through virtually every discussion of heroin use in the journals of liberal opinion during the 1960s and early 1970s. Thus the *Nation* stated: "Society must come to realize that it is a cause—perhaps the major cause—of the affliction that it now observes with such fear and revulsion." Dr. Joel Fort, writing in the *Saturday Review of Literature*, underscored the extent to which addiction was perceived as an indication of social distress by referring to heroin use as a "barometer" of the extent to which society was characterized by "poverty, segregation, slums, psychological immaturity, ignorance and misery" (1962, 30).

Typically, the response provoked by this understanding involved calls for the full range of social programs that would get at the "root causes" of deviancy—programs designed to attack chronic unemployment and the grinding poverty of the underclass. Decrying the resources devoted to interdiction by the Nixon administration, the *Nation* asked: "Why . . . doesn't President Nixon devote more resources to the elimination of the social and economic problems which permit large scale drug abuse to take root?" (1971, 421).

Given the openness of postwar liberalism to deterministic theories of behavior, arguments for the psychopathological theories of heroin use seemed particularly congenial. The influence of mental health professionals—psychiatrists, psychologists, and social workers—on liberalism's perception of drug use cannot be overstated. Not only did they offer to explain discordant behavior in terms that avoided notions of personal guilt, but they also promised a technology of rehabilitation untainted by the brutality of punishment. Thus, the disease concept of addiction provided liberals with a perfect mechanism for achieving the very corrective ends that conservative law enforcement approaches had failed to attain.

With addiction defined as the expression of an underlying psychological disease, liberals could propose a range of treatment alternatives to punitive incarceration. Outpatient clinics providing psychotherapy as well as inpatient, hospital-based treatment were to become, at different moments, the focus of the liberal and reformist approach to drug users. Although clinics might suffice if they could control the heroin user's behavior, quarantine in hospitals for the purpose of treatment might also be necessary to help the addict and to protect the community. Predisposed toward noncoercive solutions, liberalism was by no means unwilling to embrace the imposition of therapeutic solutions. Indeed, no less a figure than Justice William O. Douglas, the exemplar of liberal jurisprudence, wrote in *Robinson v. California*[1] that a state might determine that "the general health and welfare require that [addicts] be dealt with by compulsory treatment involving quarantine, confinement or sequestration."

But within a decade liberals had turned on such confinement as both expensive and ineffective. Writing in 1971, David Bazilon, the noted liberal U.S. Court of Appeals judge, who had done so much to open the legal process to psychiatry and the behavioral sciences, stated: "It certainly sounds more enlightened to treat the drug user than to punish him for his status. But my experience with the civil commitment process suggests that the differences between punishment and compulsory treatment do not justify the extravagant claims made" (Bazilon 1971, 48).

---

1. *Robinson v. California* 370 U.S. 676 (1962). This case declared that imprisonment of addicts for the status of addiction constituted cruel and unusual punishment.

Medicalization of Drug Addiction

Despite the disenchantment with compulsory closed-ward treatment—a reflection of the due process transformation that was affecting the willingness to tolerate benign confinement of juvenile and
mental patients—the hold of the deterministic perspective did not
waver (Gostin 1991). The *Robinson* decision had embraced the conception of addiction as a disease and thus had subverted the moral
foundations for the use of the criminal law. "It is unlikely that any
state at this moment would attempt to make it a criminal offense for
a person to be mentally ill, or a leper, or to be afflicted with venereal
disease. . . . Even one day in prison would be cruel and unusual
punishment for the 'crime' of having a common cold."[2] But the
Court had spoken only of the *status* of addiction. Its decision had not
extended the exculpatory perspective to the acts associated with that
status. For almost a decade, from the mid-1960s onward, legal commentators struggled with this issue and liberal analysts had sought to
broaden the meaning of *Robinson* to include those behaviors inextri-
cably linked to the "disease of addiction" (Bayer 1978a), just as they
sought to protect alcoholics from imprisonment for acts of public
drunkenness. Pharmacological duress was the doctrine employed in
the effort to extend *Robinson*. Whereas the Supreme Court had protected the addict as an addict from punishment, the proponents of
pharmacological duress sought to extend the protective scope of the
court's decision to those whose addiction compelled them to purchase illicit drugs (Lowenstein 1967). "The commission of such
offenses is merely an involuntary submission to [a] compulsion"
(Goldstein 1973, 153). Some went further and sought to extend the
doctrine to property crimes committed to obtain narcotics on the
black market (*Georgetown Law Review* 1971). Although ultimately
unsuccessful before the courts, the effort to win approval for the doc-

2. *Robinson v. California*, op. cit., 667.

trine of pharmacological duress underscored its proponents' determination to vanquish the still dominant status of the criminal law in the social response to drug use.

Paralleling the reformist assault on the theoretical and moral justifications for using criminal law in the struggle against drug abuse was a deep concern about how the efforts to incarcerate drug users and those engaged in the small-scale street-level trade in drugs were affecting the criminal justice system itself. Long a point made by the critics of prohibition, these concerns were ultimately to find expression from individuals whose commitment to the efficient functioning of the agencies of law enforcement drew them to the minimalist conception of decriminalization. "Addicts guilty of no other crime than illegal possession of narcotics are filling the jails, prisons and penitentiaries of our country," declared Judge Morris Ploscowe in an appendix to the joint American Bar Association–American Medical Association (1963) study of the narcotics problem in 1963. Almost ten years later, when the demand for a less punitive response to drug use had begun to have some impact, a state investigation in New York stated: "The Commission could only conclude that the narcotics law enforcement efforts by the police of New York City was [*sic*] a failure, and a monumental waste of time, of money and manpower. The evidence was clear and compelling that the police effort was directed at the lowest type of street violator, the addict, and that the police work was having no appreciable effect upon narcotics traffic in New York City" (New York State Temporary Commission Investigation 1973, 46).

The most striking feature of the liberal challenge to the prevailing perspective on drug abuse policy was, however, not simply its embrace of the conception of addiction as a disease, and its rejection of the centrality of law enforcement to the effort to limit drug use. Rather, it was the growing belief that efforts to prohibit the use of narcotics in the treatment of the illness of addiction were a profound mistake (Bayer 1975c). . . .

The Americanization of Narcotic Maintenance

In the period between the late 1950s and the mid-1960s reformers were increasingly vocal in their support for narcotic maintenance. That support found repeated expression in the journals of liberal opinion—*Commonweal, Commentary,* the *Nation.* The *New York Times* also spoke out editorially against the prohibitionist response to addiction. Invariably, the link between crime and drug use, so central to the prohibitionist perspective, was rejected. It was not heroin that produced crime, but rather prohibition that drove the addict to criminality. These arguments were shaped by and helped to shape the proposals of a number of reformist bodies (Berger 1956; New York Academy of Medicine 1955; American Bar Association–American Medical Association 1963). . . .

Heroin maintenance was never to become a viable political option in the United States. A sanitized version of narcotic maintenance, however, was to make striking inroads through the willingness of local, state, and, most important, federal agencies to fund the rapid expansion of methadone maintenance in the early 1970s. Methadone, a synthetic, long-acting narcotic that could be taken orally, met each of the challenges posed by reformers since the end of World War II (Dole 1965). Clinics could stabilize former heroin addicts so that they were no longer driven to seek illicit sources of narcotics; they permitted medical supervision of addicts, who in the past would have been the target of police surveillance; they could undercut the need to engage in crime to purchase heroin. It is not the least of the ironies of the methadone solution that it was given important federal support during the administration of Richard Nixon, who had denounced heroin maintenance as a "concession to weakness and defeat in the drug struggle, a concession which would surely lead to the erosion of our most cherished values for the dignity of man" (quoted in Bayer 1976, 264), and that it was ultimately, if grudgingly, accepted by many black leaders who continued to denounce proposals for heroin maintenance as genocidal.

But the reality of methadone fell far short of the promise that advocates of narcotic maintenance had held out for two decades (Epstein 1974). It soon became clear that many addicts were uninterested in medically supervised care. What they wanted from narcotics was more than the stabilization of their condition. Dr. Robert Newman, director of the New York City Methadone Maintenance Program, drew the only possible conclusion:

> When someone wants a heroin treatment program, when methadone maintenance is available that person is saying he or she is unwilling to give up the narcotic effect that heroin will give. If the person no longer wanted to get high, then it would really be strange that he or she would prefer to go four or five or six times a day into a clinic where somebody is going to try to find a vein and inject some heroin. (*Contemporary Drug Problems* 1973, 180).

The Limits of Medicalization

It thus appeared in the early 1970s that the medical conception of decriminalization—at least insofar as heroin was concerned—had reached its limits. It was under these circumstances that liberal Republican Nelson Rockefeller of New York State, an architect in the mid-1960s of New York's compulsory closed-ward treatment approach to drug use and strong supporter in the early 1970s of methadone maintenance, made a radical and sweeping proposal for severe recriminalization of the problem (Bayer 1974). It was also under these circumstances that there first emerged a proposal that represented a radical departure from the reformist thrust of the past six decades. Medicalization had been the centerpiece of the call for decriminalization. Now some began to urge the demedicalization of addiction; but it was demedicalization of a very different kind from what Rockefeller was pressing. Adults who wanted to use drugs, including heroin, should be as free to purchase them as they were free to purchase alcohol.

While liberals and other drug reformers had little difficulty in supporting the legalization of marijuana, which was widely used by middle-class youth and largely viewed as relatively benign, this was not the case for heroin and other "hard drugs." The radical conception of decriminalization posed severe problems for liberals, who had deeply committed themselves to the view that narcotic use reflected the profound inequities of American social life and who believed that legalization would result in a sharp rise in drug use. As a consequence, fissures developed between those committed to the libertarian and to the social welfare traditions of liberalism. Nevertheless the call for legalization did find expression in the journals of liberal opinion (Bayer 1975b).

In a January 1972 editorial, entitled "Society Is Hooked," the editors of the *Nation* called for the "legalization of hard drugs and marijuana." Significantly, however, instead of portraying maintenance as a humane solution to the problems of addiction, as was the case when proposed by reformers like Lindesmith, the editors acknowledged that their program would in all likelihood result in the "epidemic . . . spread[ing] still more rapidly" (*Nation* 1972, 99–100). Gone, too, from the radical challenge to drug policy was the earlier article of liberal faith that addicts given access to heroin would be normal, that enforced abstinence was responsible for their dysfunctional state. Like the proponents of "harm reduction" almost 20 years later, those who pressed for radical change hoped only to contain the damages caused by drug use. But no other option seemed viable. With a pessimistic air, the editors of the *Nation* noted that society as well as the addict were "hooked"; there were no quick "fixes."

Liberal legal theorist Herbert Packer, who had long argued that the "victimless crimes" were an inappropriate target of the criminal law, also endorsed the legalization of all drugs. In "Decriminalizing Heroin," which appeared in the *New Republic*, he wrote: "Enforcing *personal morals* through the criminal laws is one of this country's principal self-inflicted wounds. We can allow sick people—as we should allow nations to choose their own roads to hell if that is where they want to go—I should have thought that to be the most important lesson of liberalism" (Packer 1972, 11). Making drugs available to those who wanted them was no longer offered as a way of assisting the addict to live a "normal life" but, rather, as a way of giving him the option of traveling the "road to hell."

Nothing more tellingly reveals the difficulty that heroin legalization presented American liberals than the prolonged conflict it engendered within the American Civil Liberties Union. As early as 1970, some within the organization had begun to insist that John Stuart Mill's dictum on the sovereignty of the individual over his or her own self-regarding behavior be applied without modification to all drug use. Thus Jeremiah Guttman, a board member of the New York Civil Liberties Union, stated in a position paper designed to move the ACLU: "The right *not* to live should be as basic as the right to life. Whether a person chooses to end his life with a bullet through the brain, fifteen years of alcoholic indulgence, or five years of heroin should not be material" (cited in Bayer 1975b). In 1973 a committee of the board of directors of the ACLU that had considered the drug issue concluded that the libertarian commitment of the ACLU left no alternative but to endorse the freedom of adults to use narcotic and nonnarcotic drugs. The evidence it had considered had provided no justification for prohibition because no "direct" harms to others could be traced to drug use. Indeed the harm to others that could be traced to such use was a consequence of the prohibition itself. Only with those under 18 years of age was the physician to play a role as the source of a prescription for narcotics, and then only with parental consent.

This perspective, however, was not so easily accepted by the board of the ACLU, where strong social welfare concerns were raised by members fearful of the extent to which a free market in drugs would have a profound impact on the nation's ghetto poor. Three years later, after considerable debate, when the ACLU board did adopt a new policy on drugs, it was riddled with the contradictions between, on the one hand, a libertarian model of decriminalization within which heroin would be sold under a regulatory regime similar to what prevailed for alcohol, and on the other hand, a medical model, which would require the use of prescriptions. "Nothing in this policy is to be construed as placing the ACLU in opposition to reasonable restraint such as already exists with respect to the production and sale of food, liquor, cigarettes, penicillin, insulin, methadone. . . ." (cited in Bayer 1978b).

The ACLU's tortured effort to confront the problem of narcotic drugs stood in sharp contrast to the ease with which the issue was resolved by two politically conservative libertarians, Milton Friedman and Thomas Szasz. . . . At the very moment when the ACLU was struggling with the heroin issue, Friedman wrote in *Newsweek*: "Do we have the right to use force directly or indirectly to prevent a fellow adult from drinking, smoking or using drugs? [The] answer is no" (cited in Friedman and Friedman 1984, 138–9). Beyond his principled position, however, Friedman pointed out that the course of legalization was dictated by pragmatic concerns. Prohibition did not work. It did not prevent drug use; it made the life of both the addict and the nonaddict more miserable. Underscoring a point that would assume great salience two decades later, he concluded: "Legalizing drugs would simultaneously reduce the amount of crime and improve law enforcement. It is hard to conceive of any other single recourse that would accomplish so much to promote law and order."

Like Friedman, Thomas Szasz was not burdened by welfare liberalism's conception of addiction as determined by social deprivation. Thus he was able to articulate a position on drug use derived exclusively from adherence to a radically individualistic perspective.

Although reference to the social response to addiction ran throughout Szasz's earlier, often polemical, attacks on the psychiatric establishment, his first fully developed statement on the issue appeared in *Harper's Magazine* in "The Ethics of Addiction" (Szasz 1972). Starting from the premise that individuals are capable of freely choosing among differing behavioral patterns, Szasz noted that drug use and addiction were the results of just such personal decisions. Linking the freedom to use drugs with the right to exchange freely in ideas, he asserted: "In an open society it is none of the government's business what idea a man puts into his head; likewise it should be none of the government's business what drug he puts into his body" (75). For Szasz, then, the social response to addiction was a microcosm of the struggle between collectivist and individualist values. "We can choose to maximize the sphere of action of the state at the expense of the individual or the individual at the expense of the state" (79). The willingness to prohibit the use of drugs as medically unwise, and the role of physicians in enforcing prohibition and in treating drug users against their will, comprised for Szasz a paradigmatic expression of the baleful development of the "therapeutic state."

Two years later these arguments appeared in elaborated form in the book-length polemic, *Ceremonial Chemistry: The Ritual Persecution of Drug Addicts and Pushers*. Using imagery drawn from the history of religion, Szasz argued in typically hyperbolic fashion: "What exists today is nothing less than a worldwide quasi-medical pogrom against opium and the users of opiates" (45). "I regard tolerance with respect to drugs as wholly analogous to tolerance with respect to religion" (53).

It is important not to overstate the extent to which calls for the legalization of drugs had attained explicit support during the 1970s. What gave them resonance, however, was the radical ferment among intellectuals dating from the upheavals of the 1960s, a ferment that had subjected both the practice and ideology of social control to repeated attack. The "labeling" school sought to shatter the orthodox perspective on drug use and other detested forms of behavior (Becker

1963). Society created deviance out of difference (Kitsuse 1962). The process of labeling "deviant" behavior set in motion a series of events with dire consequences for people who were labeled as well as for society. Unlike the corrective posture of the "helping professions," the sociologists associated with the "labeling" school saw in behavioral diversity an intrinsic and vital aspect of social life (Matza 1969). To those drawn to the plight of psychiatric patients, the "antipsychiatrists" like Szasz and R. D. Laing suggested that medical dominance and control were every bit as repressive as the imposition of legal sanctions (Sedgwick 1972). Coercion by physicians buttressed the agencies of social control and imposed dreadful suffering on the patient.

Finally, for those concerned about the scope of the criminal law, the effort to restrict personal behaviors that posed no direct threat to others had created a "crisis of overcriminalization" (Kadish 1968). Gambling, prostitution, drug use, sexual behavior between consenting adults—the entire range of "victimless crimes"—had been mistakenly subject to the criminal law, with terrible consequences for the courts, the prisons, police departments, and the very status of the law. "The criminal law is an inefficient instrument for imposing the good life on others" (Morris and Hawkins 1970, 2).

The intellectual ferment of the 1960s and mid-1970s exhausted itself with little by way of demonstrable impact on the radical reform of drug abuse policy. The criminal law remained dominant, although the advocates of a therapeutic model had done much to reshape the social response to drug use. The most significant reflection of the effort to medicalize heroin addiction was in the methadone maintenance programs that had been provided with a niche in the clinical panoply. As the years passed, however, the initial therapeutic optimism that accompanied the rupture with the commitment to abstinence all but vanished. Methadone clinics were increasingly viewed with hostility, as community eyesores, where addicts met to engage in the commerce in drugs including methadone itself. Another change in outlook resulted when the fashion in drug use shifted from heroin to cocaine, rendering irrelevant many of the arguments for maintenance therapy rooted in the psychopharmacology of opiate use.

Finally, liberal intellectuals lost the capacity to inform the policy agenda across the full range of domestic problems as an aggressively conservative national administration came to Washington in 1980. When a renewed assault on drug use took shape—with its battle cry of "zero tolerance"—and a revitalized commitment to law enforcement took form, directed at both the international commerce in illicit psychotropic substances and at street-level trade, little by way of broad countervailing perspective was left to express the concerns that had animated the debate in earlier years.

THE REVIVAL OF THE DRUG POLICY DEBATE

Although David A. J. Richards, the legal philosopher, argued in 1981 that respect for human rights necessitated legalization of drugs, albeit under the supervision of physicians (1981), and William Buckley, the editor of the conservative *National Review*, announced his support for drug legalization in 1985 (Buckley 1985), they were the exceptions. Little sustained discussion took place until 1988, when suddenly a plethora of articles appeared calling for the decriminalization of drug use. At times these articles suggested that only outright legalization of all drugs would represent a coherent response to the crisis of drug use in America's cities. Thus Arnold Trebach of the Drug Policy Foundation, a center committed to fostering reformist thought, wrote in a special symposium issue of the *American Behavioral Scientist*:

> I am now convinced that our society would be safer and healthier if all of the illegal drugs were fully removed from the control of the criminal law tomorrow. . . . I would be very worried about the possibility of future harm if that radical change took place, but less

worried than I am about the reality of the present harm being inflicted every day by our current laws and policies. (1989, 254)

Others supported legalization for some drugs, medical control for others. Pete Hamill, the popular columnist, thus declared:

After watching the results of the plague since heroin first came to Brooklyn in the early fifties, after visiting the courtrooms and the morgues, after wandering New York's neighborhoods . . . and after consuming much of the literature on drugs, I've reluctantly come to a terrible conclusion: The only solution is the complete legalization of these drugs. (1988, 26)

. . . From across the political spectrum the call for decriminalization has drawn support. U.S. District Court Judge Robert Sweet (Kleiman and Saiger 1990) and Baltimore's mayor, Kurt Schmoke (1989), have each denounced the prohibitionist strategy. Stephen J. Gould, writing in *Dissent* (1990), and Taylor Branch, in the *New Republic* (1988), have both issued attacks on the use of the criminal law. Most remarkable and in sharp contrast to the linkage between liberalism and drug reform in the 1950s, 1960s, and 1970s, noted conservatives in surprising numbers have been drawn to the reformist banner.

Nothing more distressed the conservative proponents of decriminalization than the commitment of the Reagan and Bush administrations to the ever greater reliance on the instruments of legal repression in the "war on drugs," a strategy that could only result in the enhancement of state power and the withering of freedom. In an open letter to William Bennett, the nation's "drug czar," Milton Friedman sought to recall the common principles that united conservatives in their opposition to the statist programs of their liberal opponents:

The path you propose of more police, more jails, use of the military in foreign countries, harsh penalties for drug users and a whole panoply of repressive measures can only make a bad situation worse.

The drug war cannot be won by those tactics without undermining the human liberty and individual freedom that you and I cherish. (cited in Reinarman and Levine 1990)

To cultural conservatives who rejected the radical individualism so central to libertarians of whatever political stripe, and whose ideological roots could be traced to Burke rather than Mill, all such characterizations of the effort to repress drug use were profoundly mistaken, subverting the prospects of human virtue upon which the very existence of civic life in a democratic society was dependent (Kleiman and Saiger 1990). Thus was William Bennett archly critical of the intellectuals and fellow conservatives who would desert the struggle against drug use.

Drug use—especially heavy drug use—destroys human character. It destroys dignity and autonomy, it burns away the sense of responsibility, it makes a mockery of virtue. . . . Libertarians don't like to hear this. . . . Drugs are a threat to the life of the mind. . . . That's why I find the surrender to arguments for drug legalization so odd and so scandalous. (1990, 32).

Although their arguments are rooted in a very different political perspective on American social life, black leaders have been equally vehement in their reaction against the calls for decriminalization and especially toward the maximalist call for legalization. In part a reflection of the cultural conservatism of the black clergy, this response also reflects the despair of those who have seen their communities devastated by drug use and the drug wars and who fear that legalization would represent nothing more than the determination to write off an expendable population. Committed as they are to greater public expenditures for treatment, many leaders have denounced as genocidal the calls for legalization of drugs, and even for halfway measures motivated by the philosophy of harm reduction (Dalton 1989).

The Debate over Costs

Despite the expected ideological exchanges provoked by the call for fundamental drug policy reform, the crucial and most dramatic feature of the debate over decriminalization in the late 1980s has been the extent to which it has *not* been shaped by reference to issues of liberty and the role of the state as the guarantor of social cohesion. Rather a set of more prosaic concerns has dominated the debate: the social costs generated by the very effort to limit the social costs of drug use. Cost-benefit analysis has provided the yardstick of analysis (Warner 1991). It is the willingness to embrace that social accounting technique and to employ its apparently nonideological methods that has united the liberal and conservative critics of the status quo.

If the maximalist, radical option of legalization has drawn more support in the late 1980s than at any moment since the imposition of prohibition in the century's second decade, the structure of the argument made against the use of the criminal law has not changed much since the challenge to criminalization gained some currency in the post–World War II era. Indeed, if anything is striking about the contemporary debate, it is how reminiscent it is of earlier conflicts, despite its markedly more sophisticated character.

Although the upsurge of critical analysis had already begun, the appearance in the fall of 1989 of Ethan Nadelmann's "Drug Prohibition in the United States: Costs, Consequences and Alternatives" in *Science* marked an important juncture. Like those who preceded him, he painstakingly detailed the costs of drug prohibition. Vast expenditures—estimated at $10 billion in 1987—corruption, crime, violence, the spread of HIV infection, international misadventures could all be traced to the effort to suppress drug use and commerce. When balanced against the achievements, the price was for Nadelmann beyond all reason. But what of the potential costs that would follow upon legalization? Would drug use and, more important, the most disabling forms of drug use increase? These are questions that

Nadelmann approaches with some caution. His conclusions, however, are unmistakable: the risks of pursuing such an agenda have been exaggerated, even grossly distorted; the costs of not advancing a reform agenda—of legalizing cocaine, heroin, and "other relatively dangerous drugs"—are too great. Legalization would not only produce enormous benefits for society in general, and America's ghettos in particular, but would enhance the health and quality of life of drug users who would be assured of access to drugs whose purity could be vouchsafed through government regulation.

Nothing more tellingly distinguishes the proponents of legalization and their antagonists than the very different estimations of the potential consequences that might attend an end to prohibition (Inciardi and McBride 1990). James Q. Wilson's "Against the Legalization of Drugs," which appeared in *Commentary* magazine, represents a forthright challenge to Nadelmann's optimistic characterization. Legalization, Wilson asserts, almost certainly would produce a vast increase in drug use with devastating impacts on the most vulnerable.

The current great debate over drug prohibition is being conducted in the face of an irreducible level of uncertainty about the potential consequences of legalization. Although the antagonists each acknowledge that there are many unknowns about the consequences of taking even modest steps toward legalization, they bring fundamentally, and in most instances, unbridgeable assumptions about how the risks and benefits of reform should be weighed.

CONCLUSION

Despite the fact that the range of advocates for decriminalization is broader now than at any point in more than a decade, and that the coalition favoring a maximalist strategy of legalization is more vital than it has ever been since prohibition was instituted in the early part of the century, there is little reason to believe that the demand for radical change will have an immediate impact on policy. In fact, the prospects for even minimalist steps toward decriminalization are far weaker than in the 1970s when, under the threat of returning heroin-addicted Vietnam soldiers, the U.S. government made a major commitment to the medical management of addiction, and when middle-class pressure moved the decriminalization of marijuana use and possession toward becoming a politically viable option in a number of states and local jurisdictions. Indeed, it is no small irony that the current move for decriminalization has arisen precisely at a moment when America may have entered a neoprohibitionist era, one in which the social tolerance for the use of intoxicants—both licit and illicit—may be declining.

What, then, is the significance of the debate over decriminalization? First, and perhaps most important, the sharp assault on the contours of American drug policy has exposed the profound imbalance between public expenditures for law enforcement designed to repress drug sales and use and the funds available for the treatment of individuals whose drug dependency has resulted in personal misery. Even some who reject the need for radical change now recognize that current efforts to support the treatment of drug users who express an interest in managing their addiction to opiates through methadone maintenance or in achieving abstinence from other drug use are grossly inadequate.

Second, the decriminalization debate has forced a consideration of the rationality of policies that currently prohibit the use of a wide range of drugs. By compelling a discussion of the extent to which our conventions have brought us to define some drugs as licit and others as illicit, causing us mistakenly to lump relatively less damaging drugs with more harmful substances, the proponents of decriminalization may foster a more reasoned discussion of public policy.

Finally, the advocates of decriminalization, no matter how limited or expansive their goals, have served to underscore the enormous economic and human costs of current prohibitionist policies. In so doing they have encouraged the search for alternatives to repression: the willingness of a number of state and local governments to tolerate or fund needle exchange programs in an effort to interdict the spread of HIV infection provides a striking example of such newly found openness.

In the end, the call for decriminalization—however broadly or narrowly defined—has revitalized the public debate over the fundamental structure of American drug policy. It has thus made possible a serious examination of the appropriate role of the state in regulating the behavior of competent adults, as well as its obligation to foster the conditions necessary for the existence of civic life and to provide care for the most vulnerable and even for the most socially despised. Perhaps more important, the decriminalization debate has shattered—if only for a moment—the dead weight of tradition that for more than a decade served to close off the possibility of critical inquiry.

REFERENCES

American Bar Association and American Medical Association. 1963. Drug Addiction: Crime or Disease? *Interim and Final Reports of the Joint Committee of the American Bar Association and the American Medical Association on Narcotic Drugs.* Bloomington: Indiana University Press.

Bayer, R. 1974. Repression, Reform and Drug Abuse: An Analysis of the Response to the Rockefeller Drug Law Proposals of 1973. *Journal of Psychedelic Drugs* 6:299–309.

———. 1975a. Liberal Opinion and the Problem of Heroin Addiction: An Examination of the Organs of Cultural Expression, 1960–1973. *Contemporary Drug Problems* 4:93–112.

———. 1975b. Drug Stores, Liquor Stores, and Heroin: An Analysis of the Libertarian Debate. *Contemporary Drug Problems* 4:459–82.

———. 1975c. Heroin Maintenance, the Vera Proposal and Narcotics Reform: An Analysis of the Debate, 1971–1973. *Contemporary Drug Problems* 4:297–322.

———. 1976. Drug Addiction and Liberal Social Policy: The Limits of Reform. Ph.D. dissertation, University of Chicago. (Unpublished)

———. 1978a. Addiction, Criminal Culpability and the Penal Sanction: A Perspective on the Liberal Response to Repressive Social Policy. *Crime and Delinquency* (March):221–32.

———. 1978b. Heroin Decriminalization and the Ideology of Tolerance: A Critical View. *Law and Society Review* 12:301–18.

Bazilon, D. L. 1971. Drugs That Turn on the Law. *Journal of Social Issues* 27:47–52.

Becker, H. 1963. *The Outsiders*. New York: Free Press.

Bennett, W. J. 1990. Drug Wars: Drug Policy and the Intellectuals. *Police Chief* (May):30–6.

Berger, H. 1956. The Richmond County Medical Society's Plan for the Control of Narcotics Addiction. *New York State Journal of Medicine* 56: 888–94.

Branch, T. 1988. Let Koop Do It. *New Republic* (October 24):22.

Buckley, W. F. 1985. Does Reagan Mean It? *National Review* 37:54.

Cloward, R. A., and K. Ohlen. 1960. *Delinquency and Opportunity: A Theory of Delinquent Gangs*. New York: Free Press.

Contemporary Drug Problems. 1973. Heroin Maintenance: A Panel Discussion. (Spring):165–200.

Dalton, H. D. 1989. AIDS in Blackface. *Daedalus* 118 (Summer):205–27.

Dole, V. P. 1965. A Medical Treatment for Diacetyl-Morphine (Heroin) Addiction. *Journal of the American Medical Association* 193:646–50.

Epstein, E. J. 1974. Methadone: The Forlorn Hope. *Public Interest* (Summer):3–23.

Fort, J. 1962. Addiction: Fact or Fiction. *Saturday Review of Literature* (September 18):30–1.

Friedman, M., and R. Friedman. 1984. *The Tyranny of the Status Quo*. San Diego, Calif.: Harcourt, Brace, Jovanovich.

Georgetown Law Review. 1971. Emerging Recognition of Pharmacological Duress as a Defense to Possession of Narcotics: Watson v. United States. (February):761–76.

Goldstein, R. M. 1973. The Doctrine of Pharmacological Duress: Critical Analysis. *New York University Review of Law and Social Change* (Spring):141–58.

Gostin, L. 1991. Compulsory Treatment for Drug-dependent Persons: Justifications for a Public Health Approach to Drug Dependency. *Milbank Quarterly* 69(4):561–94.

Gould, S. J. 1990. Taxonomy as Politics: The Harm of False Classification. *Dissent* (Winter):73–8.

Hamill, P. August 15, 1988. Facing Up to Drugs: Is Legalization the Solution? *New York* (August 15):21–7.

Inciardi, J. A., and D. C. McBride. 1989. Legalization: A High-Risk Alternative in the War on Drugs. *American Behavioral Scientist* 32:259–89.

Kadish, S. 1968. The Crisis of Over-Criminalization. *American Criminal Law Quarterly* 7:18–34.

Kitsuse, J. 1962. Societal Reactions to Human Deviance. *Social Problems* 9:247–56.

Kleiman, M. A. R., and A. J. Saiger. 1990. Drug Legalization: The Importance of Asking the Right Question. *Hofstra Law Review* 18:527–65.

Lindesmith, A. 1947. *Opiate Addiction*. Bloomington, Ind.: Principia Press. (*Addiction and Opiates*, 2d ed., published in 1968. Chicago: Aldine.)

Lowenstein, R. 1967. Addiction, Insanity and Due Process of Law: An Examination of the Capacity Defense. *Harvard Civil Rights-Civil Liberties Law Review* (Fall):125–65.

Matza, D. 1969. *Becoming Deviant*. Englewood Cliffs, N.J.: Prentice-Hall.

Morris, N., and G. Hawkins. 1970. *The Honest Politician's Guide to Crime Control*. Chicago: University of Chicago Press.

Musto, D. 1973. *The American Disease: Origins of Narcotic Control*. New Haven, Conn.: Yale University Press.

Nadelmann, E. A. 1989. Drug Prohibition in the United States: Costs, Consequences, and Alternatives. *Science* 245:939–46.

Nation. 1970. The Menace and the Malady. (September 21):228–9.

———. 1971. Opium: Sweeping the Sands. (November 1):421.

———. 1972. Society Is Hooked. (January 24):99–100.

New York Academy of Medicine, Committee on Public Health. 1955. Report on Drug Addiction I. *Bulletin of the New York Academy of Medicine* 31:592–607.

New York State Temporary Commission of Investigation. 1973. Interim Report Concerning the Operation of the Special Narcotics Parts of the Supreme Court, April 29. (Mimeo)

Packer, H. L. 1972. Decriminalizing Heroin. *New Republic* (June 3):11–13.

Reinarman, C., and H. G. Levine. February 1990. A Peace Movement Has Emerged Against the War on Drugs. *Footnotes* 18(2).

Richards, D. A. J. 1981. Drug Use and the Rights of the Person: A Moral Argument for Decriminalization of Certain Forms of Drug Use. Symposium on Punishment: Critiques and Justifications. *Rutgers Law Review* 33:607–86.

Schmoke, K. L. 1989. First Word. *Omni* 11:8.

Sedgwick, P. 1972. R. D. Laing: Self, Symptom and Society. In *R. D. Laing and Anti-Psychiatry*, eds. R. Boyers and R. Orvill. New York: Harper & Row.

Szasz, T. 1972. The Ethics of Addiction. *Harper's Magazine* (April):74–79.

———. 1974. *Ceremonial Chemistry: The Ritual Persecution of Drugs, Addicts, and Pushers.* New York: Anchor Books.

Trebach, A. S. 1989. Tough Choices: The Practical Politics of Drug Policy Reform. *American Behavioral Scientist* 32:249–58.

Warner, K. E. 1991. Legalizing Drugs: Lessons from (and about) Economics. *Milbank Quarterly* 69(4):641–62.

Wilson, J. Q. February 1990. Against the Legalization of Drugs. *Commentary* (February):21–8.

Should Harm Reduction Be Our Overall Goal in Fighting Drug Abuse?

Charles Levinthal

Charles Levinthal is a professor of psychology at Hofstra University.

This selection was excerpted from "Should Harm Reduction Be Our Overall Goal in Fighting Drug Abuse?" in *Point/Counterpoint: Opposing Perspectives on Issues of Drug Policy* (Boston, MA: Allyn and Bacon, 2003).

To say that we are waging a "war on drugs" is, in effect, communicating how serious we are in dealing with the problems of drug abuse in the United States. Using the metaphor of warfare, we recognize that there is an acknowledged enemy (drug abuse), there are victims or casualties (us), there are resources at our disposal to fight the necessary battles (federal and state governments, communities, parents, etc.), and there is a high price to pay (in excess of $18 billion of federal funds each year).

The implications of this real-life struggle, such as our overall strategy and ultimate goals, are also drawn in metaphorical terms. Do we want total victory and complete annihilation of the enemy? Or do we want some kind of negotiated settlement, some type of compromise, that gives us some semblance of peace and tranquility? If it is the former, then we require a total elimination, often expressed as "zero tolerance" of abusive drug-taking behavior in America. If it is the latter, then we require a good deal less. We desire, in that case, only a reduction of the harmful consequences of abusive drug-taking behavior, knowing fully well that a total elimination is unrealistic. This is essentially our dilemma, and the core issue for this chapter.

What does the American public really want? Which way should we direct our drug policies?

The harm-reduction approach in drug policy has its historical roots in the libertarian philosophy of the nineteenth-century philosopher John Stuart Mill who argued that the state did not have the duty to protect individual citizens from harming themselves. As Mill expressed it,

> The only purpose for which power can be rightfully exercised over any member of a civilized community, against his will, is to prevent harm to others. His own good, either physical or moral, is not a sufficient warrant. . . . Over himself, over his own body and mind, the individual is sovereign.

On the other hand, it is readily evident that drug-taking behavior does indeed harm other people. We can look to the violence of illicit drug trafficking and the disruption in the lives of drug abusers' families and friends. The question, according to those advocating a harm-reduction strategy, is to look for policies that reduce the harm that drugs do, both directly to the drug user and indirectly to others.

On the opposite end of the debate are advocates for a drug policy that is based upon the goal of absolute deterrence, brought about by law enforcement. Sociologist Erich Goode has put it this way:

> . . . they do not believe simply that law enforcement is more likely to "contain" or keep a given activity at a lower level than no enforcement at all. Even further, they believe (or, at least, in their speeches, they state) that law enforcement, if not restrained by loopholes, technicalities, and restrictions, will actually reduce that activity, ideally, nearly to zero. In short, we *can* win the war on drugs, the cultural conservative asserts, if we have sufficient will, determination, and unity.

Those who argue that a reduction of the harmful consequences of abusive drug-taking behavior is the optimal strategy can be seen as following a middle path between, on one hand, those who advocate stronger law enforcement and interdiction efforts to eliminate all drugs and, on the other hand, those who advocate an approach in which presently illegal drugs are legalized and thus made available to the American public. Drug problems, as the harm-reductionists argue, are more a result of the harsh and absolutist system of prohibitions now in place than the drugs themselves. There is no doubt that the misery endured by drug-dependent individuals, their families and associates, and society in general is immense. The debate is in the strategy that is best suited to contend with the horrific conditions in which we now live. . . .

REFERENCES

Goode, Erich (1997). *Between politics and reason: The drug legalization debate.* New York: St. Martin's Press. Quotation on page 58.
How did we get here? History has a habit of repeating itself (2001, July 28– August 3). *Economist,* pp. 4–5. Quotation of John Stuart Mill on page 5.
MacCoun, Robert J. (1998). Toward a psychology of harm reduction. *American Psychologist,* 53, 1199–1208. Quotations on pages 1202 and 1203.

A New Direction for Drug Education: Harm Reduction

David F. Duncan

David F. Duncan is President of Duncan and Associates, and a Clinical Associate Professor of Community Health at Brown University School of Medicine.

This piece originally appeared in "Harm Reduction: An Emerging New Paradigm for Drug Education," *Journal of Drug Education* 24 (4): 281–289 (Amityville, N.Y.: Baywood Publishing Company, Inc., 1994).

Harm reduction is a new direction for health education that has been developing in Western Europe and Australia. Instead of trying to prevent drug use, this new direction focuses on trying to prevent the harms associated with drug use. One of the most familiar examples of harm reduction is needle exchange, which has been effective in preventing HIV/AIDS among drug users.

Over the past two decades, drug abuse prevention in Western Europe and Australia has taken a new direction that has major implications for the future of drug education and drug abuse prevention here in the United States. This new direction was given the name "harm reduction" in a report of the British Home Office (1984) that described two alternate goals for drug abuse prevention programs — either reducing drug use or reducing the harms associated with drug use.

Since that time the International Conferences on the Reduction of Drug-Related Harm, held in Liverpool, England, in 1990, Barcelona, Spain, in 1991, Melbourne, Australia, in 1992, and Rotterdam, the Netherlands, in 1993, have illustrated the rapid growth of this strategy in Western Europe and Australia while the 1994 conference in Toronto showed its recent encroachment in North America.

Earlier proposals for such an approach included the "casualty-reduction" approach to glue sniffing adopted by the Institute for the Study of Drug Dependence in 1980 and the proposal for "cultivating drug use" suggested by Duncan and Gold in 1983—using the word cultivation in the sense of promoting healthy and productive development, while weeding out tendencies toward abuse. Harm reduction has also been called damage limitation or harm minimization.

Whatever it is called, this new direction consists of a policy of preventing the potential harms related to drug use rather than focusing on preventing the drug use itself. It recognizes that as Moore and Saunders (1991, p. 29) state, "given the universality of drug use in human societies and the very real benefits that accrue from drug use, the usual prevention goal of abstinence from drug use for young people is unthinking, unobtainable and unacceptable."

Mugford (1991) says that a harm reduction approach accepts the fact that people will continue to use drugs no matter what the laws may dictate and asks how they can do so most safety. Such a strategy is consistent with human experience. Historically, all human cultures except Eskimos have accepted some form of recreational drug use and all attempts at prohibition of a drug once its use has been established have resulted in failure. . . .

Furthermore, harm reduction recognizes that measures intended to prevent drug use have often had the unintended effect of increasing the harms associated with drug use. Outlawing drugs results in the creation of black markets with associated corruption of law enforcers, violence between competing drug dealers, erosion of civil rights inevitable in policing a "victimless crime," and the seduction of youth into lucrative careers in drug dealing. A black market will sell illicit drugs to anyone regardless of their age or mental state. The strength, purity, and even the identity of drugs on the black market is uncertain, leading to adverse reactions and overdoses.

In one sense, harm reduction may be seen as a form of tertiary prevention (Duncan, 1988, pp. 50–51)—preventing the long-term harms that may result from drug abuse. Such harm reduction measures as methadone maintenance and needle exchanges constitute harm reduction in this sense.

Needle exchanges, for instance, have gained increasing support as the epidemic of HIV infection associated with intravenous drug use has motivated many public health and drug abuse authorities to rethink their priorities in dealing with IV drug use, moving them toward harm reduction. Mugford (1991), for instance, reports that Australian efforts combining needle exchange, education of drug users on proper syringe hygiene, and establishment of safe disposal points for used syringes in public restrooms have resulted in keeping the prevalence of HIV among drug users in Australia down to only 2 percent. This compares with the 50–70 percent HIV prevalence among drug users in large U.S. cities. In Switzerland, where HIV prevalence among drug users had reached nearly 50 percent, it has dropped to less than 5 percent since the Swiss adopted a harm-reduction policy (Rihs-Middel, 1993).

In another sense, however, harm reduction can be primary prevention. The essence of harm reduction in this sense is the recognition of the distinction between drug use and drug abuse. Just as it is a truth that any drug can be abused, it is a truth that any drug can be used without abuse. No drug is inherently abusive. Tobacco would appear to be the only drug for which it cannot be said that users outnumber abusers. The Epidemiologic Catchment Area Study (Anthony and Helzer, 1991, p. 124) has demonstrated that 20.3 percent of all users of illicit drugs have experienced a period of abuse at some time during their drug use history. Only 4.2 percent of current illicit drug users were dependent or abusers. The first symptoms of drug abuse typically occurred within two to three years after beginning illicit drug use and the median duration of a case of drug abuse/dependence was four to five years (pp. 133–135).

Harm reduction recognizes that preventing drug abuse is a different task from preventing drug use and may be both a more justifiable and a more achievable goal. Harm reduction can mean educating drug users on how to use drugs safely and responsibly. Duncan and Gold (1985, ch. 18) describe the types of responsibilities which drug users might be taught in harm reduction–oriented drug education. These include responsibilities regarding the situations under which drugs are used, health responsibilities, and safety-related responsibilities.

Situational responsibilities would include the responsibility for only using a drug in environments conducive to pleasant and rewarding experiences—avoiding use in hazardous or threatening environments. Another situational responsibility would be only using recreational drugs in social settings. A third would be to make provision in advance for anyone who should become severely intoxicated. Always having someone present who can assist knowledgeably in the event of untoward reactions to the drugs being used is another responsibility.

Health responsibilities would include not using recreational drugs when under severe stress or emotionally distraught. Another would be to avoid exacerbating any health problems through drug use. Drug use during pregnancy should be restricted to those drugs that will not place the unborn child at risk. Avoiding the use of drug combinations that can have dangerous interactions is another health responsibility. Another would be to avoid continued use of drugs for long periods of time.

Safety-related responsibilities would include avoiding the performance of complex tasks, such as driving or operating machinery, while using recreational drugs. Another would be to take the smallest possible dose to produce the desired effects. Altered consciousness is inappropriate in potentially dangerous or unknown settings.

Many health educators will be uncomfortable with this direction. They may see it as a surrender in the war on drugs. Others will see it as a refocusing of our efforts on what really matters for health education—the prevention of health problems. It is the proper role of health educators to help people live healthier lives, not to act as moral police.

REFERENCES

Anthony, J. C., & Helzer, J. E. (1991). Syndromes of drug abuse and dependency. In L. N. Robins and D. A. Regier (Eds.). *Psychiatric Disorders in America* (pp. 116–154). New York: Free Press.
British Home Office (1984). *Prevention: Report of the Advisory Council on the Misuse of Drugs.* London: Her Majesty's Stationery Office.
Duncan, D. F. (1988). *Epidemiology: Basis for Disease Prevention and Health Promotion.* New York: Macmillan.
Duncan, D. F., & Gold, R. S. (1983). Cultivating drug use: A strategy for the eighties. *Bulletin of the Society of Psychologists in Addictive Behaviors,* 2(3), 143–147.
Duncan, D. F., & Gold, R. S. (1985). *Drugs and the Whole Person.* New York: Macmillan.
Institute for the Study of Drug Dependence (1980). *Teaching about a Volatile Situation.* London: Author.
Moore, D., & Saunders, B. (1991). Youth drug use and the prevention of problems. *International Journal on Drug Policy,* 2(5), 13–15.
Mugford, S. (Nov. 12, 1991). Panel discussion on the topic, "Should public health adopt a harm reduction drug control strategy?" at the annual meeting of the American Public Health Association, Atlanta, GA.
Rihs-Middel, M. (July 13, 1993). Personal communication with the Coordinator of Drug Research and Evaluation, Swiss Federal Office of Public Health.
Watson, M. (1991). Harm reduction—Why do it? *International Journal on Drug Policy,* (5), 13–15.

Has the War on Drugs Reduced Crime?

Robert E. Peterson

Robert E. Peterson is an attorney and former director of drug control policy for the state of Michigan. His company, Drug Facts, provides research on drug law enforcement and legalization matters.

This selection appeared on *Close to Home Online—Viewpoints*: "Moyers on Addiction" available online at http://pbs.org/wnet/closetohome/viewpoints/html/crime.html.

Strong drug enforcement in the United States is correlated with dramatic reductions in crime, drug use, and drug addiction rates. Historically, permissive enforcement policies brought record murder and crime rates, peak drug use levels, and increased the addict population.

Drug arrest rates are not an accurate measure of how tough the nation is on drugs. There are three times as many alcohol related arrests than drug arrests—is alcohol policy three times tougher than drug policy? If we legalize drugs, we may triple the number of drug arrests. To measure drug enforcement strength one must examine what happens to those arrested. A good method is to track the number of persons incarcerated for every thousand drug arrests. Periods of weak and strong drug policy can then be compared.

Permissive drug policy was an abject failure in the United States. A drug criminal was four times more likely to serve prison time in 1960 than in 1980 and the incarceration rate plummeted 79 percent. This drug tolerant era brought a doubling of the murder rate, a 230 percent increase in burglaries, a ten-fold increase in teen drug use, and a 900 percent rise in addiction rates. The peak years for teen drug use and murder were the same years that drug incarceration rates hit an all time low point.

From 1980 to 1997, the drug incarceration rate rose over fourfold and crime and drug use began a steady unprecedented decline. Murder rates fell by more than 25 percent, burglary rates dropped 41 percent, teen drug use reduced by more than a third, and heavy cocaine and heroin use levels fell. With peak drug incarceration rates, many cities, such as New York, reached record low crime levels.

Increasing the odds of imprisonment for drugs helped lower crime and drug use rates because major drug offenders, traffickers, and repeat felons were targeted—not minor drug possessors. Urban drug defendants are more likely to be repeat criminals than violent or property offenders. The hardcore drug felon often steals not just to buy drugs but also to pay bills and survive through a career of crime. Locking up career criminals is a very cost effective policy.

More than 95 percent of state prisoners are violent and repeat criminals. Under one-tenth of one percent of inmates are non-violent, first time marijuana offenders. Most state drug prisoners are traffickers or repeat and/or violent offenders. A federal marijuana inmate was involved with 3.5 tons of the drug on average; a crack offender averaged 18,000 doses. Federal agencies have almost no jurisdiction over violent street crime; that is why most federal cases involve major cocaine and heroin drug traffickers.

Are we getting too tough? Drug prison sentences have held fairly steady the past five years and drug inmate growth is slowing. Studies show that prison growth is the result of increasing the odds of imprisonment for all criminals and not from longer sentences being served. Mandatory minimum sentences have not caused court backlogs or dramatically longer terms, but they may be in part responsible for the tremendous success demonstrated by lower crime rates. One is more likely to go to prison for a federal gambling offense than for drug possession—and a tax law violator will serve more prison time!

Tougher drug policy also reduces addiction because the criminal justice system is the number one source of treatment referrals. President Clinton credits the justice system for saving his brother's life and many treatment centers would shut down, and addicts would die, if drug laws were repealed. In 1991, a quarter of a million inmates received their most recent drug treatment while in prison.

History indicates that increasing the odds of hardcore drug criminals going to prison has been an extremely effective way to reduce violent and property crime and to lower addiction and drug use rates. The nation is still recuperating from twenty years of permissive drug policy. Current enforcement efforts must be sustained.

We may have found a good balance, and neither tougher nor weaker policy is called for. The real problem is that of the minor drug offender, who now often escapes any consequences at all. Zero tolerance through alternative sanctions must be applied, such as abstinence enforced through drug testing, fines, civil liability, loss of driving and other privileges, and treatment modalities to deter these users before they reach the hardcore criminal stage.

Reducing Harm: Treatment and Beyond

Drug Policy Alliance

This selection is available online at http://www.drugpolicy.org/reducingharm/treatmentvsi/.

Recent developments in criminal justice indicate the emergence of a national movement in favor of treating, rather than incarcerating, non-violent drug possession offenders. These developments include drug courts, local policies that favor treatment, and statewide ballot initiatives that divert nonviolent drug offenders to treatment instead of incarceration.

Public health approaches towards drug offenders have gained national attention and public support. In a recent survey sponsored by the Open Society Institute, "Changing Attitudes Towards the Criminal Justice Systems," 63 percent of Americans consider drug abuse a problem that should be addressed primarily through counseling and treatment, rather than the criminal justice system.

Arizona

In 1996, Arizonans voted in favor of Proposition 200, the Drug Medicalization Prevention and Control Act of 1996, which sends first and second time nonviolent drug offenders to treatment rather than incarceration. According to a recent report conducted by the Supreme Court of Arizona, Proposition 200 saved Arizona taxpayers $6.7 million in 1999. In addition, 62 percent of probationers successfully completed the drug treatment ordered by the court.

California

In November 2000, 61 percent of California voters passed Proposition 36, the Substance Abuse and Crime Prevention Act of 2000 (SACPA), an initiative aimed at rehabilitating rather than incarcerating nonviolent drug possession offenders. Under SACPA, certain persons convicted of nonviolent drug possession offenses are given an opportunity to receive community-based drug treatment in lieu of incarceration.

Prior to its passage, the independent Legislative Analyst's Office (LAO) predicted that by treating rather than incarcerating low level drug offenders, SACPA would save California taxpayers approximately $1.5 billion over the next five years and prevent the need for a new prison slated for construction, avoiding an expenditure of approximately $500 million. LAO estimated that SACPA would annually divert as many as 36,000 probationers and parolees from incarceration into community-based treatment.

Already, progress reports show that tens of thousands of offenders have been placed in community-based treatment instead of jail thereby improving public health and saving the state hundreds of thousands of dollars. Regulation of treatment facilities has resulted in increased quality and accountability for hundreds of treatment programs, and the overall capacity of these facilities has increased.

Maryland

Maryland's new treatment law immediately diverts several thousand prisoners into drug treatment, saving the state's taxpayers millions of dollars a year in the process. It also provides $3 million in additional funding for treatment and gives judges new discretion in sentencing.

Washington, DC

In November 2002, an overwhelming 78 percent of DC voters passed the drug treatment initiative, Measure 62. Under Measure 62 the city will provide substance abuse treatment instead of conviction or imprisonment to nonviolent defendants charged with illegal possession or use of drugs (except those drugs classified as Schedule I); provide a plan for rehabilitation to individuals accepted for substance abuse treatment; and provide for dismissal of legal proceedings for defendants upon successful completion of the treatment program. In addition to dealing with a lawsuit by the DC Corporation Council the measure will have to go through several steps before becoming law. Meanwhile, implementation strategies will take place outlining how treatment instead of incarceration may become a successful model in Washington, DC.

PART FIVE

What about Marijuana?

Even if one takes every reefer madness allegation of the prohibitionists at face value, marijuana *prohibition* has done far more harm to far more people than marijuana ever could.

William F. Buckley, Jr.
New York Post
February 27, 1999

No drug matches the threat posed by marijuana.

John Walters
Office of National Drug Control Policy
November 2003

An End to Marijuana Prohibition: The Drive to Legalize Picks Up

Ethan A. Nadelmann

Ethan A. Nadelmann is the founder and director of the Drug Policy Alliance.

This selection first appeared in *National Review*, July 12, 2004.

Never before have so many Americans supported decriminalizing and even legalizing marijuana. Seventy-two percent say that for simple marijuana possession, people should not be incarcerated but fined: the generally accepted definition of "decriminalization."[1] Even more Americans support making marijuana legal for medical purposes. Support for broader legalization ranges between 25 and 42 percent, depending on how one asks the question.[2] Two of every five Americans—according to a 2003 Zogby poll—say "the government should treat marijuana more or less the same way it treats alcohol: It should regulate it, control it, tax it, and only make it illegal for children."[3]

Close to 100 million Americans—including more than half of those between the ages of 18 and 50—have tried marijuana at least

   1. Joel Stein, "The New Politics of Pot," *Time*, 4 November 2002. Available online at http://www.time.com/time/covers/1101021104/story.html. For more polling information, see http://www.drugpolicy.org/library/publicopinio/.

   2. Ibid.; "Poll Finds Increasing Support For Legalizing Marijuana," *Alcoholism and Drug Abuse Weekly*, 15, No. 27 (2003): 8; Zogby International, "National Views on Drug Policy" (Utica, New York: Zogby, April 2003). The poll was conducted during April 2003. Forty-one percent of respondents stated that marijuana should be treated in a similar manner as alcohol.

   3. Ibid.

once.[4] Military and police recruiters often have no choice but to ignore past marijuana use by job seekers.[5] The public apparently feels the same way about presidential and other political candidates. Al Gore,[6] Bill Bradley,[7] and John Kerry[8] all say they smoked pot in days past. So did Bill Clinton, with his notorious caveat.[9] George W. Bush won't deny he did.[10] And ever more political, business, religious, intellectual, and other leaders plead guilty as well.[11]

The debate over ending marijuana prohibition simmers just below the surface of mainstream politics, crossing ideological and partisan boundaries. Marijuana is no longer the symbol of sixties rebellion and seventies permissiveness, and it's not just liberals and libertarians who say it should be legal, as William F. Buckley Jr. has demonstrated better than anyone. As director of the country's leading drug policy reform organization, I've had countless conversations with police and prosecutors, judges and politicians, and hundreds of others who quietly agree that the criminalization of marijuana is costly, foolish, and destructive. What's most needed now is principled conservative leadership. Buckley has led the way, and New Mexico's former

4. Substance Abuse and Mental Health Services Administration, Department of Health and Human Services, *National Survey on Drug Use and Health*, 2002 (Maryland: U.S. Department of Health and Human Services, 2003): Table 1.31A.

5. Jesse Katz, "Past Drug Use, Future Cops," *Los Angeles Times*, 18 June 2000; "Alcohol and drug disqualifications," *Military.com*, Military Advantage, 2004, *http://www.military.com/Recruiting/Content/0,13898.rec_step07_DQ_alcohol_drug.00.html* (17 June 2004).

6. Yvonne Abraham, "Campaign 2000/McCain: Crime and Drugs the Topic in South Carolina," *The Boston Globe*, 9 February 2000.

7. Greg Freeman, "Blagojevich's Pot Use Is Raising Eyebrows, But It Isn't Big News," *St. Louis Post-Dispatch*, 19 September 2002.

8. Bob Dart, "Democrat Hopefuls Pin Hearts on Sleeves; Political 'Oprahization' Means That Confession Is Good for the Poll," *The Austin American Statesman*, 8 December 2003.

9. John Stossel and Sam Donaldson, "Give Me a Break: Politicians Don't Always Do What They Say Or What They Do," *20/20 Friday*, ABC News, 25 August 2000.

10. Ibid.

11. See http://www.norml.org/index.cfm?Group_ID=3461.

governor, Gary Johnson, spoke out courageously while in office. How about others?

A SYSTEMIC OVERREACTION

Marijuana prohibition is unique among American criminal laws. No other law is both enforced so widely and harshly and yet deemed unnecessary by such a substantial portion of the populace.

Police make about 700,000 arrests per year for marijuana offenses.[12] That's almost the same number as are arrested each year for cocaine, heroin, methamphetamine, Ecstasy, and all other illicit drugs combined.[13] Roughly 600,000, or 87 percent, of marijuana arrests are for nothing more than possession of small amounts.[14] Millions of Americans have never been arrested or convicted of any criminal offense except this.[15] Enforcing marijuana laws costs an estimated $10 to 15 billion in direct costs alone.[16]

Punishments range widely across the country, from modest fines to a few days in jail to many years in prison. Prosecutors often contend that no one goes to prison for simple possession—but tens, perhaps hundreds, of thousands of people on probation and parole are locked up each year because their urine tested positive for marijuana or because they were picked up in possession of a joint. Alabama currently locks up people convicted three times of marijuana *possession*

12. Federal Bureau of Investigation, Division of Uniform Crime Reports, *Crime in the United States: 2002* (Washington, D.C.: U.S. Government Printing Office, 2003): 234. Available online at http://www.fbi.gov/ucr/02cius.htm.

13. 840,000 arrests were made for all other drugs combined. Ibid.

14. Ibid.

15. There have been more than 11 million marijuana arrests made in the U.S. since 1970. See Federal Bureau of Investigation, *Uniform Crime Reports*, Washington, D.C.: Department of Justice; 1966–2002.

16. See http://www.norml.org/index.efm?Group_ID=4444&wtm_format=print/pro hibcost. See also Marijuana Policy Project, "Marijuana Prohibition Facts 2004," 2004, http://mpp.org/pdf/prohfact.pdf (18 June 2004); Mitch Earleywine, *Understanding Marijuana: A New Look at the Scientific Evidence* (New York: Oxford University Press, 2002): 235.

for 15 years to life.[17] There are probably—no firm estimates exist—100,000 Americans behind bars tonight for one marijuana offense or another.[18] And even for those who don't lose their freedom, simply being arrested can be traumatic and costly. A parent's marijuana use can be the basis for taking away her children and putting them in foster care.[19] Foreign-born residents of the United States can be deported for a marijuana offense no matter how long they have lived in this country, no matter if their children are U.S. citizens, and no matter how long they have been legally employed.[20] More than half the states revoke or suspend driver's licenses of people arrested for marijuana possession even though they were not driving at the time of arrest.[21] The federal Higher Education Act prohibits student loans to young people convicted of any drug offense;[22] all other criminal offenders remain eligible.[23]

17. The Alabama Sentencing Commission, *Recommendations for Reform of Alabama's Criminal Justice System 2003 Report* (Alabama: Alabama Sentencing Commission, March 2003): 22, 23.

18. Estimated by Marijuana Policy Project, based on Bureau of Justice Statistics, *Prisoners in 2001*, U.S. Department of Justice (Washington, D.C.: U.S. Government Printing Office, 2002); Bureau of Justice Statistics, U.S. Department of Justice, *Prison and Jail Inmates at Midyear 2001* (Washington, D.C.: U.S. Government Printing Office, 2002); Bureau of Justice Statistics, U.S. Department of Justice, *Profile of Jail Inmates, 1996* (Washington, D.C.: U.S. Government Printing Office, 1998); Bureau of Justice Statistics, U.S. Department of Justice, *Substance Abuse and Treatment, State and Federal Prisoners 1997* (Washington, D.C.: U.S. Government Printing Office, 1999). All reports available online at http://www.ojp.usdoj.gov/bjs/pubalp2.htm.

19. Judy Appel and Robin Levi, *Collateral Consequences: Denial of Basic Social Services Based on Drug Use* (California: Drug Policy Alliance, June 2003). Available online at http://www.drugpolicy.org/docUploads/Postincarceration_abuses_memo.pdf.

20. Carl Hiaasen, "New Rules Trap Immigrants with Old Secrets," *The Miami Herald*, 30 May 2004.

21. Paul Samuels and Debbie Mukamal, *After Prison: Roadblocks to Reentry: A Report on State Legal Barriers Facing People With Criminal Records* (New York: Legal Action Center, 2004). Available online at http://www.lac.org/lac/upload/lacreport/LAC_Print Report.pdf.

22. *Higher Education Act of 1998, U.S. Code*. Title 20, Sec. 1091.

23. According to data from the Department of Education analyzed by Students for Sensible Drug Policy, over 150,000 students have lost aid thus far due to the provision.

This is clearly an overreaction on the part of government. No drug is perfectly safe, and every psychoactive drug can be used in ways that are problematic. The federal government has spent billions of dollars on advertisements and anti-drug programs that preach the dangers of marijuana—that it's a gateway drug, and addictive in its own right, and dramatically more potent than it used to be, and responsible for all sorts of physical and social diseases as well as international terrorism.[24,25] But the government has yet to repudiate the 1988 finding of the Drug Enforcement Administration's own administrative law judge, Francis Young, who concluded after extensive testimony that "marijuana in its natural form is one of the safest therapeutically active substances known to man."[26]

Is marijuana a gateway drug? Yes, insofar as most Americans try marijuana before they try other illicit drugs. But no, insofar as the vast majority of Americans who have tried marijuana have never gone on to try other illegal drugs, much less get in trouble with them, and most have never even gone on to become regular or problem marijuana users.[27] Trying to reduce heroin addiction by preventing marijuana use, it's been said, is like trying to reduce motorcycle fatalities

See Greg Winter, "A Student Aid Ban for Past Drug Use Is Creating a Furor," the *New York Times*, 13 March 2004; Alexandra Marks, "No Education Funds for Drug Offenders," *Christian Science Monitor*, 24 April 2001; John Kelly, "Students Seeking Aid Not Answering Drug Questions," *Associated Press*, 21 March 2000.

24. See http://www.mediacampaign.org/mg/index.html.

25. Theresa Howard, "U.S. Crafts Anti-Drug Message," *USA Today*, 15 March 2004.

26. Drug Enforcement Administration, *In the Matter of Marijuana Rescheduling Petition* [Docket #86–22] (Washington, D.C.: U.S. Department of Justice, 6 September 1988): 57.

27. Based on data from *National Household Survey on Drug Abuse: Population Estimates 1994* (Rockville, MD: U.S. Department of Health and Human Services, 1995); *National Household Survey on Drug Abuse: Main Findings 1994* (Rockville, MD: U.S. Department of Health and Human Services, 1996). See also D. B. Kandel and M. Davies, "Progression to Regular Marijuana Involvement: Phenomenology and Risk Factors for Near-Daily Use," *Vulnerability to Drug Abuse*, Eds. M. Glantz and R. Pickens (Washington, D.C.: American Psychological Association, 1992): 211–253.

by cracking down on bicycle riding.[28] If marijuana did not exist, there's little reason to believe that there would be less drug abuse in the U.S.; indeed, its role would most likely be filled by a more dangerous substance.

Is marijuana dramatically more potent today? There's certainly a greater variety of high-quality marijuana available today than 30 years ago. But anyone who smoked marijuana in the 1970s and 1980s can recall smoking pot that was just as strong as anything available today.[29] What's more, one needs to take only a few puffs of higher-potency pot to get the desired effect, so there's less wear and tear on the lungs.[30]

Is marijuana addictive? Yes, it can be, in that some people use it to excess, in ways that are problematic for themselves and those around them, and find it hard to stop. But marijuana may well be the least addictive and least damaging of all commonly used psycho-active drugs, including many that are now legal.[31] Most people who smoke marijuana never become dependent.[32] Withdrawal symptoms pale compared with those from other drugs. No one has ever died from a marijuana overdose, which cannot be said of most other drugs.[33] Marijuana is not associated with violent behavior and only

28. Lynn Zimmer and John P. Morgan, *Marijuana Myths, Marijuana Facts: A Review of the Scientific Evidence* (New York: Drug Policy Alliance, 1997): 37–38.

29. Ibid., 134–141.

30. Mitch Earleywine, *Understanding Marijuana: A New Look at the Scientific Evidence* (New York: Oxford University Press, 2002): 130.

31. Janet E. Joy, Stanley J. Watson Jr., and John A. Benson Jr., Eds., *Marijuana and Medicine: Assessing the Science Base* (Washington, D.C.: National Academy of Sciences Institute of Medicine, 1999): 89–91. Available online at http://books.nap.edu/html/marimed/.

32. See the findings of the Canadian Committee on Illegal Drugs, available at http://www.parl.gc.ca/37/1/perlbus/commbus/senate/com-e/ille-e/rep-e/summary-e.pdf.   Pierre Claude Nolin, Chair, Senate Special Committee on Illegal Drugs, *Cannabis: Our Position for a Canadian Public Policy: Summary Report* (Ontario: Senate of Canada, 2002).

33. I. Greenberg, "Psychiatric and Behavioral Observations of Casual and Heavy Marijuana Users," *Annals of the New York Academy of Sciences*, 282 (1976): 72–84; N. Solowij et al., "Biophysical Changes Associated with Cessation of Cannabis Use: A Single Case

minimally with reckless sexual behavior.[34] And even heavy marijuana smokers smoke only a fraction of what cigarette addicts smoke. Lung cancers involving only marijuana are rare.[35]

The government's most recent claim is that marijuana abuse accounts for more people entering treatment than any other illegal drug. That shouldn't be surprising, given that tens of millions of Americans smoke marijuana while only a few million use all other illicit drugs.[36] But the claim is spurious nonetheless. Few Americans who enter "treatment" for marijuana are addicted. Fewer than one in five people entering drug treatment for marijuana do so voluntarily.[37] More than half were referred by the criminal justice system.[38] They go because they got caught with a joint or failed a drug test at school or work (typically for having smoked marijuana days ago, not

Study of Acute and Chronic Effects, Withdrawal and Treatment," *Life Sciences* 56 (1995): 2127–2135; A. D. Bensusan, "Marihuana Withdrawal Symptoms," *British Journal of Medicine* 3 (1971): 112.

34. Numerous government commissions investigating the relationship between marijuana and violence have concluded that marijuana does not cause crime. See National Commission on Marihuana and Drug Abuse, *Marihuana: A Signal of Understanding* (Washington, D.C.: U.S. Government Printing Office, 1972): 77; Pierre Claude Nolin, Chair, Senate Special Committee on Illegal Drugs, *Cannabis: Our Position for a Canadian Public Policy: Summary Report* (Ontario: Senate of Canada, 2002). See also Lynn Zimmer and John P. Morgan, *Marijuana Myths, Marijuana Facts: A Review of the Scientific Evidence* (New York: Drug Policy Alliance, 1997): 7, 88–91.

35. S. Sidney, C. P. Quesenberry, G. D. Friedman, and I. S. Tekawa, "Marijuana Use and Cancer Incidence," *Cancer Cause and Control* 8 (1997): 722–728; Lynn Zimmer and John P. Morgan, *Marijuana Myths, Marijuana Facts: A Review of the Scientific Evidence* (New York: Drug Policy Alliance, 1997): 7, 112–116; Mitch Earleywine, *Understanding Marijuana: A New Look at the Scientific Evidence* (New York: Oxford University Press, 2002): 155–158.

36. Substance Abuse and Mental Health Services Administration, Department of Health and Human Services, *National Survey on Drug Use and Health*, 2002 (Maryland: U.S. Department of Health and Human Services, 2003): 4, 5.

37. Substance Abuse and Mental Health Services Administration, *2003 Treatment Episode Data Set: 1992–2001*, National Admissions to Substance Abuse Treatment Services, DASIS Series: S-20 (Maryland: U.S. Department of Health and Human Services, 2003): 122.

38. Ibid.

for being impaired), or because they were caught by a law-enforcement officer—and attending a marijuana "treatment" program is what's required to avoid expulsion, dismissal, or incarceration.[39] Many traditional drug treatment programs shamelessly participate in this charade to preserve a profitable and captive client stream.[40]

Even those who recoil at the "nanny state" telling adults what they can or cannot sell to one another often make an exception when it comes to marijuana—to "protect the kids." This is a bad joke, as any teenager will attest. The criminalization of marijuana for adults has not prevented young people from having better access to marijuana than anyone else. Even as marijuana's popularity has waxed and waned since the 1970s, one statistic has remained constant: More than 80 percent of high school students report it's easy to get.[41] Meanwhile, the government's exaggerations and outright dishonesty easily backfire. For every teen who refrains from trying marijuana because it's illegal (for adults), another is tempted by its status as "forbidden fruit."[42] Many respond to the lies about marijuana by disbelieving warnings about more dangerous drugs. So much for protecting the kids by criminalizing the adults.

39. Ibid.

40. Substance Abuse and Mental Health Services Administration, Department of Health and Human Services, "Coerced Treatment Among Youths: 1993 to 1998," *The DASIS Report*, 21 September 2001.

41. L. D. Johnston, P. M. O'Malley, and J. G. Bachman, *Monitoring the Future: National Results on Adolescent Drug Use: Overview of Key Findings, 2003* (Bethesda, Maryland: National Institute on Drug Abuse, 2004); Ann L. Pastore and Kathleen Maguire, Eds., U.S. Department of Justice, Bureau of Justice Statistics, *Sourcebook of Criminal Justice Statistics 2001* (Washington, D.C.: U.S. Government Printing Office, 2002): 173.

42. Svetlana Kolchik, "More Americans Used Illegal Drugs in 2001, U.S. Study Says," *USA Today*, 6 September 2002; Corky Newton, *Generation Risk: How to Protect Your Teenager from Smoking and Other Dangerous Behaviors* (New York: M. Evans and Company, 2001).

THE MEDICAL DIMENSION

The debate over medical marijuana obviously colors the broader debate over marijuana prohibition. Marijuana's medical efficacy is no longer in serious dispute. Its use as a medicine dates back thousands of years.[43] Pharmaceutical products containing marijuana's central ingredient, THC, are legally sold in the U.S., and more are emerging.[44,45,46] Some people find the pill form satisfactory, and others consume it in teas or baked products. Most find smoking the easiest and most effective way to consume this unusual medicine,[47] but non-smoking consumption methods, notably vaporizers, are emerging.[48]

Federal law still prohibits medical marijuana.[49] But every state ballot initiative to legalize medical marijuana has been approved, often by wide margins—in California, Washington, Oregon, Alaska,

---

43. Ernest Abel, *Marijuana: The First Twelve Thousand Years* (New York: McGraw Hill, 1982); Martin Booth, *Cannabis: A History* (London: Doubleday, 2003); Janet E. Joy, Stanley J. Watson Jr., and John A. Benson Jr., Eds., *Marijuana and Medicine: Assessing the Science Base* (Washington, D.C.: National Academy of Sciences Institute of Medicine, 1999): 19. Available online at http://books.nap.edu/html/marimed/.

44. Janet E. Joy, Stanley J. Watson Jr., and John A. Benson Jr., Eds., *Marijuana and Medicine: Assessing the Science Base* (Washington, D.C.: National Academy of Sciences Institute of Medicine, 1999): 16. Available online at http://books.nap.edu/html/marimed/.

45. "Marijuana-Based Drug Developed to Treat MS," *Calgary Sun*, 12 May 2004.

46. Heather Stewart, "Late Again: GW's Cannabis-Based Painkiller," *The Guardian*, 1 May 2004.

47. See Janet E. Joy, Stanley J. Watson Jr., and John A. Benson Jr., Eds., *Marijuana and Medicine: Assessing the Science Base* (Washington, D.C.: National Academy of Sciences Institute of Medicine, 1999): 27–29; and Mitch Earleywine, *Understanding Marijuana: A New Look at the Scientific Evidence* (New York: Oxford University Press, 2002): 171.

48. Dale Gieringer, Joseph St. Laurent, and Scott Goodrich, "Cannabis Vaporizer Combines Efficient Delivery of THC with Effective Suppression of Pyrolytic Compounds," *Journal of Cannabis Therapeutics* 4 (2004): 7–27. A British pharmaceutical company, GW Pharmaceuticals, has developed an oral spray to dispense cannabis to medical-marijuana patients. See http://gwpharm.co.uk/ for more information.

49. *Schedules of Controlled Substances, U.S. Code*, Title 21, Sec. 812.

Colorado, Nevada, Maine, and Washington, D.C.[50] State legislatures in Vermont,[51] Hawaii,[52] and Maryland[53] have followed suit, and many others are now considering their own medical marijuana bills — including New York,[54] Connecticut,[55] Rhode Island,[56] and Illinois.[57] Support is often bipartisan, with Republican governors like Gary Johnson and Maryland's Bob Ehrlich taking the lead.[58,59] In New York's 2002 gubernatorial campaign, the conservative candidate of the Independence party, Tom Golisano, surprised everyone by campaigning heavily on this issue.[60] The medical marijuana bill now before the New York legislature is backed not just by leading Republicans but even by some Conservative party leaders.[61]

The political battleground increasingly pits the White House — first under Clinton and now Bush — against everyone else. Majorities in virtually every state in the country would vote, if given the chance, to legalize medical marijuana.[62] Even Congress is beginning to turn;

50. Bill Piper et al., *State of the States: Drug Policy Reforms: 1996–2002* (New York: Drug Policy Alliance, 2003): 42. Available online at http://states.drugpolicy.org.

51. David Gram, "Vermont's Medical Marijuana Bill to Be Law," *Associated Press*, 20 May 2004.

52. Associated Press, "Hawaii Becomes First State to Approve Medical Marijuana Bill," the *New York Times*, 15 June 2000.

53. Craig Whitlock and Lori Montgomery, "Ehrlich Signs Marijuana Bill; Maryland Governor Weighs Independence, GOP Loyalty," the *Washington Post*, 23 May 2003; Angela Potter, "Maryland Governor Signs Medical Marijuana Bill Into Law," *Associated Press*, 22 May 2003.

54. Ellis Henican, "High Hopes for Pot," *Newsday*, 16 June 2004.

55. Ken Dixon, "State Urged to Legalize Medical Marijuana Use," *Connecticut Post*, 2 April 2004.

56. "Medical Marijuana in Rhode Island," the *Providence Journal*, 19 May 2004.

57. "Medical Marijuana Debate on Hold," the *State Journal-Register*, 3 March 2004.

58. Matthew Miller, "He Just Said No to the Drug War," the *New York Times Magazine*, 20 August 2000.

59. Richard Willing, "Attitudes Ease Toward Medical Marijuana," *USA Today*, 22 May 2003.

60. Seanne Adcox, "Golisano Proposes Medical Use of Marijuana," *New York Newsday*, 17 October 2002.

61. John H. Wilson, "Medical Marijuana Helps Seriously Ill," *Albany Times Union*, 24 March 2004.

62. See Janet E. Joy, Stanley J. Watson Jr., and John A. Benson Jr., Eds., *Marijuana*

last summer about two-thirds of House Democrats and a dozen Republicans voted in favor of an amendment co-sponsored by Republican Dana Rohrabacher to prohibit federal funding of any Justice Department crackdowns on medical marijuana in the states that had legalized it.[63,64] (Many more Republicans privately expressed support, but were directed to vote against.) And federal courts have imposed limits on federal aggression: first in *Conant* v. *Walters*,[65] which now protects the First Amendment rights of doctors and patients to discuss medical marijuana, and more recently in *Raich* v. *Ashcroft*[66] and *Santa Cruz* v. *Ashcroft*,[67] which determined that the federal government's power to regulate interstate commerce does not provide a basis for prohibiting medical marijuana operations that are entirely local and noncommercial. (The Supreme Court let the *Conant* decision stand,[68] but has yet to consider the others.)

State and local governments are increasingly involved in trying to regulate medical marijuana, notwithstanding the federal prohibition. California, Oregon, Hawaii, Alaska, Colorado, and Nevada have created confidential medical marijuana patient registries, which pro-

---

and Medicine: Assessing the Science Base (Washington, D.C.: National Academy of Sciences Institute of Medicine, 1999): 18; and Richard Schmitz and Chuck Thomas, *State-By-State Medical Marijuana Laws: How to Remove the Threat of Arrest* (Washington, D.C.: Marijuana Policy Project, 2001): Appendix D. Available at http://www.mpp.org/statelaw/app_d.html. For a list of polls results, see http://www.drugpolicy.org/library/publicopinio/.

63. Edward Epstein, "Bill to Protect Medicinal Pot Users Falls Short in House," *San Francisco Chronicle*, 24 July 2003.

64. In July 2004, a similar amendment was voted on and once again fell short of passage. See http://www.drugpolicy.org/news/07_08_04bincheyvote.cfm.

65. See http://www.drugpolicy.org/marijuana/medical/challenges/cases/conant/index.cfm.

66. The U.S. Supreme Court will hear *Raich* v. *Ashcroft* this fall. See http://www.drugpolicy.org/library/legalmateria/wamm_raich_facts.cfm; Eric Bailey, "Stage Set for Legal Showdown Over Pot," *Los Angeles Times*, 19 May 2004.

67. "Leave Medical Marijuana Group Alone, Judge Tells Government," the *New York Times*, 22 April 2004. See also http://www.drugpolicy.org/law/marijuana/santacruz/.

68. Linda Greenhouse, "Supreme Court Roundup; Justices Say Doctors May Not Be Punished for Recommending Medical Marijuana," the *New York Times*, 15 October 2003.

tect bona fide patients and caregivers from arrest or prosecution.[69] Some municipal governments are now trying to figure out how to regulate production and distribution.[70] In California, where dozens of medical marijuana programs now operate openly, with tacit approval by local authorities, some program directors are asking to be licensed and regulated.[71,72] Many state and local authorities, including law enforcement, favor this but are intimidated by federal threats to arrest and prosecute them for violating federal law.[73]

The drug czar and DEA spokespersons recite the mantra that "there is no such thing as medical marijuana," but the claim is so specious on its face that it clearly undermines federal credibility.[74] The federal government currently provides marijuana—from its own production site in Mississippi—to a few patients who years ago were recognized by the courts as bona fide patients.[75] No one wants to

69. National Organization for the Reform of Marijuana Laws, "Summary of Active State Medical Marijuana Programs," July 2002, http://www.norml.org/index.cfm?Group_ID=3391 (June 2004).

70. Laura Counts, "Oakland to Limit Marijuana Outlets," Tri-Valley Herald, 18 April 2004. Also see information on San Francisco's Proposition S, available at http://www.drugpolicy.org/news/11_06_02props.cfm.

71. Amy Hilvers, "'Pot Club' Thrives in Oildale," the Bakersfield Californian, 26 May 2004.

72. Laura Counts, "Medical Marijuana Merchant Defies Oakland Order to Close," the Oakland Tribune, 2 June 2004.

73. Doug Bandow, "Where's the Compassion?," National Review Online, 19 December 2003. Available at http://www.mapine.org/drugnews/v03/n1964/a06.html. See also Michael Gougis, "Medical Marijuana Tug of War: Lenient Sentences Underscore Conflicting State and Federal Pot Laws," Daily News of Los Angeles, 12 December 2003; Clarence Page, "Drug Warriors Trampling Rights of Medical Marijuana Proponents," Salt Lake Tribune, 12 February 2003.

74. Andrea Barthwell, "Haze of Myths Clouds Value of Medical 'Pot,'" the Republican, 27 July 2003; Alan W. Bock, "UNSPIN//Marijuana, Medicine, and Ed Rosenthal: The Issue: Medical Marijuana and Federal Law," Orange County Register, 9 February 2003; Ian Ith and Carol M. Ostrom, "Feds Pose Challenge to Use of Medical Marijuana," the Seattle Times, 16 September 2002; and Josh Richman, "Drug Czar Coolly Received in Bay Area; Federal Stance on Medical Marijuana Won't Be Relaxed, Walters Says," the Daily Review, 18 November 2003.

75. David Brown, "NIH Panel Cautiously Favors Medical Study of Marijuana," the

debate those who have used marijuana for medical purposes, be it Santa Cruz medical-marijuana hospice founder Valerie Corral or *National Review*'s Richard Brookhiser.[76] Even many federal officials quietly regret the assault on medical marijuana. When the DEA raided Corral's hospice in September 2002, one agent was heard to say, "Maybe I'm going to think about getting another job sometime soon."

THE BROADER MOVEMENT

The bigger battle, of course, concerns whether marijuana prohibition will ultimately go the way of alcohol Prohibition, replaced by a variety of state and local tax and regulatory policies with modest federal involvement.[77] Dedicated prohibitionists see medical marijuana as the first step down a slippery slope to full legalization.[78] The voters who approved the medical-marijuana ballot initiatives (as well as the wealthy men who helped fund the campaigns[79]) were roughly divided

---

Washington Post, 21 February 1997; Ray Delgado, "Many Patients Call Government Marijuana Weak; Medicinal Cigarettes Loaded With Stems, Seeds, Researchers Say," *San Francisco Chronicle*, 16 May 2002; Lester Grinspoon and James B. Bakalar, *Marihuana: The Forbidden Medicine* (Connecticut: Yale University Press, 1997): 45–66.

76. Richard Brookhiser, "Drug Warriors Are Repeating Earlier Errors; Considering His Past Abuse, Bush Should Be Sympathetic to Reforms," *Chicago Sun-Times*, 25 May 2001; Richard Brookhiser, "In Dull Election, My Vote Is Going to Marijuana Man," *New York Observer*, 4 November 2002; Richard Brookhiser, "Madness of Pot Prohibition Claims Yet Another Victim," *New York Observer*, 24 July 2000; Richard Brookhiser, "The Sick Shouldn't Be Victims of the Drug War," *Buffalo News*, 20 July 2003; Richard Brookhiser, "Why I Support Medical Marijuana," Congressional Testimony, House Judiciary committee, Subcommittee on Crime, 6 March 1996. Available online at http://www.norml.org/index.cfm?Group_ID=4451.

77. Raymond B. Fosdick, *Toward Liquor Control* (New York: Harper, 1933); David E. Kyvig, *Repealing National Prohibition*, 2nd Edition (Ohio: Kent State University Press, 2000).

78. John L. Mica, "Should the Federal Government Study the Effects of Medical Marijuana? Do Not Waste Taxpayers' Dollars," *Roll Call*, 21 June 1999.

79. George Soros, "The Drug War 'Cannot Be Won': It's Time to Just Say No to Self-Destructive Prohibition," the *Washington Post*, 2 February 1997.

between those who support broader legalization and those who don't, but united in seeing the criminalization and persecution of medical marijuana patients as the most distasteful aspect of the war on marijuana. (This was a point that Buckley made forcefully in his columns about the plight of Peter McWilliams, who likely died because federal authorities effectively forbade him to use marijuana as medicine.[80])

The medical marijuana effort has probably aided the broader antiprohibitionist campaign in three ways. It helped transform the face of marijuana in the media, from the stereotypical rebel with long hair and tie-dyed shirt to an ordinary middle-aged American struggling with MS or cancer or AIDS.[81] By winning first Proposition 215, the 1996 medical-marijuana ballot initiative in California, and then a string of similar victories in other states, the nascent drug policy reform movement demonstrated that it could win in the big leagues of American politics.[82] And the emergence of successful models of medical marijuana control is likely to boost public confidence in the possibilities and virtue of regulating nonmedical use as well.

In this regard, the history of Dutch policy on cannabis (i.e., marijuana and hashish) is instructive. The "coffee shop" model in the Netherlands, where retail (but not wholesale) sale of cannabis is de facto legal, was not legislated into existence. It evolved in fits and starts following the decriminalization of cannabis by Parliament in 1976, as consumers, growers, and entrepreneurs negotiated and collaborated with local police, prosecutors, and other authorities to find an acceptable middle-ground policy.[83] "Coffee shops" now operate

80. William F. Buckley, Jr., "The Legal Jam," *National Review Online*, 15 May 2001; William F. Buckley, Jr., "Peter McWilliams, R.I.P.," *National Review*, 17 July 2000; William F. Buckley, Jr., "Reefer Madness," *National Review*, 14 July 2003.

81. Compare the photographs that accompany the following two articles: Tom Morganthau et al., "Should Drugs Be Legal?," *Newsweek*, 30 May 1988; Geoffrey Cowley et al., "Can Marijuana Be Medicine?," *Newsweek*, 3 February 1997.

82. Bill Piper et al., *State of the States: Drug Policy Reforms: 1996–2002* (New York: Drug Policy Alliance, 2003). Available online at http://states.drugpolicy.org.

83. Robert J. MacCoun and Peter Reuter, *Drug War Heresies: Learning from Other Vices, Times, and Places* (New York: Cambridge University Press, 2001): 238–264.

throughout the country, subject to local regulations.[84] Troublesome shops are shut down, and most are well integrated into local city cultures. Cannabis is no more popular than in the U.S. and other Western countries, notwithstanding the effective absence of criminal sanctions and controls.[85] Parallel developments are now underway in other countries.

Like the Dutch decriminalization law in 1976, California's Prop 215 in 1996 initiated a dialogue over how best to implement the new law.[86] The variety of outlets that have emerged—ranging from pharmacy-like stores to medical "coffee shops" to hospices, all of which provide marijuana only to people with a patient ID card or doctor's recommendation—play a key role as the most public symbol and manifestation of this dialogue. More such outlets will likely pop up around the country as other states legalize marijuana for medical purposes and then seek ways to regulate distribution and access. And the question will inevitably arise: If the emerging system is successful in controlling production and distribution of marijuana for those with a medical need, can it not also expand to provide for those without medical need?

Millions of Americans use marijuana not just "for fun" but because they find it useful for many of the same reasons that people drink alcohol or take pharmaceutical drugs. It's akin to the beer, glass of wine, or cocktail at the end of the workday, or the prescribed drug to alleviate depression or anxiety, or the sleeping pill, or the aid to sexual function and pleasure.[87] More and more Americans are apt to

84. A. C. M. Jansen, "The Development of a 'Legal' Consumers' Market for Cannabis—The 'Coffee Shop' Phenomenon," *Between Prohibition and Legalization: The Dutch Experiment in Drug Policy*, E. Leuw and I. Haen Marshall, Eds. (New York: Kugler Publications, 1996).

85. Craig Reinarman, Peter D. A. Cohen, and Hendrien L. Kaal, "The Limited Relevance of Drug Policy: Cannabis in Amsterdam and in San Francisco," *American Journal of Public Health* 94 (2004): 836–842.

86. Michael Pollan, "Living With Medical Marijuana," *New York Times Magazine*, 20 July 1997.

87. See Pierre Claude Nolin, Chair, Senate Special Committee on Illegal Drugs,

describe some or all of their marijuana use as "medical" as the definition of that term evolves and broadens. Their anecdotal experiences are increasingly backed by new scientific research into marijuana's essential ingredients, the cannabinoids.[88] Last year, a subsidiary of the *Lancet*, Britain's leading medical journal, speculated whether marijuana might soon emerge as the "aspirin of the 21st century," providing a wide array of medical benefits at low cost to diverse populations.[89]

Perhaps the expansion of the medical-control model provides the best answer—at least in the United States—to the question of how best to reduce the substantial costs and harms of marijuana prohibition without inviting significant increases in real drug abuse. It's analogous to the evolution of many pharmaceutical drugs from prescription to over-the-counter, but with stricter controls still in place. It's also an incrementalist approach to reform that can provide both the control and the reassurance that cautious politicians and voters desire.

In 1931, with public support for alcohol Prohibition rapidly waning, President Hoover released the report of the Wickersham Commission.[90] The report included a devastating critique of Prohibition's failures and costly consequences, but the commissioners, apparently fearful of getting out too far ahead of public opinion, opposed

Cannabis: Our Position for a Canadian Public Policy: Summary Report (Ontario: Senate of Canada, 2002); Mitch Earleywine, *Understanding Marijuana: A New Look at the Scientific Evidence* (New York: Oxford University Press, 2002).

88. J. M. McPartland and E. B. Russo, "Cannabis and Cannabis Extracts: Greater Than the Sum of Their Parts?," *Journal of Cannabis Therapeutics* 1 (2001): 103–132; R. Mechoulam, L. A. Parker, and R. Gallily, "Cannabidiol: An Overview of Some Pharmacological Aspects," *Journal of Clinical Pharmacology*, 42 (2002): 11S–19S; R. G. Pertwee, "The Pharmacology and Therapeutic Potential of Cannabidiol," *Cannabinoids*, Ed. V. DiMarzo (The Netherlands: Kluwer Academic Publishers, 2004).

89. David Baker, Alan Thompson, et al., "The Therapeutic Potential of Cannabis," *The Lancet Neurology*, 2 (2003): 294.

90. See http://www.drugtext.org/library/reports/wick/Default.htm for the complete text of the Commission's report.

repeal.[91] Franklin P. Adams of the *New York World* neatly summed up their findings:

> Prohibition is an awful flop.
>> We like it.
> It can't stop what it's meant to stop.
>> We like it.
> It's left a trail of graft and slime
> It don't prohibit worth a dime
> It's filled our land with vice and crime,
>> Nevertheless, we're for it.[92]

Two years later, federal alcohol Prohibition was history.

What support there is for marijuana prohibition would likely end quickly absent the billions of dollars spent annually by federal and other governments to prop it up. All those anti-marijuana ads pretend to be about reducing drug abuse, but in fact their basic purpose is sustaining popular support for the war on marijuana. What's needed now are conservative politicians willing to say enough is enough: Tens of billions of taxpayer dollars down the drain each year. People losing their jobs, their property, and their freedom for nothing more than possessing a joint or growing a few marijuana plants. And all for what? To send a message? To keep pretending that we're protecting our children? Alcohol Prohibition made a lot more sense than marijuana prohibition does today—and it, too, was a disaster.

91. David E. Kyvig, *Repealing National Prohibition*, 2nd Edition (Ohio: Kent State University Press, 2000): 111–115.

92. As cited in David E. Kyvig, *Repealing National Prohibition*, 2nd Edition (Ohio: Kent State University Press, 2000): 114.

No Surrender: The Drug War Saves Lives

John P. Walters

John P. Walters is the director of the White House Office of National Drug Control Policy.

This article originally appeared in *National Review*, September 27, 2004.

The prospect of a drug-control policy that includes regulated legalization has enticed intelligent commentators for years, no doubt because it offers, on the surface, a simple solution to a complex problem. Reasoned debate about the real consequences usually dampens enthusiasm, leaving many erstwhile proponents feeling mugged by reality; not so Ethan Nadelmann, whose version of marijuana legalization ("An End to Marijuana Prohibition," *National Review*, July 12) fronts for a worldwide political movement, funded by billionaire George Soros, to embed the use of all drugs as acceptable policy. Unfortunately for Nadelmann, his is not a serious argument. Nor is it attached to the facts.

To take but one example, Nadelmann's article alleges the therapeutic value of smoked marijuana by claiming: "Marijuana's medical efficacy is no longer in serious dispute." But he never substantiates this sweeping claim. In fact, smoked marijuana, a Schedule I controlled substance (Schedule I is the government's most restrictive category), has no medical value and a high risk of abuse. The Food and Drug Administration notes that marijuana has not been approved for any indication, that scientific studies do not support claims of marijuana's usefulness as a medication, and that there is a lack of accepted safety standards for the use of smoked marijuana.

The FDA has also expressed concern that marijuana use may

worsen the condition of those for whom it is prescribed. Legalization advocates such as Nadelmann simply ignore these facts and continue their promotion, the outcome of which will undermine drug-prevention and treatment efforts, and put genuinely sick patients at risk. The legalization scheme is also unworkable. A government-sanctioned program to produce, distribute, and tax an addictive intoxicant creates more problems than it solves. First, drug use would increase. No student of supply-and-demand curves can doubt that marijuana would become cheaper, more readily available, and more widespread than it currently is when all legal risk is removed and demand is increased by marketing.

Second, legalization will not eliminate marijuana use among young people any more than legalizing alcohol eliminated underage drinking. If you think we can tax marijuana to where it costs more than the average teenager can afford, think again. Marijuana is a plant that can be readily grown by anyone. If law enforcement is unable to distinguish "legal" marijuana from illegal, growing marijuana at home becomes a low-cost (and low-risk) way to supply your neighborhood and friends. "Official marijuana" will not drive out the black market, nor will it eliminate the need for tough law enforcement. It will only make the task more difficult. In debating legalization, the burden is to consider the costs and benefits both of keeping strict control over dangerous substances and of making them more accessible.

The Soros position consistently overstates the benefits of legalizing marijuana and understates the risks. At the same time, drug promoters ignore the current benefits of criminalization while dramatically overstating the costs. Government-sanctioned marijuana would be a bonanza for trial lawyers (the government may wake up to find that it has a liability for the stoned trucker who plows into a school bus). Health-care and employment-benefits costs will increase (there is plenty of evidence that drug-using employees are less productive, and less healthy), while more marijuana use will further burden our education system.

The truth is, there are laws against marijuana because marijuana is harmful. With every year that passes, medical research discovers greater dangers from smoking it, from links to serious mental illness to the risk of cancer, and even dangers from in utero exposure. In fact, given the new levels of potency and the sheer prevalence of marijuana (the number of users contrasted with the number of those using cocaine or heroin), a case can be made that marijuana does the most social harm of any illegal drug. Marijuana is currently the leading cause of treatment need: Nearly two-thirds of those who meet the psychiatric criteria for needing substance-abuse treatment do so because of marijuana use. For youth, the harmful effects of marijuana use now exceed those of all other drugs combined.

Remarkably, over 40 percent of youths who are current marijuana smokers meet the criteria for abuse or dependency. In several states, marijuana smoking exceeds tobacco smoking among young people, while marijuana has become more important than alcohol as a factor in treatment for teenagers. Legalizers assert that the justice system arrests 700,000 marijuana users a year, suggesting that an oppressive system is persecuting the innocent. This charge is a fraud. Less than 1 percent of those in prison for drug violations are low-level marijuana offenders, and many of these have "pled down" to the marijuana violation in the face of other crimes.

The vast majority of those in prison on drug convictions are true criminals involved in drug trafficking, repeat offenses, or violent crime. The value of legal control is that it enables judicial discretion over offenders, diverting minor offenders who need it into treatment while retaining the authority to guard against the violent and incorrigible. Further, where the sanction and supervision of a court are present, the likelihood of recovery is greatly increased. Removing legal sanction endangers the public and fails to help the offender. Proponents of legalization argue that because approximately half of the referrals for treatment are from the criminal-justice system, it is the law and not marijuana that is the problem.

Yet nearly half of all referrals for alcohol treatment likewise derive from judicial intervention, and nobody argues that drunk drivers do not really have a substance-abuse problem, or that it is the courts that are creating the perception of alcoholism. Marijuana's role in emergency-room cases has tripled in the past decade. Yet no judge is sending people to emergency rooms. They are there because of the dangers of the drug, which have greatly increased because of soaring potency. Legalization advocates suggest that youth will reduce their smoking because of this new potency. But when tobacco companies were accused of deliberately "spiking" their product with nicotine, no one saw this as a public-health gesture intended to reduce cigarette consumption.

The deliberate effort to increase marijuana potency (and market it to younger initiates) should be seen for what it is—a steeply increased threat of addiction. Proponents of legalization argue that the fact that 100 million Americans admit on surveys that they have tried marijuana in their lifetime demonstrates the public's acceptance of the drug. But the pertinent number tells a different story. There are approximately 15 million Americans, mostly young people, who report using marijuana on a monthly basis.

That is, only about 6 percent of the population age twelve and over use marijuana on a regular basis. To grasp the impact of legal control, contrast that figure with the number of current alcohol users (approximately 120 million). Regular alcohol use is eight times that of marijuana, and a large part of the difference is a function of laws against marijuana use. Under legalization, which would decrease the cost (now a little-noticed impediment to the young) and eliminate the legal risk, it is certain that the number of users would increase.

Can anyone seriously argue that American democracy would be strengthened by more marijuana smoking? The law itself is our safeguard, and it works. Far from being a hopeless battle, the drug-control tide is turning against marijuana. We have witnessed an 11 percent reduction in youth marijuana use over the last two years, while perceptions of risk have soared. Make no mistake about what is going on here: Drug legalization is a worldwide movement, the goal of which is to make drug consumption—including heroin, cocaine, and methamphetamine—an acceptable practice. Using the discourse of rights without responsibilities, the effort strives to establish an entitlement to addictive substances.

The impact will be devastating. Drug legalizers will not be satisfied with a limited distribution of medical marijuana, nor will they stop at legal marijuana for sale in convenience stores. Their goal is clearly identifiable: tolerated addiction. It is a travesty to suggest, as Ethan Nadelmann has done, that it is consistent with conservative principles to abandon those who could be treated for their addiction, to create a situation in which government both condones and is the agent of drug distribution, and to place in the hands of the state the power to grant or not grant access to an addictive substance. This is not a conservative vision. But it is the goal of George Soros.

Western States Back Medical Marijuana

MSNBC

This selection originally appeared on MSNBC.com on November 4, 2004 (available online at http://msnbc.msn.com/id/6406453/).

With Montana's approval of a medical marijuana initiative, nearly three-fourths of Western states now have such laws—while only two of the 37 states outside the West have adopted them.

Why is the West so much more receptive to the idea?

From a procedural standpoint, it's just easier to get pot issues on Western ballots because most states in the region allow such initiatives. Nationwide, just 24 states allow citizens to put issues on the ballot by petition, bypassing the Legislature. Eleven of those states are in the West.

But activists and political scientists also say Westerners are less willing than other Americans to tell their neighbors what they can and can't do. And historically, Western states tend to be in front on social trends.

"I would guess many of the people that voted for it probably don't use marijuana, but they don't want to say their neighbors can't," said Steven Stehr, political science professor at Washington State University.

"Westerners have a stronger belief in a kind of individualism in the old-fashioned frontier sense," said Sven Steinmo, a University of Colorado political scientist and board member for the Center of the American West.

The population also is newer than the rest of the country and states don't have deeply ingrained traditions, said David Olson, political scientist at the University of Washington.

"Our politics in the West are much less constrained . . . and it gives opportunities for initiatives like the death with dignity issue in Oregon or medicinal marijuana. You name it," Olson said.

Oregon Rejects Ambitious Program

Montana has become the eleventh state in the country—and the ninth Western state—to allow medical marijuana. The approval came even as Montana voted by wide margins to ban gay marriage and to re-elect President Bush, a Republican.

"We always say in Montana we're extraordinarily independent, so we'll vote for contradictory things," said Jerry Calvert, political science professor at Montana State University in Bozeman.

The Montana initiative passed 62 percent to 38 percent, support that marijuana reform groups say was the highest ever for a medical marijuana ballot initiative.

Oregon voters rejected a measure that would have dramatically expanded its existing medical marijuana program. That may have been too ambitious even for the West, said Bruce Mirken, spokesman for the Marijuana Policy Project.

Alaska, which also has an existing medical marijuana law, rejected a measure to decriminalize the drug, though marijuana groups were impressed that 43 percent of voters there supported it.

Outside the region, voters in Ann Arbor, Mich., and Columbia, Mo., approved local medical marijuana measures.

The 9th U.S. Circuit Court of Appeals in San Francisco has ruled that states are free to adopt medical marijuana laws so long as the marijuana is not sold, transported across state lines or used for non-medicinal purposes. The ruling covers only those Western states in the circuit. The Bush administration has appealed the ruling to the U.S. Supreme Court.

Besides the favorable initiative process in the West, the region is also usually the start of progressive political movements that work their way East, said Keith Stroup, executive director of the National Organization for the Reform of Marijuana Laws.

In addition to Montana, Western states that allow medical marijuana are Alaska, California, Colorado, Hawaii, Nevada, Oregon and Washington state. Arizona has a law permitting marijuana prescriptions, but no active program.

Maine and Vermont are the only states outside the West with existing medical marijuana laws.

For now, medical marijuana has not only found acceptance in the West, but the region may set the tone for proposals across the country.

"As medical marijuana becomes more regulated and institutionalized in the West, that may provide a model for how we ultimately make marijuana legal for all adults," said Ethan Nadelmann, executive director for the Drug Policy Alliance.

PART SIX

A European Outlook

Now what I contend is that my body is my own, at least I
have always so regarded it. If I do harm through my
experimenting with it, it is I who suffers, not the state.

Mark Twain
The *New York Times*
February 28, 1901

The existing variation in drug policy among EU countries
constitutes a series of natural experiments that should be
carefully studied. The results could tell us a great deal about
what is likely to work under what conditions. At the very
least, the evidence to date suggests the need for a full
democratic discussion of the Dutch model and all other
drug policy options.

Craig Reinarman
The drug policy debate in Europe:
The case of Califano vs. The Netherlands.
International Journal of Drug Policy (1997)

Drug Intelligence Brief: The Changing Face of European Drug Policy

Drug Enforcement Administration

This report was prepared by the DEA Intelligence Division, Office of International Intelligence, Europe, Asia, Africa Strategic Unit. The report reflects information prior to February 2002.

This selection is available online at http://usdoj.gov/dea/pubs/intel/02023/02023p.html.

Drug policy in Western Europe has always been experimental, but, in recent years, several countries have joined the Netherlands and Switzerland in their pursuit of alternative methods for dealing with the drug epidemic. Many Western European nations are refocusing efforts on the social welfare aspect of drug use and reducing their focus on the law enforcement response, while imposing stricter penalties on those organizations that supply illegal drugs. Some of the alternative measures that are gaining momentum in Western Europe include legalization, decriminalization, and harm reduction.

The U.S. Drug Enforcement Administration (DEA) defines "legalization" as "making legal what is currently illegal." At present, drug use is not a criminal offense in Austria, Belgium, Germany, Ireland, and the United Kingdom with only minor exceptions.[1] While some nations have taken steps authorizing referendums on the issue of legalization, as Switzerland did in 1998, most have preferred to

Reprinted with permission from the DEA.

1. In Belgium private drug use is not an offense, unless it occurs within a group. In Ireland and the United Kingdom, drug use becomes an offense only in reference to prepared opium.

approach the drug legalization issue by focusing on decriminalization.

DEA defines "decriminalization" as "the removal of, or reduction
in, criminal penalties for particular acts." Decriminalization of drug
use and/or possession is a policy that is widely supported in most of
Western Europe. Many nations' drug policies have been a policy of
de facto decriminalization for many years, but it is only recently that
governments are changing their legislation to officially reduce or
remove criminal penalties for acts such as drug use and possession.
In several Western European nations, possession of small quantities
of drugs will no longer result in a prison sentence, but rather in
administrative sanctions that could include a fine and/or confiscation
of driver's license or passport.

Harm reduction is another policy option finding increasing popularity in Europe. Harm reduction can take on many forms and,
according to the DEA, "is often used to describe specific programs
that attempt to diminish the potential harmful consequences associated with a particular behavior." Some of those programs include
needle exchange, substitution treatment, maintenance treatment, and
injection rooms. The degree to which these programs are incorpo-
rated into society depends on the country in question, with many
nations developing pilot programs in an attempt to ascertain the
advantages of such programs.

DRUG POLICY

While there are many similarities between drug policies, there is currently no consistent policy or law throughout Europe. The variety of
laws and policies in place at the national levels makes it difficult to
create a uniform European drug policy for the European Union
(EU).[2] The EU has served as more of a forum of discussion or

2. Current EU member nations are: Austria, Belgium, Denmark, Finland, France,
Germany, Greece, Ireland, Italy, Luxembourg, the Netherlands, Portugal, Spain, Sweden,
and the United Kingdom.

exchange of ideas rather than a resource or guide for individual government policy.

All EU member nations are signatories of the 1961, 1971, and 1988 United Nations (U.N.) Conventions.[3] Additionally, non-EU member nations, such as Norway and Switzerland, incorporate the regulations set out in the U.N. Conventions. However, through decentralized drug policy, decriminalization, and harm reduction measures, many nations have been able to relax drug laws without directly violating the conventions.

TRENDS IN DRUG POLICY

Decriminalization

While there are a variety of drug laws and policies in Western Europe, several trends are noteworthy. The trend toward the decriminalization of drug use and possession has become an important force in Europe. Although some countries, such as Belgium, Greece, Luxembourg, and Switzerland, took steps to remove criminal penalties for cannabis possession in the past year, other countries, such as Portugal, decriminalized all drug use and possession for personal use.

The decriminalization of minor drug offenses has resulted in much international criticism from organizations such as the DEA and the United Nations International Narcotics Control Board. However, decriminalization is not as radical a concept in Europe as may appear at first glance. A common misconception is equating decriminalization to legalization. In the Netherlands, for instance, cannabis possession is not legal, only tolerated by Dutch authorities. Based upon

3. The 1961 U.N. Single Convention on Narcotic Drugs places international control on more than 116 narcotic drugs. The 1971 U.N. Convention on Psychotropic Substances was designed to create a universal control on psychotropic substances, or mood-altering synthetic substances. The 1988 U.N. Convention against Illicit Trafficking in Narcotics and Psychotropic Substances was designed to combat trafficking in illicit substances.

the concept of the separation of markets,[4] "coffeeshops" began to emerge throughout the Netherlands in 1976, offering cannabis products for sale. While possession and sale of cannabis are not legal, coffeeshops are permitted to exist under certain restrictions.[5]

In 2001, Belgium, Finland, Greece, Luxembourg, Portugal, and Switzerland drafted, proposed, or approved legislation for the decriminalization of minor drug use and possession offenses—in most cases, for cannabis. The United Kingdom debated reclassification of cannabis in 2001, to lower penalties for cannabis possession. That same year, the Lambeth and Brixton areas of South London implemented a pilot program decriminalizing minor cannabis possession. Several other countries including Austria, France, and Italy decriminalized minor drug use and possession in the past decade. Ireland was one of the first countries to decriminalize drug possession with the inception of the Misuse of Drugs Act in 1977, which decriminalized minor cannabis possession. While not all European countries have changed their laws to reduce or remove penalties for minor offenses, all have taken steps to offer a variety of treatment and harm reduction measures.

Treatment and Harm Reduction

The prevailing belief in Europe is that drug addiction is an illness, not a crime. European countries, including those that have not formally decreased criminal penalties for offenses, are searching for alternatives to prison. In many cases, addicts have an option for treatment instead of penalties. Even Sweden, which has some of the most strin-

---

4. Under the concept of the separation of markets, the Dutch government is attempting to separate the hard drug market from the soft drug market to prevent soft drug users from interacting with hard drugs.

5. Coffeeshop restrictions include a limit of no more than 5 grams sold to a person at any one time, no alcohol or hard drugs, no minors, no advertising, and the shop must not cause a nuisance.

gent policies against drugs, offers a suspension of sentence for minor drug offenses in return for treatment under a treatment contract.

Treatment options are no longer limited to detoxification or methadone reduction. Several European nations, including Switzerland, offer maintenance programs. While the ultimate goal of treatment is abstinence, maintenance treatment, like other harm reduction measures, is designed to regulate the drug use of those who are not willing to seek traditional forms of treatment. Maintenance programs can consist of methadone, morphine, heroin, or another opiate. Methadone maintenance is the most common, but several countries, including Germany, are experimenting with distributing heroin itself.

In the 1970s, Switzerland pioneered methadone treatment for opiate addicts. Today, treatment for opiate addiction has expanded to include morphine treatment and, in 1994, heroin distribution for addicts. While Swiss heroin distribution has received international criticism, the Swiss public supports the program and, in 1999, overwhelmingly supported the program in a national referendum.

The rapid spread of the HIV virus among intravenous drug users in the 1980s forced governments to look for measures that would reduce the harmful effects of drug use for those who refused treatment. A wide variety of harm reduction measures have developed throughout Europe. Some of the most common measures include needle-exchange programs and consumption rooms. Countries such as Germany and Switzerland have created extensive harm reduction programs to include social reintegration skills for the addict; however, even the more conservative country of Finland is beginning to experiment with harm reduction measures.

The increased focus on health issues related to drug use has resulted in a flurry of proposals and programs to increase harm reduction measures across Western Europe. All regions in Belgium are implementing drug hotlines and HIV and hepatitis prevention programs. Needle exchange programs are widely used in France. In

1991, the French government approved an experiment allowing for the testing of methylenedioxymethamphetamine (MDMA), commonly known as Ecstasy, and other synthetic drugs at "rave parties." In Luxembourg, substitution treatment, needle exchange, and consumption rooms now have a legal basis since the passage of the law of April 27, 2001.

Since 1958, Norwegian law has allowed treatment as an alternative to prison for those convicted of drug offenses and, in 1991, introduced compulsory treatment for offenders. In 1996, the Norwegian government went a step further to include compulsory treatment for pregnant drug or alcohol users. Under the new provisions, the unborn child's safety and health are placed above the abuser's freedom to choose whether to seek treatment. To reduce the potential harm to the unborn child, a user may be kept in treatment for the duration of the pregnancy without her consent, provided voluntary treatment is not an option.

In 1988, Swedish law changed to allow for compulsory treatment of addicts. Under this law and the Care of Young Persons Special Provisions Act of 1990, the court may order treatment in the case of adult and juvenile offenders. In 2001, Dutch legislation went into effect regulating the Penal Care Facility for Addicts, a compulsory treatment facility for repeat offenders. The facility is based upon research favoring mandatory confinement for treatment, when voluntary treatment has failed.

Greek law also allows for detained compulsory treatment for addicts, but, in practice, the facilities do not exist, so addicts remain in prison. The criminal justice system also seems to be reluctant to order mandatory treatment, so many of Greece's harm reduction methods remain underutilized.

ALTERNATIVES FOR THOSE IN THE PENAL SYSTEM

Removing addicts from penal institutions is only part of the problem. Dealing with the addict population already inside penal institutions is another problem. Spain, among other European countries, has implemented many of the same treatment and harm reduction measures—inside penal institutions as well as outside—to combat the drug epidemic. Methadone treatment and needle exchange programs are now available inside the Spanish prison system to address the inmate addict population.

Attempting to address drug issues in all strata of society, the Swiss government is taking steps to combat drug addiction inside the prison system. According to the Swiss Federal Office of Public Health, approximately one quarter of those in prisons or jails inject drugs. Some prisons have established drug-free wings, where inmates are voluntarily segregated from the prison populace and refrain from drug use; other prisons have installed methadone treatment programs; and some are experimenting with medically supervised heroin use. For addicts who do not seek treatment, the prison system offers several harm reduction measures including needle exchange, materials to disinfect needles, and distribution of condoms.

A pilot program, similar to the program in Switzerland, is underway in Belgium's prison system. Under this program, "drug free" sections or wings are established in prisons to segregate non-users in an attempt to prevent an increase in users in the penal system. Harm reduction measures are also imposed in prison facilities throughout Italy, where inmates with substance abuse problems may apply for treatment in place of their prison sentence. This measure can be used for inmates to start or re-start treatment.

Other countries, such as Portugal, are only looking at the feasibility of implementing programs in the prison system. Currently, there are no harm reduction measures available in the Portuguese prison system. A review of the Spanish prison system, and the harm reduction measures in place there, has forced the Portuguese government to review the possibility of implementing a needle exchange program within its prison system.

INCREASED PENALTIES FOR TRAFFICKING

While focusing on treating and reducing the harm to the addict population, European nations are also focusing effort and funds against the supply of illicit drugs, increasing penalties against those who traffic in illicit substances. In countries such as Austria, France, Greece, Luxembourg, and the United Kingdom, drug trafficking can result in sentences up to life imprisonment. Europeans, while relaxing penalties against addicts, are focusing their attention on the dismantlement of organized drug trafficking organizations.

Drug trafficking is a serious offense in Western Europe resulting in a wide range of penalties. Leaders of drug trafficking organizations in Austria could be sentenced to 10 to 20 years in prison, but with the implementation of new legislation in 2001, they will now face the possibility of life imprisonment. In Luxembourg, if a trafficker supplies drugs to minors, the law allows for penalties up to lifelong forced labor, and in Norway, the most serious drug offenses are classified as those having "very aggravating circumstances." This categorization is usually reserved for the leaders of large international trafficking organizations; it contains a penalty (equivalent to murder) of up to 21 years in prison.

Over the past decade, the United Kingdom has continued to increase penalties for drug trafficking. In 1995, the 1994 Drug Trafficking Act was implemented and replaced the Drug Trafficking Offenses Act of 1986. While this Act applies only to England and Wales, Scotland and Northern Ireland have similar laws.[6] Under the

6. Similar regulations are contained in Scotland's Proceeds of Crime Act 1995, the Criminal Law (Consolidation) Scotland Act 1995, and Northern Ireland's Proceeds of Crime Order 1996.

Maximum Trafficking Penalties[a]

Country	Penalty	Country	Penalty
Austria	Life	Luxembourg	Lifelong
Belgium	20 years		forced labor
Denmark	10 years	Netherlands	16 years
Finland	10 years	Norway	21 years
France	Life	Portugal	25 years
Germany	15 years	Spain	23 years
Greece	Life	Sweden	18 years
Ireland	Life	Switzerland	20 years
Italy	20 years	United Kingdom	Life

[a]The maximum penalties may not be applicable in all cases. In many cases, the maximum penalty applies to extenuating circumstances, such as the death of a user.

Drug Trafficking Act, the court assumes that all current assets, including any owned by the offender during the previous 6 years, are the result of trafficking offenses. Unless the offender can prove otherwise, the court may seize these assets. The penal procedure (summary judgment or indictment) and the drug classification determine the trafficking penalties in the United Kingdom. The 1971 Misuse of Drugs Act divides controlled substances into three classes, A, B, and C.[7] Class A drug trafficking is punishable by up to life imprisonment and, in 2000, the Powers of the Criminal Courts Act established a minimum 7-year sentence for a third conviction of Class A drug trafficking. In 2001, the Criminal Justice and Police Act enabled the courts to strengthen controls on convicted traffickers. Through this act, the court can place a ban on all overseas travel of a convicted trafficker for up to 4 years, in an attempt to reduce his opportunity to re-engage in trafficking activities.

7. Under the Misuse of Drugs Act, substances are divided into 3 classes, A, B, and C. Class A substances are those considered to be the most dangerous, including opiates, cocaine, Ecstasy, and LSD. Class B substances are considered to be less dangerous and include cannabis, sedatives, less potent opiates, and synthetic stimulants. Class C substances are the least regulated and include tranquilizers and some less potent stimulants.

France has also consistently increased penalties for drug trafficking offenses. A 1986 law distinguished between penalties for trafficking and low-level drug dealing or selling, and a 1987 law increased the penalties for those who sell drugs to minors. This law expanded the focus of those prosecutable for drug trafficking offenses to include those who launder drug money. In 1994, the new Penal Code imposed the possibility of life in prison for leaders of organized drug trafficking organizations and up to 30 years for other members of the organization. The French government continued to expand its attack on drug trafficking with the imposition of a 1996 law that allows the boarding and inspection of vessels on the high seas that are believed to be involved in drug trafficking.

CONCLUSION

In several European countries, including Germany, Switzerland, and the United Kingdom, drug policy is implemented at the regional level, resulting in a diverse system throughout the country. Many of these alternative policies are relatively new and require more time to evaluate their effectiveness.

Nevertheless, the trend throughout Europe continues to be a relaxation of criminal penalties for minor drug offenses and an increase in penalties for trafficking, while improving treatment and harm reduction. According to Dutch authorities, harm reduction measures have resulted in significantly lowering their HIV infection rate and drug-related death rate. Unless time shows that these alternative policies have failed, Europe will continue to look toward decriminalization, harm reduction, treatment, and increased trafficking penalties to combat its current drug problems.

Recent Increases in Trafficking Penalties

Country	Year	Penalty
Austria	2001	Penalty increased to life in prison
Finland	1998	Those aware of an aggravated narcotics offense, but who do not alert authorities are punishable by up to 10 years[a]
France	1994	Penalties for leaders of organizations increased up to life
Greece	1993 & 1997	'93: Increased penalties for trafficking and penalized trafficking in precursors '97: Penalties increased up to life for recidivist trafficker and dealing to minors[b]
Ireland	1996 & 1999	'96: Allows a person suspected of trafficking to be detained for a maximum of 7 days '99: Increased the penalty for trafficking in quantities worth more than 10,000 Irish pounds to life and an unlimited fine[c]
Switzerland	1995	Introduced a tougher law aimed at foreign drug traffickers, allowing the detention of illegal residents for up to 9 months
United Kingdom	2000 & 2001	'00: Established a minimum 7-year sentence for a third conviction of Class A drug trafficking '01: Allows the government to ban all overseas travel for convicted traffickers for up to 4 years

[a]An aggravated narcotics offense is one that involves a "very dangerous" substance or large quantities of it; considerable financial profit; the offender acts as a member of an organized drug trafficking group; serious danger is caused to the life or health of several people; or narcotics distributed to minors.

[b]In 1999, Greece made a slight switch, offering leniency to addicts who traffic to support their habit.

[c]Also introduced a minimum mandatory sentence of 10 years for such a trafficking offense. According to the United States Department of State's INCSR 2001, during the first half of 2000, 6 cases fell under the purview of the 1999 Act and in not one case was the mandatory minimum sentence imposed.

Europe's More Liberal Drug Policies Are Not the Right Model for America

Drug Enforcement Administration

This selection was excerpted from "Speaking Out Against Drug Legalization," U.S. Department of Justice, Drug Enforcement Administration (March 2003).

Over the past decade, European drug policy has gone through some dramatic changes toward greater liberalization. The Netherlands, considered to have led the way in the liberalization of drug policy, is only one of a number of West European countries to relax penalties for marijuana possession. Now several European nations are looking to relax penalties on all drugs—including cocaine and heroin—as Portugal did in July 2001, when minor possession of all drugs was decriminalized.

There is no uniform drug policy in Europe. Some countries have liberalized their laws, while others have instituted strict drug control policies. Which means that the so-called "European Model" is a misnomer. Like America, the various countries of Europe are looking for new ways to combat the worldwide problem of drug abuse.

The Netherlands has led Europe in the liberalization of drug policy. "Coffee shops" began to emerge throughout the Netherlands in 1976, offering marijuana products for sale. Possession and sale of marijuana are not legal, but coffee shops are permitted to operate and sell marijuana under certain restrictions, including a limit of no more than 5 grams sold to a person at any one time, no alcohol or hard drugs, no minors, and no advertising. In the Netherlands, it is illegal to sell or possess marijuana products. So coffee shop operators must purchase their marijuana products from illegal drug trafficking organizations.

Apparently, there has been some public dissatisfaction with the government's policy. Recently the Dutch government began considering scaling back the quantity of marijuana available in coffee shops from 5 to 3 grams.

Furthermore, drug abuse has increased in the Netherlands. From 1984 to 1996, marijuana use among 18–25 year olds in Holland increased two-fold. Since legalization of marijuana, heroin addiction levels in Holland have tripled and perhaps even quadrupled by some estimates.

The increasing use of marijuana is responsible for more than increased crime. It has widespread social implications as well. The head of Holland's best-known drug abuse rehabilitation center has described what the new drug culture has created: The strong form of marijuana that most of the young people smoke, he says, produces "a chronically passive individual—someone who is lazy, who doesn't want to take initiatives, doesn't want to be active—the kid who'd prefer to lie in bed with a joint in the morning rather than getting up and doing something."

Marijuana is not the only illegal drug to find a home in the Netherlands. The club drug commonly referred to as Ecstasy (methylenedioxymethamphetamine or MDMA) also has strong roots in the Netherlands. The majority of the world's Ecstasy is produced in clandestine laboratories in the Netherlands and, to a lesser extent, Belgium.

The growing Ecstasy problem in Europe, and the Netherlands' pivotal role in Ecstasy production, has led the Dutch government to look once again to law enforcement. In May 2001, the government announced a "Five-Year Offensive against the Production, Trade, and Consumption of Synthetic Drugs." The offensive focuses on more cooperation among the enforcement agencies with the Unit Synthetic Drugs playing a pivotal role.

Recognizing that the government needs to take firm action to deal with the increasing levels of addiction, in April 2001 the Dutch government established the Penal Care Facility for Addicts. Like American drug treatment courts, this facility is designed to detain and treat addicts (of any drug) who repeatedly commit crimes and have failed voluntary treatment facilities. Offenders may be held in this facility for up to two years, during which time they will go through a three-phase program. The first phase focuses on detoxification, while the second and third phases focus on training for social reintegration.

The United Kingdom has also experimented with the relaxation of drug laws. Until the mid-1960s, British physicians were allowed to prescribe heroin to certain classes of addicts. According to political scientist James Q. Wilson, "a youthful drug culture emerged with a demand for drugs far different from that of the older addicts." Many addicts chose to boycott the program and continued to get their heroin from illicit drug distributors. The British government's experiment with controlled heroin distribution, says Wilson, resulted in, at a minimum, a 30-fold increase in the number of addicts in ten years.

Switzerland has some of the most liberal drug policies in Europe. In the late 1980s, Zurich experimented with what became known as Needle Park, where addicts could openly purchase drugs and inject heroin without police intervention. Zurich became the hub for drug addicts across Europe, until the experiment was ended, and "Needle Park" was shut down.

Many proponents of drug legalization or decriminalization claim that drug use will be reduced if drugs are legalized. However, history has not shown this assertion to be true. According to an October 2000 CNN report, marijuana, the illegal drug most often decriminalized, is "continuing to spread in the European Union, with one in five people across the 15-state bloc having tried it at least once."

It's not just marijuana use that is increasing in Europe. According to the 2001 *Annual Report on the State of the Drugs Problem in the*

European Union, there is a Europe-wide increase in cocaine use. The report also cites a new trend of mixing "base/crack" cocaine with tobacco in a joint at nightspots. With the increase in use, Europe is also seeing an increase in the number of drug users seeking treatment for cocaine use.

Drug policy also has an impact on general crime. In a 2001 study, the British Home Office found violent crime and property crime increased in the late 1990s in every wealthy country except the United States.

Not all of Europe has been swept up in the trend to liberalize drug laws. Sweden, Finland, and Greece have the strictest policies against drugs in Europe. Sweden's zero-tolerance policy is widely supported within the country and among the various political parties. Drug use is relatively low in the Scandinavian countries.

In April 1994, a number of European cities signed a resolution titled "European Cities Against Drugs," commonly known as the Stockholm resolution. It states: "The demands to legalize illicit drugs should be seen against the background of current problems, which have led to a feeling of helplessness. For many, the only way to cope is to try to administer the current situation. But the answer does not lie in making harmful drugs more accessible, cheaper, and socially acceptable. Attempts to do this have not proved successful. By making them legal, society will signal that it has resigned to the acceptance of drug abuse. The signatories to this resolution therefore want to make their position clear by rejecting the proposals to legalize illicit drugs."

Does Europe Do It Better?

Robert J. MacCoun and Peter Reuter

Robert J. MacCoun is Professor of Law and Public Policy at the Richard and Rhoda Goldman School of Public Policy at the University of California at Berkeley. Peter Reuter is Professor in the School of Public Policy and in the Department of Criminology at the University of Maryland.

This selection first appeared in The Nation September 20, 1999.

Listen to a debate among drug policy advocates and you're likely to hear impassioned claims about the brilliant success (or dismal failure) of more "liberal" approaches in certain European countries. Frequently, however, such claims are based on false assumptions. For example, we are told that marijuana has been legalized in the Netherlands. Or that addicts receive heroin by prescription in Great Britain.

Pruned of erroneous or excessive claims, the experience in Europe points to both the feasibility of successful reform of U.S. drug laws and the drawbacks of radical change. What follows are descriptions of some innovative approaches being tried over there, with judgments of their applicability over here. They fall into three broad categories: eliminating user sanctions (decriminalization), allowing commercial sales (legalization) and medical provision of heroin to addicts (maintenance).

DECRIMINALIZING MARIJUANA:
THE CASE OF THE DUTCH COFFEE SHOPS

Dutch cannabis policy and its effects are routinely mischaracterized by both sides in the U.S. drug debate. Much of the confusion hinges on a failure to distinguish between two very different eras in Dutch policy. In compliance with international treaty obligations, Dutch law states unequivocally that cannabis is illegal. Yet in 1976 the Dutch adopted a formal written policy of nonenforcement for violations involving possession or sale of up to thirty grams (five grams since 1995) of cannabis—a sizable quantity, since one gram is sufficient for two joints. Police and prosecutors were forbidden to act against users, and officials adopted a set of rules that effectively allowed the technically illicit sale of small amounts in licensed coffee shops and nightclubs. The Dutch implemented this system to avoid excessive punishment of casual users and to weaken the link between the soft and hard drug markets; the coffee shops would allow marijuana users to avoid street dealers, who may also traffic in other drugs. Despite some recent tightenings in response to domestic and international pressure (particularly from the hard-line French), the Dutch have shown little intention of abandoning their course.

In the initial decriminalization phase, which lasted from the mid-seventies to the mid-eighties, marijuana was not very accessible, sold in a few out-of-the-way places. Surveys show no increase in the number of Dutch marijuana smokers from 1976 to about 1984. Likewise, in the United States during the seventies, twelve U.S. states removed criminal penalties for possession of small amounts of marijuana, and studies indicate that this change had at most a very limited effect on the number of users. More recent evidence from South Australia suggests the same.

From the mid-eighties Dutch policy evolved from the simple decriminalization of cannabis to the active commercialization of it. Between 1980 and 1988, the number of coffee shops selling cannabis in Amsterdam increased tenfold; the shops spread to more prominent and accessible locations in the central city and began to promote the drug more openly. Today, somewhere between 1,200 and 1,500 coffee shops (about one per 12,000 inhabitants) sell cannabis products in the Netherlands; much of their business involves tourists. Coffee shops account for perhaps a third of all cannabis purchases among minors and supply most of the adult market.

As commercial access and promotion increased in the eighties, the Netherlands saw rapid growth in the number of cannabis users, an increase not mirrored in other nations. Whereas in 1984 15 percent of 18- to 20-year-olds reported having used marijuana at some point in their life, the figure had more than doubled to 33 percent in 1992, essentially identical to the U.S. figure. That increase might have been coincidental, but it is certainly consistent with other evidence (from alcohol, tobacco and legal gambling markets) that commercial promotion of such activities increases consumption. Since 1992 the Dutch figure has continued to rise, but that growth is paralleled in the United States and most other rich Western nations despite very different drug policies—apparently the result of shifts in global youth culture.

The rise in marijuana use has not led to a worsening of the Dutch heroin problem. Although the Netherlands had an epidemic of heroin use in the early seventies, there has been little growth in the addict population since 1976; indeed, the heroin problem is now largely one of managing the health problems of aging (but still criminally active) addicts. Cocaine use is not particularly high by European standards, and a smaller fraction of marijuana users go on to use cocaine or heroin in the Netherlands than in the United States. Even cannabis commercialization does not seem to increase other drug problems.

TREATING HEROIN ADDICTS IN BRITAIN

The British experience in allowing doctors to prescribe heroin for maintenance has been criticized for more than two decades in the United States. In a 1926 British report, the blue-ribbon Rolleston Committee concluded that "morphine and heroin addiction must be regarded as a manifestation of disease and not as a mere form of vicious indulgence," and hence that "the indefinitely prolonged administration of morphine and heroin" might be necessary for such patients. This perspective—already quite distinct from U.S. views in the twenties—led Britain to adopt, or at least formalize, a system in which physicians could prescribe heroin to addicted patients for maintenance purposes. With a small population of several hundred patients, most of whom became addicted while under medical treatment, the system muddled along for four decades with few problems. Then, in the early sixties, a handful of physicians began to prescribe irresponsibly and a few heroin users began taking the drug purely for recreational purposes, recruiting others like themselves. What followed was a sharp relative increase in heroin addiction in the mid-sixties, though the problem remained small in absolute numbers (about 1,500 known addicts in 1967).

In response to the increase, the Dangerous Drugs Act of 1967 greatly curtailed access to heroin maintenance, limiting long-term prescriptions to a small number of specially licensed drug-treatment specialists. At the same time, oral methadone became available as an alternative maintenance drug. By 1975, just 12 percent of maintained opiate addicts were receiving heroin; today, fewer than 1 percent of maintenance clients receive heroin. Specialists are still allowed to maintain their addicted patients on heroin if they wish; most choose not to do so—in part because the government reimbursement for heroin maintenance is low, but also because of a widespread reluctance to take on a role that is difficult to reconcile with traditional norms of medical practice. Thus, one can hardly claim that heroin maintenance was a failure in Britain. When it was the primary mode of treatment, the heroin problem was small. The problem grew larger even as there was a sharp decline in heroin maintenance, for many reasons unrelated to the policy.

"HEROIN-ASSISTED TREATMENT": THE SWISS EXPERIENCE

What the British dropped, the Swiss took up. Although less widely known, the Swiss experience is in fact more informative. By the mid-eighties it was clear that Switzerland had a major heroin problem, compounded by a very high rate of HIV infection. A generally tough policy, with arrest rates approaching those in the United States, was seen as a failure. The first response was from Zurich, which opened a "zone of tolerance" for addicts at the so-called "Needle Park" (the Platzspitz) in 1987. This area, in which police permitted the open buying and selling of small quantities of drugs, attracted many users and sellers, and was regarded by the citizens of Zurich as unsightly and embarrassing. The Platzspitz was closed in 1992.

Then in January 1994 Swiss authorities opened the first heroin maintenance clinics, part of a three-year national trial of heroin maintenance as a supplement to the large methadone maintenance program that had been operating for more than a decade. The motivation for these trials was complex. They were an obvious next step in combating AIDS, but they also represented an effort to reduce the unsightliness of the drug scene and to forestall a strong legalization movement. The program worked as follows: Each addict could choose the amount he or she wanted and inject it in the clinic under the care of a nurse up to three times a day, seven days a week. The drug could not be taken out of the clinic. Sixteen small clinics were scattered around the country, including one in a prison. Patients had to be over 18, have injected heroin for two years and have failed at least two treatment episodes. In fact, most of them had more than ten years of heroin addiction and many treatment failures. They were among the most troubled heroin addicts with the most chaotic lives.

By the end of the trials, more than 800 patients had received heroin on a regular basis without any leakage into the illicit market. No overdoses were reported among participants while they stayed in the program. A large majority of participants had maintained the regime of daily attendance at the clinic; 69 percent were in treatment eighteen months after admission. This was a high rate relative to those found in methadone programs. About half of the "dropouts" switched to other forms of treatment, some choosing methadone and others abstinence-based therapies. The crime rate among all patients dropped over the course of treatment, use of nonprescribed heroin dipped sharply and unemployment fell from 44 to 20 percent. Cocaine use remained high. The prospect of free, easily obtainable heroin would seem to be wondrously attractive to addicts who spend much of their days hustling for a fix, but initially the trial program had trouble recruiting patients. Some addicts saw it as a recourse for losers who were unable to make their own way on the street. For some participants the discovery that a ready supply of heroin did not make life wonderful led to a new interest in sobriety.

Critics, such as an independent review panel of the World Health Organization (also based in Switzerland), reasonably asked whether the claimed success was a result of the heroin or the many additional services provided to trial participants. And the evaluation relied primarily on the patients' own reports, with few objective measures. Nevertheless, despite the methodological weaknesses, the results of the Swiss trials provide evidence of the feasibility and effectiveness of this approach. In late 1997 the Swiss government approved a large-scale expansion of the program, potentially accommodating 15 percent of the nation's estimated 30,000 heroin addicts.

Americans are loath to learn from other nations. This is but another symptom of "American exceptionalism." Yet European drug-policy experiences have a lot to offer. The Dutch experience with decriminalization provides support for those who want to lift U.S. criminal penalties for marijuana possession. It is hard to identify differences between the United States and the Netherlands that would make marijuana decriminalization more dangerous here than there. Because the Dutch went further with decriminalization than the few states in this country that tried it—lifting even civil penalties—the burden is on U.S. drug hawks to show what this nation could possibly gain from continuing a policy that results in 700,000 marijuana arrests annually. Marijuana is not harmless, but surely it is less damaging than arrest and a possible jail sentence; claims that reduced penalties would "send the wrong message" ring hollow if in fact levels of pot use are unlikely to escalate and use of cocaine and heroin are unaffected.

The Swiss heroin trials are perhaps even more important. American heroin addicts, even though most are over 35, continue to be the source of much crime and disease. A lot would be gained if heroin maintenance would lead, say, the 10 percent who cause the most harm to more stable and socially integrated lives. Swiss addicts may be different from those in the United States, and the trials there are not enough of a basis for implementing heroin maintenance here. But the Swiss experience does provide grounds for thinking about similar tests in the United States.

Much is dysfunctional about other social policies in this country, compared with Europe—the schools are unequal, the rate of violent crime is high and many people are deprived of adequate access to health services. But we are quick to draw broad conclusions from apparent failures of social programs in Europe (for example, that the cost of an elaborate social safety net is prohibitive), while we are all too ready to attribute their successes to some characteristic of their population or traditions that we could not achieve or would not want—a homogeneous population, more conformity, more intrusive government and the like. It's time we rose above such provincialism.

The benefits of Europe's drug policy innovations are by no means decisively demonstrated, not for Europe and surely not for the United States. But the results thus far show the plausibility of a wide range of variations—both inside and at the edges of a prohibition framework—that merit more serious consideration in this country.

CONCLUSION

If opponents of the drug war want to have an impact, rather than focusing on the perfect policy or waiting for revolutions in the public's thinking, we have to reach out to new people, find working compromises, and advance concrete proposals. . . . At the same time, if it is true that any successful challenge to the drug war, even on a relatively narrow issue, threatens an overly rigid paradigm, so much the better. We can't count on overthrowing the generals with modest peace offerings. But in the very strange world of U.S. drug policy, it might just happen.

Dave Fratello
"The Medical Marijuana Menace"
Reason Online, March 1998

I do not have the answer to the drug-policy dilemma other than to keep moving ahead pretty much as we have been. . . . If we are going to make policy for this difficult and tragic problem with simplistic solutions that can fit into 30 second TV sound bytes, then I would definitely prefer a real drug war, with swift and certain punishment of casual drug users, to a drug legalization surrender.

Joel W. Hay
"The Harm They Do to Others: A Primer on the External Cost of Drug Abuse," in Melvyn B. Krauss and Edward P. Lazear, eds., Searching for Alternatives: Drug-Control Policy in the United States (1991).

A Blueprint for Peace: Ending the War on Drugs

Ted Galen Carpenter

Ted Galen Carpenter is vice president for defense and foreign policy studies at the Cato Institute.

The following selection originally appeared in "A Blueprint for Peace: Ending the War on Drugs" in *Bad Neighbor Policy: Washington's Futile War on Drugs in Latin America* (New York, NY: Palgrave Macmillan, 2003).

The United States has waged an intense war on drugs both at home and abroad for more than three decades. Throughout that period, domestic support for the effort has been consistent and strong. Although there have been a few prominent critics in the United States, their voices usually have been drowned out by calls for the expenditure of more funds and the adoption of ever-harsher measures to overcome the scourge of drugs. Latin American critics have been even rarer and quieter. Few wanted to incur Washington's wrath by criticizing the drug war, and the fate of the handful of individuals who dared to do so did not encourage emulation.

There are signs, though, that the strategy of intimidation used by drug warriors is beginning to lose its effect. For the first time since the late 1970s, there appears to be a reasonable chance that the pro-hibitionist strategy eventually could be overturned. Such prominent businessmen as financier George Soros, Peter Lewis, the chairman of Progressive Insurance, Inc. (the nation's fifth largest auto insurer), and John Sperling, a wealthy entrepreneur, have funded a variety of initiatives that challenge the sacred cows of the drug war. They have promoted various measures that embody a strategy of "harm reduction" and treatment, not jail. As the *Wall Street Journal* noted, since 1996 the three men have spent more than $20 million "on a state-by-state campaign to chip away at the hard-line policies" of the war on drugs.[1] Most of their efforts have focused on two issues: allowing the medical use of marijuana and curbing the authority of law enforcement agencies to seize property from accused drug law violators without a conviction for that crime.

Their financial support has enabled opponents of the drug war to put referenda on the ballots in various states permitting the use of marijuana (and in some cases other now-illegal drugs) for medical purposes. Indeed, by the end of 2000, nine states—Alaska, Arizona, California, Colorado, Hawaii, Maine, Nevada, Oregon, and Washington—had adopted such measures. One of the more revealing pieces of evidence of waning public enthusiasm for an across-the-board prohibitionist strategy is that initiatives on making medical exceptions to the drug laws were approved by voters—and usually adopted by wide margins—in state after state. Another indicator was the approval by California voters in the November 2000 elections of Proposition 36, an even more ambitious proposal that sought to bar state judges from sending people to prison after their first or second conviction for drug use or possession. Instead, such nonviolent offenders would be directed into treatment programs.

Signs of change are surfacing elsewhere as well. At the beginning of 2001, the government of Jamaica appointed a commission to examine the possible legalization of marijuana; interestingly, a majority of people appearing before the commission favored legalization. Among those who testified were representatives of the Medical Association of Jamaica, the Scientific Research Council, the Jamaica Manufacturers Association, and the National Democratic Movement, the country's

---

1. David Bank, "Counterattack: Soros, Two Rich Allies Fund a Growing War on the War on Drugs," *Wall Street Journal*, May 30, 2001, p. A1.

third largest political party.[2] In September 2001 the commission issued a report recommending the decriminalization of marijuana, despite U.S. warnings that passage of such a measure by Jamaica's parliament could lead to the country's decertification under the 1988 Drug Abuse Act and the imposition of economic sanctions.[3]

In addition to the growing roster of domestic critics in the United States, some Latin American officials are beginning to advocate an end to the drug war, even though they risk denunciation and harassment from Washington for doing so. One prominent convert is Uruguayan president Jorge Batlle. "During the past 30 years [the drug war] has grown, grown, grown, every day more problems, every day more violence, every day more militarization," Batlle told a nationwide radio audience in February 2001. "This has not gotten people off drugs. And what's more, if you remove the economic incentive of [the drug trade] it loses strength, it loses size, it loses people who participate."[4] Although the president pledged continued cooperation with antidrug efforts until the laws are changed, having a head of state condemn the logic of the drug war caused Washington no small amount of concern.

Although few other Latin American officials are as bold as Batlle, several have dared to criticize the drug war as a failure and hint at their support for legalization. A little more than a year before he became Mexico's foreign minister, Jorge Castañeda wrote a scathing commentary in *Newsweek* proclaiming the war a failure. "It's hard to find a place where the war on drugs is being won," Castañeda concluded. "Indeed, the time is uniquely propitious for a wide-ranging debate between North and Latin Americans on this absurd war that

2. "Jamaica Looks at Crime of Marijuana Use," Reuters, May 23, 2001.

3. Canute James, "U.S. Worried as Jamaica Rethinks Marijuana Stance," *Financial Times*, September 4, 2001, p. 3; and David Gonzalez, "Panel Urges Legalization of Marijuana in Jamaica," *New York Times*, September 30, 2001, p. A9.

4. Quoted in Sebastian Rotella, "Uruguayan Leader Urges Legalizing Drugs," *Philadelphia Inquirer*, February 11, 2001, online edition.

no one really wants to wage." Moreover, "In the end, legalization of certain substances may be the only way to bring prices down, and doing so may be the only remedy to some of the worst aspects of the drug plague: violence, corruption, and the collapse of the rule of law."[5]

Perhaps the most surprising critique came from Castañeda's boss, Mexican president Vicente Fox, in a March 2001 interview in the newspaper *Unomasuno*. Alluding to the violence and corruption that drug trafficking has spawned, Fox stated that the solution might be eventually to legalize drugs. He added an important caveat, however. "When the day comes that it is time to adopt the alternative of lifting punishment for consumption of drugs, it would have to come from all over the world because we would gain nothing if Mexico did it but the production and traffic of drugs . . . continued here" for lucrative markets where the substances remained illegal.[6] Even with that caveat, Fox's comments caused more than a little consternation in official Washington.

Perhaps most significant, at "ground zero" in the war on drugs (Colombia), criticism of the prohibitionist strategy is mounting. Some of the critics are now openly advocating the legalization of drugs. In the summer of 2001 Liberal Party senator Viviane Morales submitted a bill to the Colombian congress calling for legalization. "The main ally of narcotrafficking is prohibition," Morales states bluntly. Another influential Colombian politician, Guillermo Gaviria, governor of powerful Antioquia province, insists that his country should lead an international debate on legalization. Although there is little chance that Morales's legislation will pass in the near future, the fact that a serious legalization campaign in Colombia surfaced at all in the face

5. Jorge G. Castañeda, "How We Fight a Losing War," *Newsweek*, September 6, 1999, electronic version.

6. Quoted in John Rice, "Mexican President Vicente Fox Discusses Drug Legalization in Newspaper Interview," Associated Press, March 19, 2001.

of vehement opposition from the United States and the Pastrana government is remarkable.

A few countries are abandoning the prohibitionist strategy, despite pressure from Washington not to do so. The Netherlands has had de facto decriminalization of marijuana for years, even though that policy has been a frequent target of wrath from U.S. officials.[7] Indeed, Dutch authorities in one town now plan to open "drive-through" drug shops to better accommodate the drug tourists who flock to that country from jurisdictions (especially Germany) with far more restrictive drug laws.[8] Recently the government of Belgium decided to legalize the possession of small quantities of marijuana for personal consumption. Growing marijuana plants for personal use also would be permitted.[9] The government of Canada is seriously considering the decriminalization of marijuana, making possession a civil rather than a criminal offense. In May 2001 the House of Commons established a committee to examine the merits of decriminalization, and Justice Minister Anne McLellan is openly encouraging the debate. Advocates of decriminalization include members of the principal conservative political party, the Canadian Alliance, as well as the Royal Canadian Mounted Police.[10] Two months later the Canadian government made it legal for terminally ill patients, as well as some patients with

7. For a discussion of the Netherlands policy and U.S. hostility toward it, see Ineke Haen Marshall and Henk Van De Bunt, "Exporting the Drug War to the Netherlands and Dutch Alternatives," in Jurg Gerber and Eric L. Jensen, eds., *Drug War American Style: The Internationalization of Failed Policies and Its Alternatives* (New York: Gardner, 2001), pp. 197–217; and Robert J. MacCoun and Peter Reuter, *Drug War Heresies: Learning from Other Vices, Times, and Places* (Cambridge: Cambridge University Press, 2001), pp. 238–264.

8. "Dutch to Open Drug Drive-Thru Shops," Associated Press, May 1, 2001; "Dutch Approve Coffee and Pot for German Tourists," Reuters, May 31, 2001; and Suzanne Daley, "The New Reefer Madness: Drive-Through Shops," *New York Times*, May 28, 2001, p. A4.

9. "Belgium Agrees to Legalize Cannabis," Associated Press, January 19, 2001.

10. Joel Baglole, "O Cannabis: Ottawa May Soon Ease Up on Its Marijuana Laws," *Wall Street Journal*, June 5, 2001, p. A18.

chronically debilitating conditions such as multiple sclerosis, to use marijuana to alleviate their symptoms.[11]

Even Portugal, not known as a bastion of radical libertarian thinking on law enforcement issues, is rethinking its position on the drug war. Although the government maintains a harsh policy toward traffickers, it has adopted a far less punitive approach to drug users. A new law that went into effect in July 2001 eliminates the threat of prison for possession of small quantities of any drug, not merely marijuana. Punishment is confined to fines or mandatory community service. While the Portuguese law does not constitute legalization or even true decriminalization, it is a major step for a socially conservative country.

Potentially as significant as the episodes of reform overseas and the adoption of medical marijuana initiatives in the United States is the evidence of growing ambivalence about the drug war itself on the part of the American people. Underlying that ambivalence is the widespread belief that the drug war has been a failure. A detailed public opinion survey conducted by the Pew Research Center in February 2001 confirmed that point. Not only did 74 percent of respondents agree that the drug war is being lost, but the same percentage agreed with the statement that "demand is so high we will never stop drug use."[12] Equally revealing, only 6 percent considered illegal drug use to be the nation's most pressing problem. That compared to 37 percent in a similar survey conducted in 1990.[13]

Respondents also were less than enthusiastic about the supply-side campaign. Some 68 percent believed that Latin America would never be able to control the outflow of drugs. When asked whether

11. Jim Burns, "Canada Legalizes Marijuana for Medicinal Purposes," CNS News.Com, July 30, 2001, E-Brief@topica.email-publisher.com.

12. Pew Research Center for the People and the Press, "74% Say Drug War Being Lost," February 2001, part 1, p. 1.

13. Ibid., p. 3.

the U.S. government should provide more, less, or about the same amount of financial assistance to help drug-producing countries stem the flow, only 11 percent wanted to give more aid; 42 percent advocated giving less aid. Their response was only slightly more favorable when queried specifically about military aid: 23 percent favored giving more aid; 28 percent wanted to reduce the level of assistance.[14]

Although despondency about the drug war did not necessarily translate into a surge of support for outright legalization, there were also signs of softening public attitudes about criminalizing drug use. As many respondents (47 percent) agreed with the statement that "too many people are put in jail for drug offenses" as disagreed. And by a narrow plurality (47 percent to 45 percent) respondents thought that eliminating mandatory jail sentences would be "a good thing."[15] In addition, only 49 percent favored retaining criminal penalties for possessing small quantities of marijuana, and by better than a three-to-one margin (73 percent to 21 percent), respondents supported permitting doctors to prescribe marijuana to their patients.[16] That result suggests that the victory of medical marijuana initiatives in several states was not a fluke.

Although such survey data hardly reveal a popular mandate for drug legalization, they do reveal the profile of a public that is war weary, pessimistic about the efficacy of drug-war tactics in the future, and supportive of a limited legalization of some drugs under some conditions—especially medical marijuana. That is not the profile of American public opinion likely to gladden the hearts of committed drug warriors. It suggests a public that is gradually becoming receptive to alternative policies.

An admission by former DEA chief Jack Lawn underscores one reason why the drug war should be ended: "With all of our efforts, with the military in their aircraft and Coast Guard cutters and heli-

14. Ibid., part 2, p. 4.
15. Ibid., p. 1.
16. Ibid., part 1, pp. 2–3.

copters, traffickers will just move to a third country to get things done. They don't lose money. They don't lose hours. I don't think they have lost anything substantial in the last 20 years."[17]

Laws and other policy initiatives must be judged by their consequences, not their intentions. By that measure, the war on drugs over the past three decades has been a colossal failure. The international drug traffickers have been barely inconvenienced while societies in drug-producing and drug-transiting countries have experienced a massive upsurge in corruption and violence. In at least one drug-source country (Colombia), the entire social and political system is in peril. On the domestic front, the sole achievement has been a decline in recreational use of illegal drugs by casual, occasional users. Even assuming that the decline is the result of the prohibitionist strategy and not the effect of educational campaigns about the health consequences of drug abuse, the benefit has been achieved at enormous cost. We have filled our prisons with drug offenders, diverted criminal justice resources and personnel away from serious crimes to wage the drug war, and badly damaged the Fourth Amendment and other portions of the Bill of Rights.[18]

The only realistic way out of this policy morass is to adopt a regime of drug legalization. And contrary to the alarmists in the prohibitionist camp, that option is not a venture into terra incognita, replete with unimaginable horrors. Although the fact is largely forgotten, now-illicit drugs were once legal in America. At the beginning of the twentieth century, there were virtually no restrictions on opiates, cocaine, or marijuana.

Even the first "antidrug measure" approved by Congress was quite modest and reasonable. In 1906 Congress enacted the Pure Food and Drug Act, which required that labels on medicine list any narcotic content. (Some American consumers had unwittingly become

17. "Drug Wars: Part 2," PBS, *Frontline*, October 10, 2000, transcript, p. 35.
18. For a good, concise discussion, see "Collateral Damage: The Drug War Has Many Casualties," the *Economist*, July 28, 2001, pp. 12–13.

dependent on patent medicines containing opiates or cocaine.) It was not until the adoption of the Harrison Narcotic Act in 1914 that the United States took a major step toward drug prohibition. (It may be more than coincidental that it was about this same time that the movement for a national prohibition of alcoholic beverages also began to gather steam.) Yet although the Harrison Act outlawed normal commerce in opiates and cocaine, even that legislation permitted medically prescribed uses of those drugs, and addicts were still able to obtain drugs legally from physicians and clinics. Only after a dubious decision by the U.S. Supreme Court in 1919, ruling that providing morphine to an addict with no intention to cure him violated the Harrison Act, and the passage of subsequent amendments to the law by Congress, did prohibition become complete with regard to opiates and cocaine.[19]

Marijuana remained legal even longer. Not until the passage of the Marijuana Tax Act in 1937 did that drug join the rank of banned substances.

Granted, America was not free of drug-related problems under a regime of legalization. For example, in the early years of the twentieth century there were an estimated 300,000 opiate addicts—often individuals who had become dependent on patent medicines.[20] Yet that was still a relatively small portion of the population. And America was certainly not plagued with the violence, corruption, economic distortions, and abasement of the Bill of Rights that have accompanied the prohibitionist regime. Legalization may not be a panacea, but it certainly beats the alternative.

It is time to terminate the prohibitionist strategy. We need an

---

19. The definitive accounts of early twentieth century drug policies are David T. Courtwright, *Dark Paradise: Opiate Addiction in America Before 1940* (Cambridge, MA: Harvard University Press, 1982); and David F. Musto, *The American Disease: Origins of Narcotics Control*, expanded edition (New York: Oxford University Press, 1987).

20. Mathea Falco, *The Making of a Drug-Free America: Programs That Work* (New York: Times Books, 1992), p. 17.

entirely new policy, not merely an effort to repackage the war on drugs as a "compassionate crusade," as Asa Hutchinson, the new head of the Drug Enforcement Administration, seeks to do. The first step ought to be to end the browbeating of our neighbors in the Western Hemisphere to take actions that create massive problems for their societies and undermine the stability of democratic institutions. It is bad enough if we inflict the many follies of prohibition on ourselves; we should at least have the decency not to inflict them on others.

Washington's supply-side campaign against drugs has not worked, is not working, and, given economic realities, will not work. That is not to suggest that the influence of the drug trade is a benign one or that Latin American countries would not be better off if the trafficking organizations were less powerful. The exaggerated importance that the drug trade has acquired is an economic distortion caused by foolish policies adopted in Washington and the drug-source countries themselves. Immediate steps can and should be taken to eliminate that distortion.

Latin American governments should move more aggressively to deregulate their economies and spur economic growth, thereby creating new opportunities for those people who are now involved in the lower echelons of the drug trade. Although some governments took promising steps in that direction during the 1990s, the trend has stalled and in some places (e.g., Venezuela, Peru, and Argentina) even reversed. Adopting policies that promoted real growth in the private sector of the economy (as opposed to sterile government-directed economic development programs funded by U.S. aid dollars) would give new options to those who now see drug trafficking as the only path to prosperity.

The United States also can take steps to reinforce the benefits of such reforms. The adoption of the North American Free Trade Agreement provided important new economic opportunities for Mexico. Creating a hemispheric free trade agreement would extend such opportunities to other societies. Latin American representatives have long complained that U.S. import quotas on sugar, textiles, and an array of other products have retarded the development of their economies. Although those officials often ignore the fact that many of the problems with their economies are self-inflicted, their complaints have some validity. U.S. import restrictions needlessly injure Latin American business enterprises as well as U.S. consumers, and a hemispheric free trade zone would be an important step toward eliminating such inequities. More than a decade ago economist Scott MacDonald aptly observed, "Protectionism, in itself, is a dangerous force, but in the drug trade, it is negative reinforcement in the movement from legal products to illicit products."[21]

Certainly Latin American leaders recognize the importance of more open access to the U.S. market for their legal products. In arguing for renewal and expansion of the Andean Trade Preferences Act, Peru's vice president, Raúl Diez Canseco, told a forum in Colombia that such a deal could lift his country's exports to the United States to some $2.5 billion within five years. That growth in turn would create 140,000 jobs in Peru's apparel industry and up to 400,000 new jobs in the agricultural sector. Foreign Minister Diego García Sayán added that it was absolutely essential that textiles be included in the renewed pact, arguing that in many former drug-producing areas, textiles were becoming an alternate economic way of life.[22]

Yet even if the governments of drug-source countries enact the most comprehensive and worthwhile economic reforms and Washington adopts unusually enlightened trade policies, drug commerce will continue to play a disproportionate role in many Latin American countries unless the United States ends its futile experiment in drug prohibition. Without that action, drug trafficking still will carry a risk

21. Scott MacDonald, *Dancing on a Volcano: The Latin American Drug Trade* (New York: Praeger, 1988), p. 150.
22. Jude Webber, "Peru to Push Powell for New Anti-Drug Flights," Reuters, August 21, 2001; see also George Gedda, "Colombia Chief Seeks Trade Benefits," Associated Press, November 8, 2001.

premium that drives up the price and the profit margin. Traffickers still will be able to pay farmers more than they can make from alternative crops or alternative occupations. Because ruthless individuals who do not fear the law tend to dominate black markets, the drug trade, in both its international and domestic incarnations, will remain largely the domain of violence-prone criminal organizations. Without legalization in the United States, the threat that such organizations pose to the governments and societies of source countries will abate only marginally, even if other reforms are enacted.

Drug legalization—treating currently illicit drugs as alcohol and tobacco are now treated—would provide important benefits to the United States: It would eliminate a significant portion of the crime and violence that plagues the streets of our major cities. It would halt the clogging of the court system with charges against nonviolent drug offenders and the clogging of our prisons with such inmates. Most important, abandoning the drug war would stop the alarming erosion of civil liberties.

Ending the war on drugs also would aid the effort against a real threat to America's security and well-being: the threat posed by international terrorism. Terminating the prohibitionist strategy would deprive terrorist organizations of an important source of revenue. (. . . the Taliban regime in Afghanistan, for example, derived a substantial portion of its income from narcotics trafficking.) Equally important, ending our latest fling with prohibition would free up thousands of personnel and billions of dollars for waging the war against terrorism. Imagine if all the well-trained personnel working for the DEA (to say nothing of the talent being wasted in state and local antidrug units) could be reassigned to antiterrorism missions.

The long-term benefits to Latin American societies from abandoning a prohibitionist strategy also would be substantial, although the short-term economic effects of a price decline might be adverse. No longer would Latin American nations suffer the massive distortions to their economies, the political corruption, and the escalating violence that accompany the lucrative black market in drugs. No longer would the governments of those countries have to dissemble in a futile attempt to satisfy the conflicting demands of the United States and their own citizens. No longer would Washington engage in the demeaning spectacle of alternately bribing and threatening its neighbors to get them to do the impossible.

Compassionate Crusade

Asa Hutchinson

Asa Hutchinson recently served as administrator of the Drug Enforcement Administration and currently serves as undersecretary for Border and Transportation Security at the Department of Homeland Security.

The following selection is an excerpt from a speech given at the 2001 Drug Abuse Resistance Education Conference in Los Angeles, California (August 1, 2001).

In my view, there is not a more important issue facing our nation than how to solve the drug problem. That's one reason why I said "Yes" to the President, gave up a Congressional seat, and took on this responsibility. I can't think of a better way to serve the American people than serving in the fight against drugs.

I have seen the problem of drugs as a member of Congress and as a federal prosecutor and I personally know the toll drugs take on families and communities.

When I was a teenager in the late 1960s, I thought drug abuse was something that happened in New York, and Chicago, and Los Angeles. Not in Springdale, Arkansas. The only time I heard drugs mentioned was when I turned on the evening news. Today, drugs are in every nook and cranny of America, whether it is Ecstasy in the teen scene, heroin in the city or meth in the heartland. . . .

I learned that you can't escape the drug problem by moving to rural America. In today's America there is no place in which drugs are not readily available. If you live in America, you can't escape drugs. The best thing you can do, the only thing you can do, is stand your ground, lock arms with your neighbors, and fight.

I might be new to the DEA, but I'm not a stranger to this effort. From my experience as a prosecutor, parent, and Congressman, I know two things I want to emphasize as DEA's Administrator. One is a greater sense of urgency; the second is a greater sense of balance.

Let me begin by telling you what I mean by a greater sense of urgency. As a Congressman for the past five years, I've been concerned that America is losing its sense of urgency in the fight against drugs.

There was a time when we called it a "war" against drugs. In the mid-1980s, when many neighborhoods were devastated by crack cocaine, when University of Maryland basketball star Len Bias died of a drug overdose on the eve of what could have been a brilliant pro career, when DEA Special Agent Kiki Camarena was tortured and murdered by traffickers in Mexico: that's when this nation decided to give its drug policies a battlefield intensity.

Guess what? The greater sense of urgency worked. From 1985 to 1992, drug use was cut in half. But somewhere along the line we lost that sense of urgency. Too many people who should have known better got complacent.

And I am sure you felt the results of that complacency. You can't be expected to do the tough work you do on the front lines without the material and moral support you need to get the job done. What's more, it's tough for you to walk into a classroom of young people and tell them about the dangers of drugs if the entertainment and fashion industries are glamorizing drug use, and if well-known political and opinion leaders are recommending legalization.

Let me tell you what America needs—What America needs is a new crusade against drugs, a crusade with equal intensity and compassion. Each year, about 50,000 Americans lose their lives from drug-related causes. That's almost as many Americans as lost their lives in eight-and-a-half years in the Vietnam War.

There are a lot of threatening issues out there that should concern us—issues like declining test scores in education and terrorism at home. But no issue presents such a serious and immediate threat to this country as the resurgence of some illegal drugs (e.g., Ecstasy, LSD) among America's young people. We simply cannot continue to allow 50,000 of our fellow Americans to die every year as a result in part of the greed of international traffickers: those who traffic in human misery to satisfy their own quest for illegal profits at the expense of the next generation.

But the problem extends beyond individual traffickers and users. When an addict injects heroin into his veins, he is not only changing the chemistry of his body. Little by little, he is changing the values of society.

I'm often asked why it's necessary to pick on some harmless addict who is just going to go off by himself and shoot up drugs. What's the harm? All he wants is a little pleasure in this world.

But the fact is, the image of the lone drug user is a myth. Drugs destroy families, they destroy neighborhoods, and if we don't get a grip on them, they can destroy the character of this nation.

You may remember a news story from 1987. It concerned a lawyer and his companion, who was a book editor and author. They lived in a New York City apartment with two adopted children. The news story related a horrifying case of physical abuse. The lawyer was charged with throwing his six-year-old adopted daughter against a wall, then sitting in front of the girl, smoking cocaine with his companion, while the girl lapsed into a coma and eventually died.

When police arrived at the apartment, they also found a 17-month-old boy, soaked in urine, encrusted with dirt, tethered by rope to a filthy playpen. The incident got a lot of press coverage because it involved two people—a lawyer and a book editor—who you'd think would know better.

I'll bet virtually everyone in this room could draw on their own experience in law enforcement to tell me a similar story. The individuals involved may not have had the high profiles to get them into the *New York Times*. But the moral of each one of those stories is the same: You can't serve your addictions and serve your family or other people at the same time.

The message our young people should be getting is clear: Drug use hurts you, and it hurts everyone around you. And we will do everything we can to help you resist the temptation to experiment with drugs.

When I say "do everything we can," I mean a crusade calling on every sector of society and using every resource that is available. This is a crusade with three fronts. There is always the debate between supply and demand resources.

When it comes to resources, we don't need a competitive fight, we need a cooperative strategy—one that uses enforcement, prevention, and treatment in a coordinated approach. I pledge to work to bring that balanced approach and assure cooperation.

Let me emphasize: Prevention and treatment cannot get the job done without enforcement. Enforcement is absolutely necessary. Enforcement sends the right signals to people who are tempted to try drugs. Young people should know their government believes drug use is a serious problem for them and for the society around them—that it's not just an alternative lifestyle. The law is our great moral teacher, and if we fail to enforce the law, we fail to teach and we succeed only in diminishing the character of this nation.

If young people get the message that society winks at drug use, then America will have surrendered to the weaknesses of our culture.

Recently, there's been a lot of talk about treatment, and there should be. I think there is a real need for more treatment facilities, and especially for efforts to make treatment programs as effective as possible. We all know there is a treatment gap, and we do not have the facilities for all who need help, especially young people. To help remedy this problem, I can tell you that President Bush included $3.4 billion in the '02 budget for treatment.

There are now roughly 1.5 million people using cocaine at least once a month. Another 350,000 are hard-core meth users. And about 200,000 use heroin. For them, treatment is a must. But availability of treatment does not necessarily result in treatment.

Some of you may have seen the film *Traffic*. The message that came out of that film was that enforcement isn't working, that the only solution is treatment.

Yet, the man who wrote the film had been a drug addict himself. In an interview with the *New York Times*, he said that he entered treatment only after his heroin dealer, his back-up dealer, and his back-up, back-up dealer were arrested on the same weekend. Treatment was important for the screenwriter, but it was enforcement that convinced him to seek treatment. His case is a perfect illustration of why we need a balanced policy in the fight against drugs. Enforcement and treatment work together.

Treatment works for some people, as it did for the screenwriter. But all too often it takes repeated stays in clinics over a period of years to finally cure an addiction to drugs. In the meantime, those who go through it are wasting the best, most productive years of their lives on overcoming addictions when they should be establishing careers and building families.

That's why I fully support drug courts. I had the opportunity to visit some here in Los Angeles a while back, and I saw how effective they are in helping those people who need help the most. The long, intensive counseling period is monitored by the courts. Relapses in drug use are punishable by imprisonment, which provides a powerful incentive for staying on the straight and narrow. These drug courts have an incredible success rate, and many lives are made whole again. It's important to remember that law enforcement triggers this whole drug court process.

Why is this battle—this compassionate crusade—worth fighting? I've heard it said that a man's character will determine his future, and so it is for the nation. What we do on the drug issue will impact not only families and communities, but also the character of our nation.

INDEX

ACLU (American Civil Liberties Union), 91, 123, 163, 189; on drug treatments, 144

Adams, Franklin P., 235

addiction, 44; dopamines and, 148–49; to heroin, 132, 136–37; marijuana and, 224; medicalization of, 184–85, 187; narcotic maintenance and, 186–87; opium, population of (1900), 5–6; scientific control of, 149

adolescence, drug use and, 141, 211–12; marijuana use during, 226, 239

African-Americans, drug abuse attitudes of, xii; drug use by, influences on, 106–7; heroin use by, 132–33. *See also* racism

"Against the Legalization of Drugs" (Wilson, James Q.), 197

alcohol, 146–49; Alcoholics Anonymous and, 147; 18th Amendment and, 105; health risks for, 147; prohibition of, 129, 173; "victimless crimes" and, 148. *See also* 18th Amendment

Alcoholics Anonymous, 147

Ambrose, Myles, 17

American Bar Association–American Medical Association, 185

American Behavioral Scientist, 193–94

American Civil Liberties Union. *See* ACLU

The American Disease: Origins of Narcotic Control, 106

Andean Trade Preferences Act, 283

Anderson, Jack, x

Anderson, Rose-Marie, x

Anglin, Doug, 144

Annual Report on the State of Drugs Problem in the European Union, 261

Anti–Drug Abuse Act (1986), 24

anti-drug groups, Anti–Drug Abuse Act and, 24; on Internet, 34. *See also* prevention programs, drugs

Arellano-Felix, Ramon, 29

armed services, U.S., heroin use by, 133

Australia, harm reduction in, 206; needle exchange programs in, 208

Austria, drug decriminalization in, 227; drug trade penalties in, 254

ballot propositions (U.S.), Measure 62, 216; for medical marijuana, 227–28, 241–43; Proposition 36, 215; Proposition 200, 214; Proposition 215, 232–33

Barca Vargas, Virgilio, 27

Basketball Diaries, 4

Battle, Jorge, 275

Bazilon, David, 183

Becker, Gary, xvii, 101

Belgium, drug decriminalization in, 227, 249–50; harm reduction programs in, 253; HIV prevention programs in, 251

"benefits of illegality," 143–49

Bennett, Georgette, 90

Bennett, William, 26, 31, 45–46, 53, 57, 60, 96, 164, 169, 194–95; Friedman letter to, 85–87

Bentham, John, 34

Besharov, Douglas, 138

Betancur, Belisario, 22

Bias, Len, 24, 287

Billings, Josh, 53

BNDD (Bureau of Narcotics and Dangerous Drugs), 17

Boaz, David, 91, 121–22, 166–67

Bone, Kathie, xvii

Bone, William, xvii

Bourne, Peter, 20

Boyle, John, 132

Bradley, Bill, 220

Branch, Taylor, 194

Brookhiser, Richard, 231

Brownsville Agreement, 29

Brunswick, Ann, 132

Buckley, William F., 88, 166, 193, 217, 220; on legalizing drugs, 90, 101, 160